SPIDER-MAN

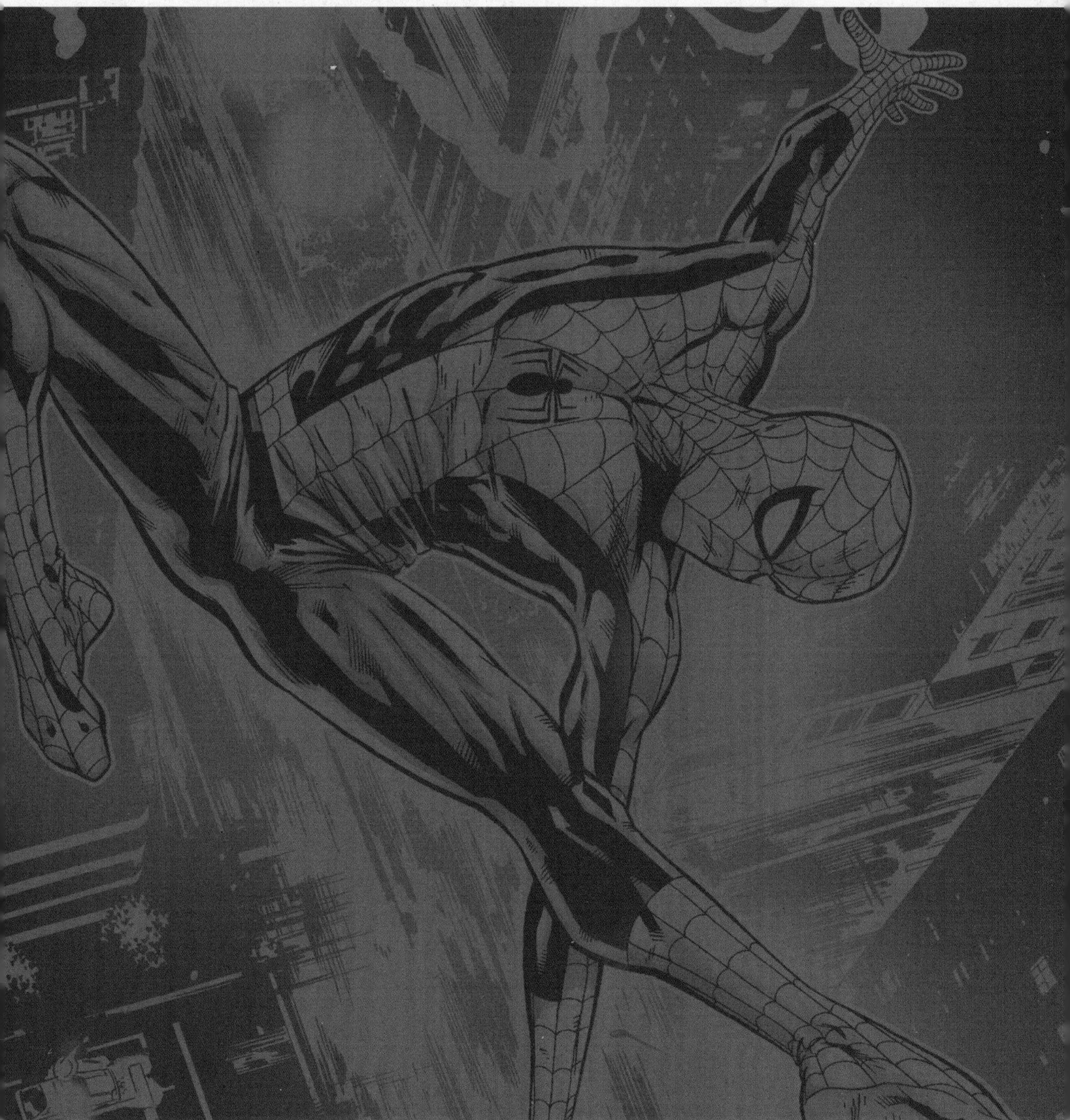

COLLECTION EDITOR: **JENNIFER GRÜNWALD**
ASSISTANT EDITOR: **CAITLIN O'CONNELL**
ASSOCIATE MANAGING EDITOR: **KATERI WOODY**
EDITOR, SPECIAL PROJECTS: **MARK D. BEAZLEY**
VP PRODUCTION & SPECIAL PROJECTS: **JEFF YOUNGQUIST**
SVP PRINT, SALES & MARKETING: **DAVID GABRIEL**
BOOK DESIGN: **JEFF POWELL**

EDITOR IN CHIEF: **AXEL ALONSO**
CHIEF CREATIVE OFFICER: **JOE QUESADA**
PRESIDENT: **DAN BUCKLEY**
EXECUTIVE PRODUCER: **ALAN FINE**

SPIDER-MAN: AMAZING ORIGINS. Contains material originally published in magazine form as SPIDER-MAN: SEASON ONE and SPIDEY #1. First printing 2017. ISBN# 978-0-7851-5821-9. Published by WORLDWIDE, INC., a subsidiary of MARVEL ENTERTAINMENT, LLC. OFFICE OF PUBLICATION: 135 West 50th Street, New York, NY 10020. **Printed in Canada.** DAN BUCKLEY, P Marvel Entertainment; JOE QUESADA, Chief Creative Officer; TOM BREVOORT, SVP of Publishing; DAVID BOGART, SVP of Business Affairs & Operations, Publishing & Partnership; C.B. CEBULSKI, VP of Brand Man & Development, Asia; DAVID GABRIEL, SVP of Sales & Marketing, Publishing; JEFF YOUNGQUIST, VP of Production & Special Projects; DAN CARR, Executive Director of Publishing Technology; ALEX MORALES, D Publishing Operations; SUSAN CRESPI, Production Manager; STAN LEE, Chairman Emeritus. For information regarding advertising in Marvel Comics or on Marvel.com, please contact Vit DeBellis, Integrated Sales at vdebellis@marvel.com. For Marvel subscription inquiries, please call 888-511-5480. **Manufactured between 4/14/2017 and 5/16/2017 by SOLISCO PRINTERS, SCOTT, QC, CANADA.**

10 9 8 7 6 5 4 3 2

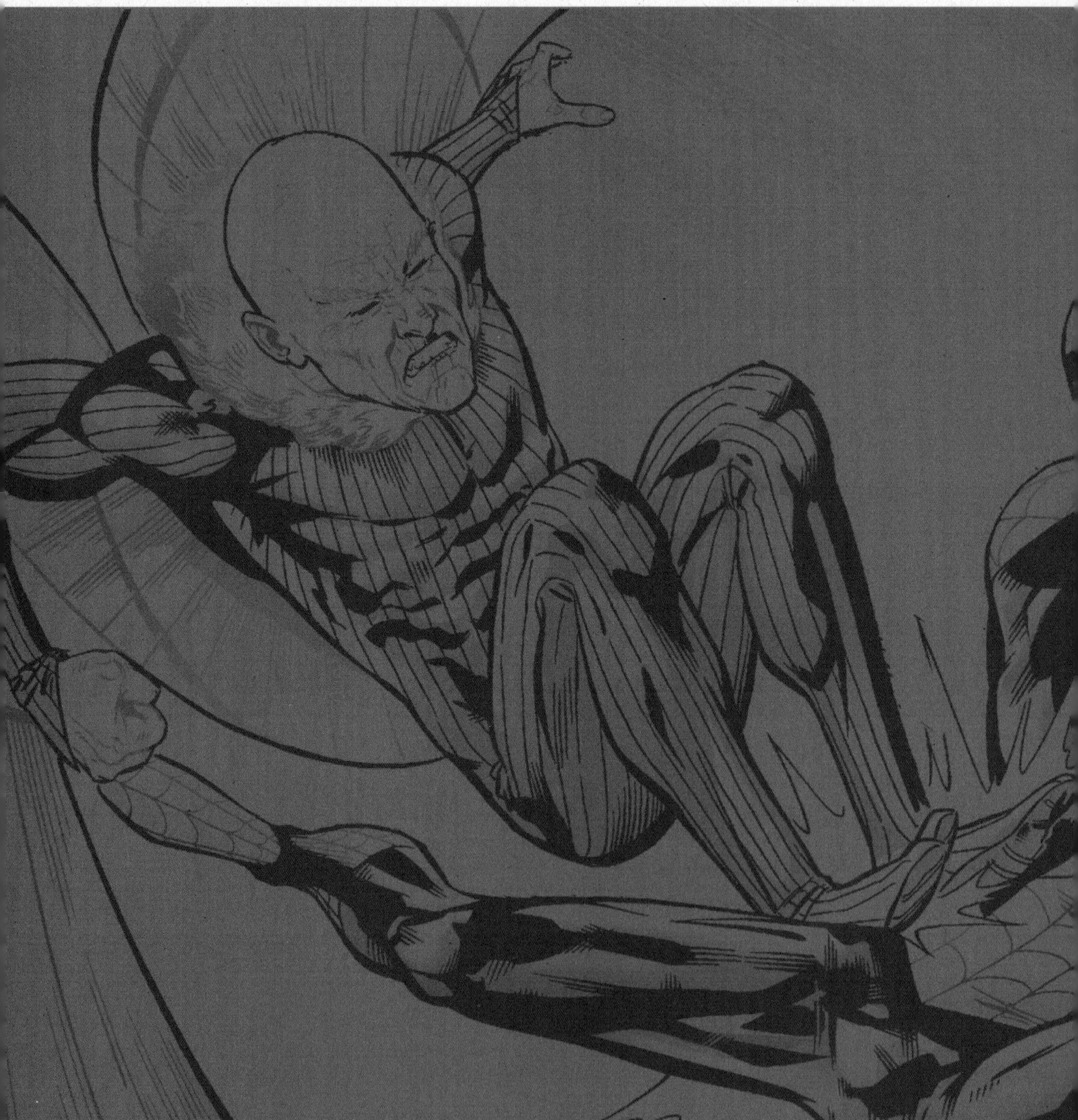

SPIDER-MAN

WRITER
CULLEN BUNN
PENCILER
NEIL EDWARDS
INKER
KARL KESEL
COLORIST
DAVID CURIEL
LETTERER
VC'S CLAYTON COWLES

COVER ARTIST
JULIAN TOTINO TEDESCO

ASSISTANT EDITOR
ELLIE PYLE
& RACHEL PINNELAS
EDITOR
STEPHEN WACKER
EXECUTIVE EDITOR
TOM BREVOORT

SPIDER-MAN CREATED BY
STAN LEE & STEVE DITKO

AMAZING ORIGINS

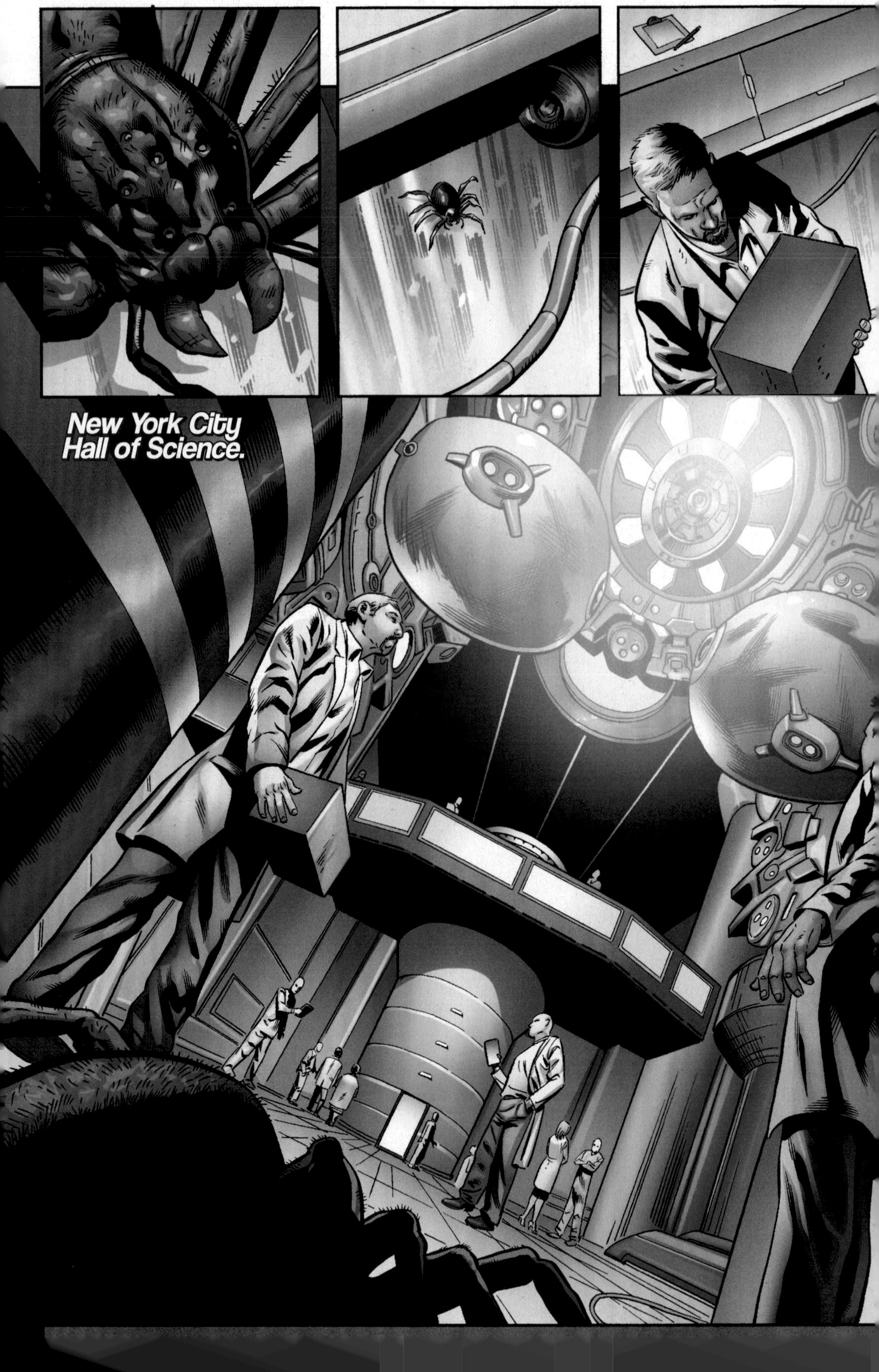
New York City
Hall of Science.

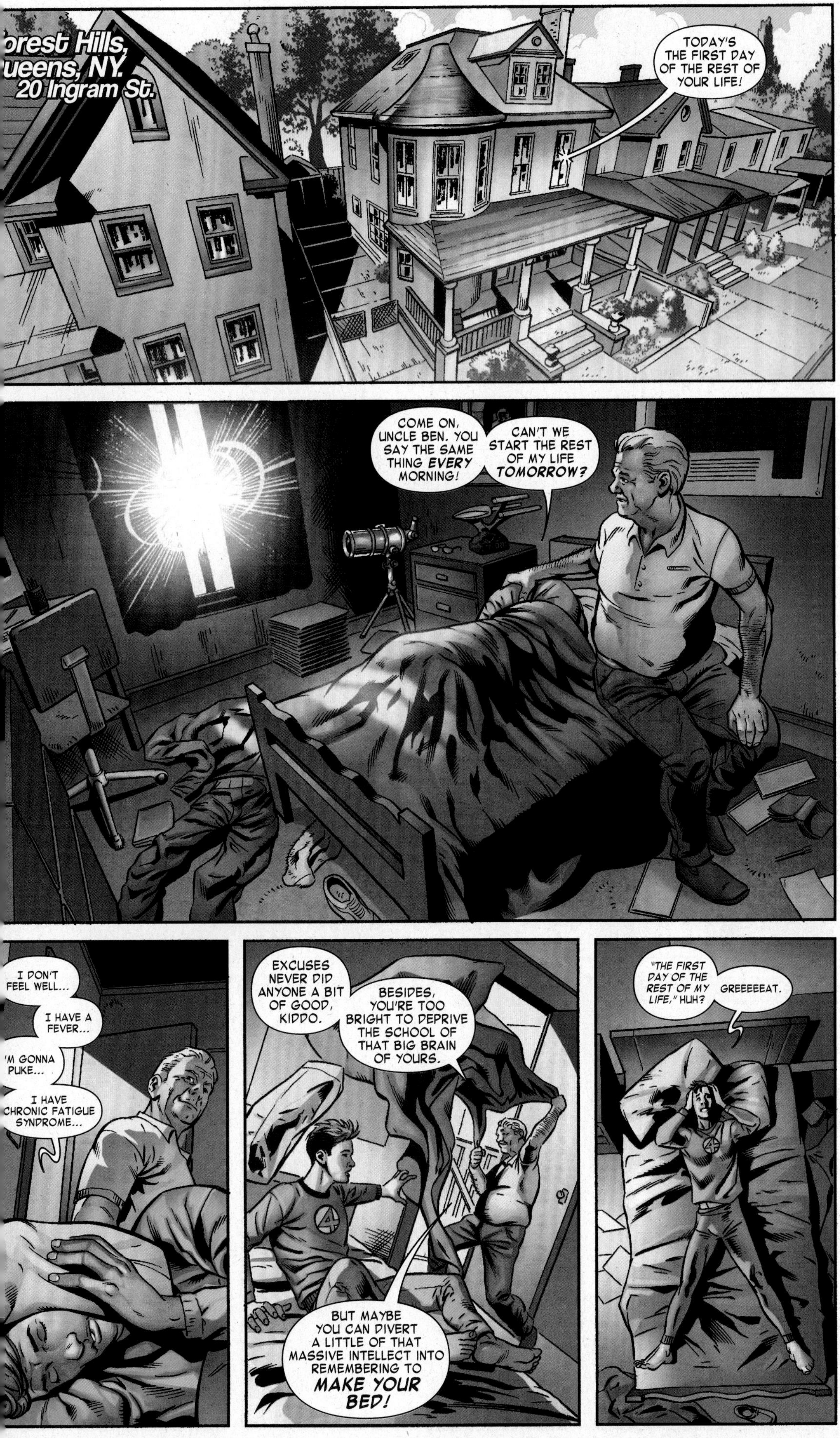
orest Hills,
ueens, NY.
20 Ingram St.
TODAY'S THE FIRST DAY OF THE REST OF YOUR LIFE!
COME ON, UNCLE BEN. YOU SAY THE SAME THING EVERY MORNING!
CAN'T WE START THE REST OF MY LIFE TOMORROW?
I DON'T FEEL WELL...
I HAVE A FEVER...
'M GONNA PUKE...
I HAVE CHRONIC FATIGUE SYNDROME...
EXCUSES NEVER DID ANYONE A BIT OF GOOD, KIDDO.
BESIDES, YOU'RE TOO BRIGHT TO DEPRIVE THE SCHOOL OF THAT BIG BRAIN OF YOURS.
BUT MAYBE YOU CAN DIVERT A LITTLE OF THAT MASSIVE INTELLECT INTO REMEMBERING TO MAKE YOUR BED!
"THE FIRST DAY OF THE REST OF MY LIFE," HUH?
GREEEEEAT.

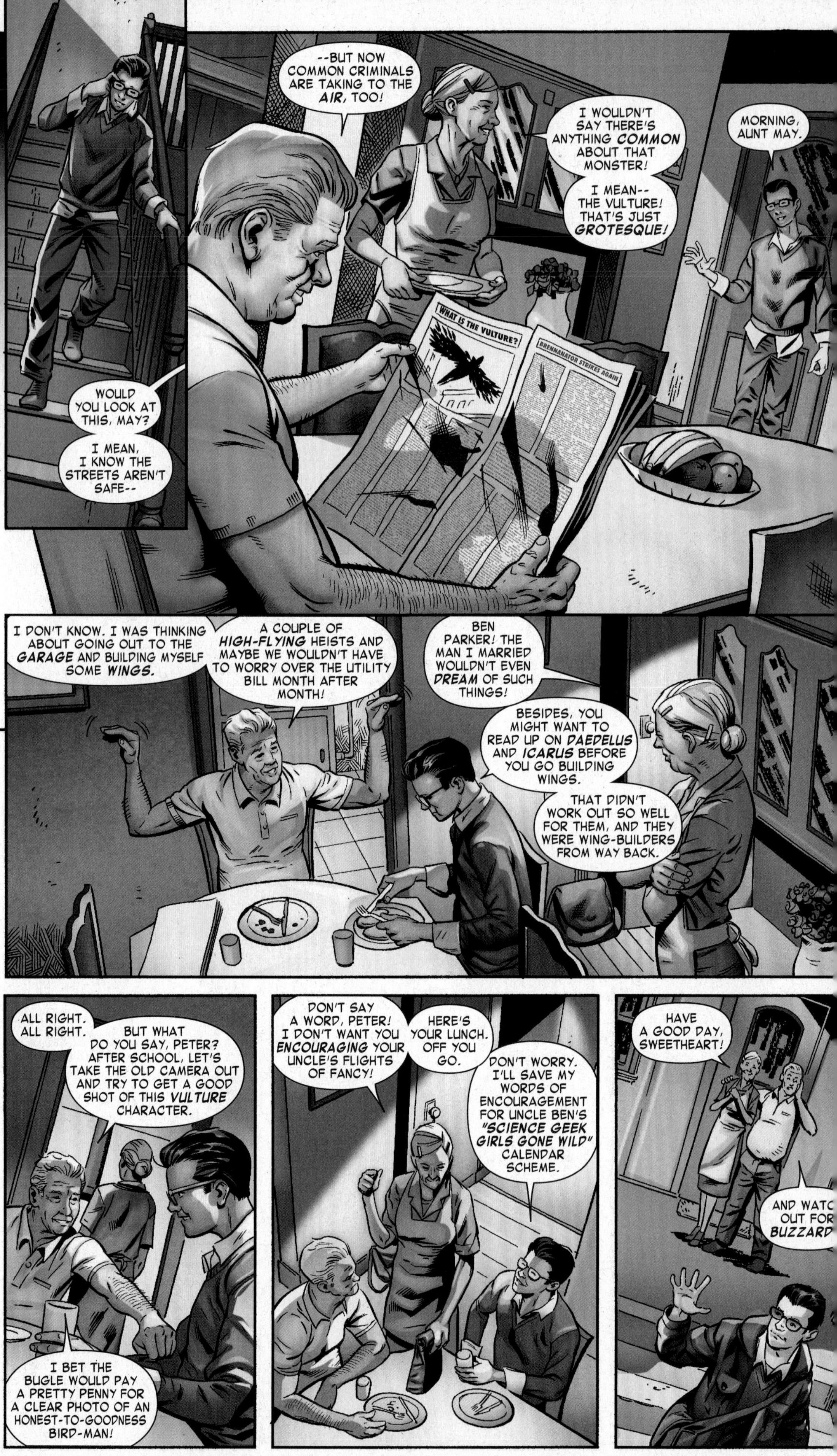
WOULD YOU LOOK AT THIS, MAY?
I MEAN, I KNOW THE STREETS AREN'T SAFE--
--BUT NOW COMMON CRIMINALS ARE TAKING TO THE AIR, TOO!
WHAT IS THE VULTURE?
BRENNANATOR STRIKES AGAIN
I WOULDN'T SAY THERE'S ANYTHING COMMON ABOUT THAT MONSTER!
I MEAN-- THE VULTURE! THAT'S JUST GROTESQUE!
MORNING, AUNT MAY.
I DON'T KNOW. I WAS THINKING ABOUT GOING OUT TO THE GARAGE AND BUILDING MYSELF SOME WINGS.
A COUPLE OF HIGH-FLYING HEISTS AND MAYBE WE WOULDN'T HAVE TO WORRY OVER THE UTILITY BILL MONTH AFTER MONTH!
BEN PARKER! THE MAN I MARRIED WOULDN'T EVEN DREAM OF SUCH THINGS!
BESIDES, YOU MIGHT WANT TO READ UP ON DAEDELUS AND ICARUS BEFORE YOU GO BUILDING WINGS.
THAT DIDN'T WORK OUT SO WELL FOR THEM, AND THEY WERE WING-BUILDERS FROM WAY BACK.
ALL RIGHT. ALL RIGHT.
BUT WHAT DO YOU SAY, PETER? AFTER SCHOOL, LET'S TAKE THE OLD CAMERA OUT AND TRY TO GET A GOOD SHOT OF THIS VULTURE CHARACTER.
I BET THE BUGLE WOULD PAY A PRETTY PENNY FOR A CLEAR PHOTO OF AN HONEST-TO-GOODNESS BIRD-MAN!
DON'T SAY A WORD, PETER! I DON'T WANT YOU ENCOURAGING YOUR UNCLE'S FLIGHTS OF FANCY!
HERE'S YOUR LUNCH. OFF YOU GO.
DON'T WORRY. I'LL SAVE MY WORDS OF ENCOURAGEMENT FOR UNCLE BEN'S "SCIENCE GEEK GIRLS GONE WILD" CALENDAR SCHEME.
HAVE A GOOD DAY, SWEETHEART!
AND WATC OUT FOR BUZZARD

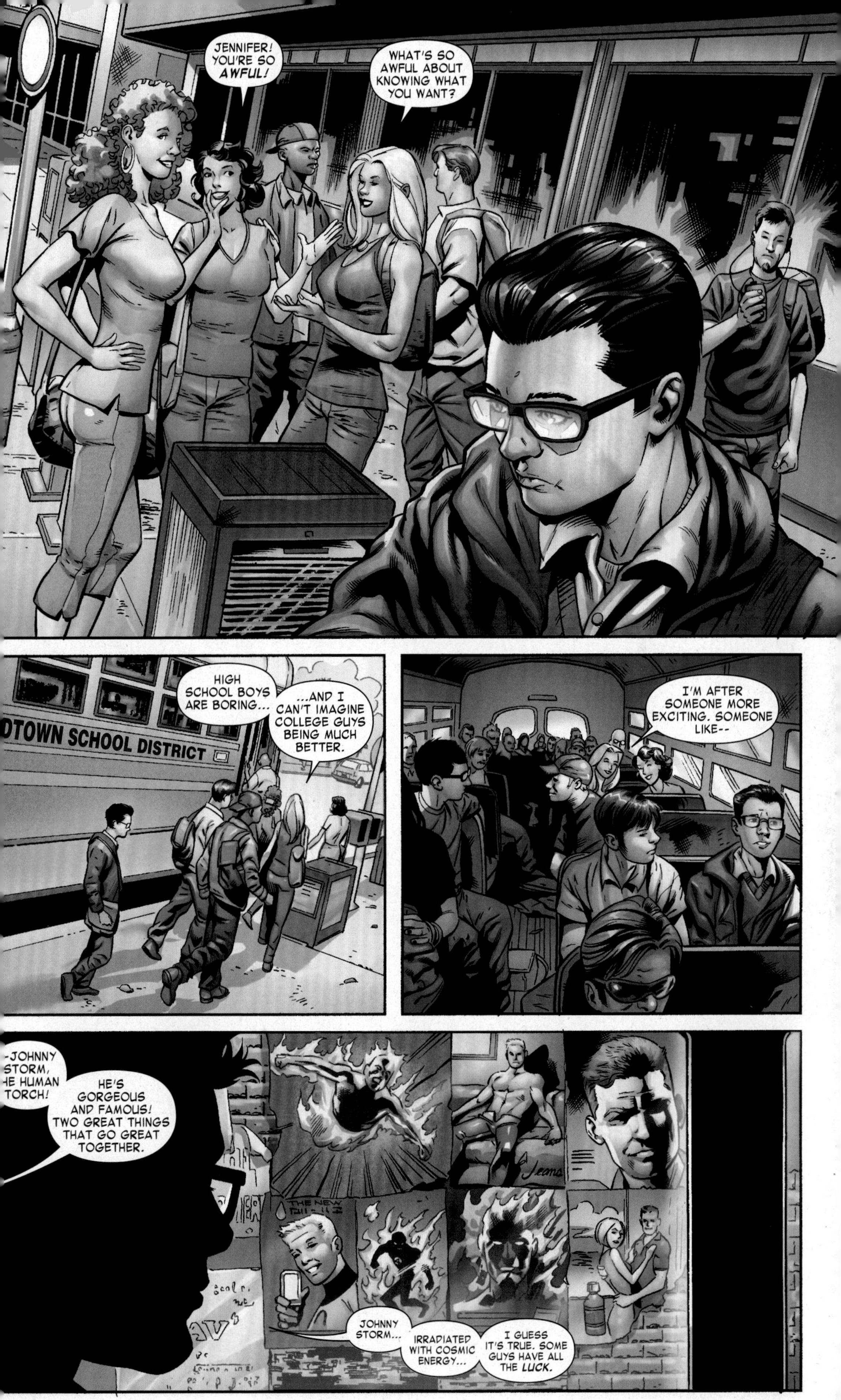
JENNIFER! YOU'RE SO AWFUL!
WHAT'S SO AWFUL ABOUT KNOWING WHAT YOU WANT?
DTOWN SCHOOL DISTRICT
HIGH SCHOOL BOYS ARE BORING...
...AND I CAN'T IMAGINE COLLEGE GUYS BEING MUCH BETTER.
I'M AFTER SOMEONE MORE EXCITING. SOMEONE LIKE--
-JOHNNY STORM, HE HUMAN TORCH!
HE'S GORGEOUS AND FAMOUS! TWO GREAT THINGS THAT GO GREAT TOGETHER.
JOHNNY STORM...
IRRADIATED WITH COSMIC ENERGY...
I GUESS IT'S TRUE. SOME GUYS HAVE ALL THE LUCK.

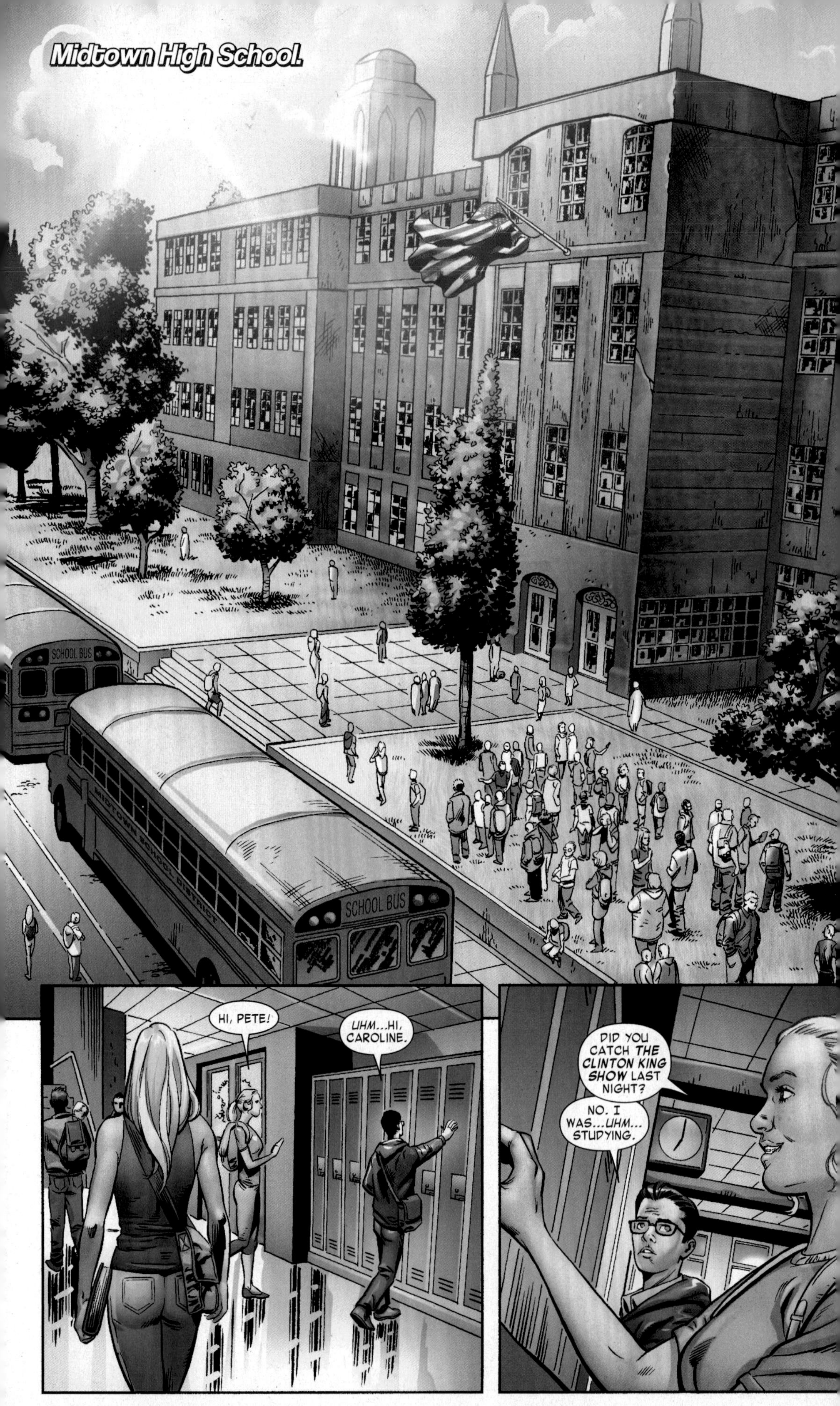
Midtown High School.
SCHOOL BUS
MIDTOWN SCHOOL DISTRICT
SCHOOL BUS
HI, PETE!
UHM...HI, CAROLINE.
DID YOU CATCH **THE CLINTON KING SHOW** LAST NIGHT?
NO. I WAS...UHM... STUDYING.

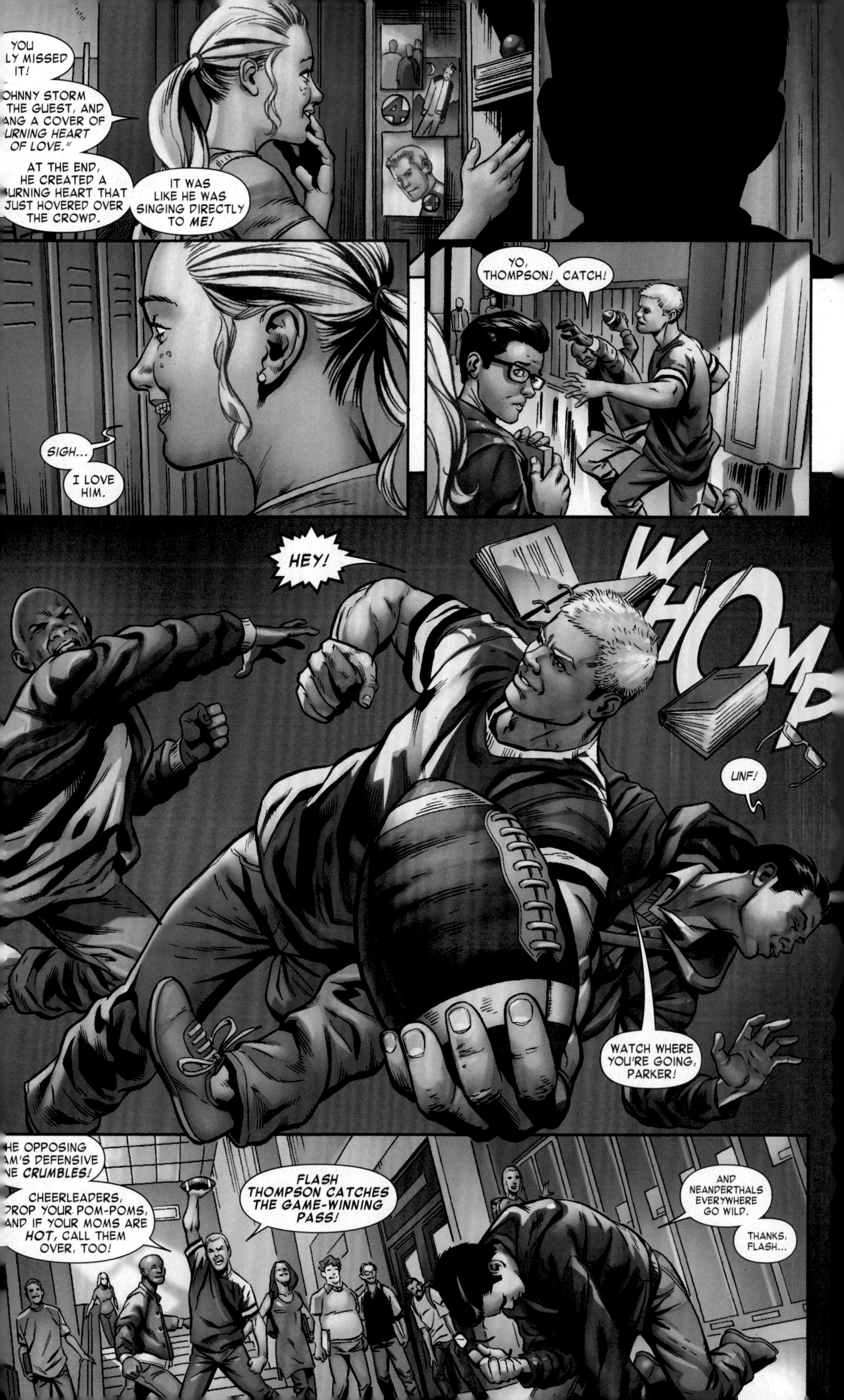

YOU
LY MISSED
IT!
OHNNY STORM
THE GUEST, AND
ANG A COVER OF
URNING HEART
OF LOVE."
AT THE END,
HE CREATED A
URNING HEART THAT
JUST HOVERED OVER
THE CROWD.
IT WAS
LIKE HE WAS
SINGING DIRECTLY
TO ME!
SIGH...
I LOVE
HIM.
YO,
THOMPSON!
CATCH!
HEY!
WHOMP
UNF!
WATCH WHERE
YOU'RE GOING,
PARKER!
HE OPPOSING
AM'S DEFENSIVE
NE CRUMBLES!
CHEERLEADERS,
DROP YOUR POM-POMS,
AND IF YOUR MOMS ARE
HOT, CALL THEM
OVER, TOO!
FLASH
THOMPSON CATCHES
THE GAME-WINNING
PASS!
AND
NEANDERTHALS
EVERYWHERE
GO WILD.
THANKS,
FLASH...

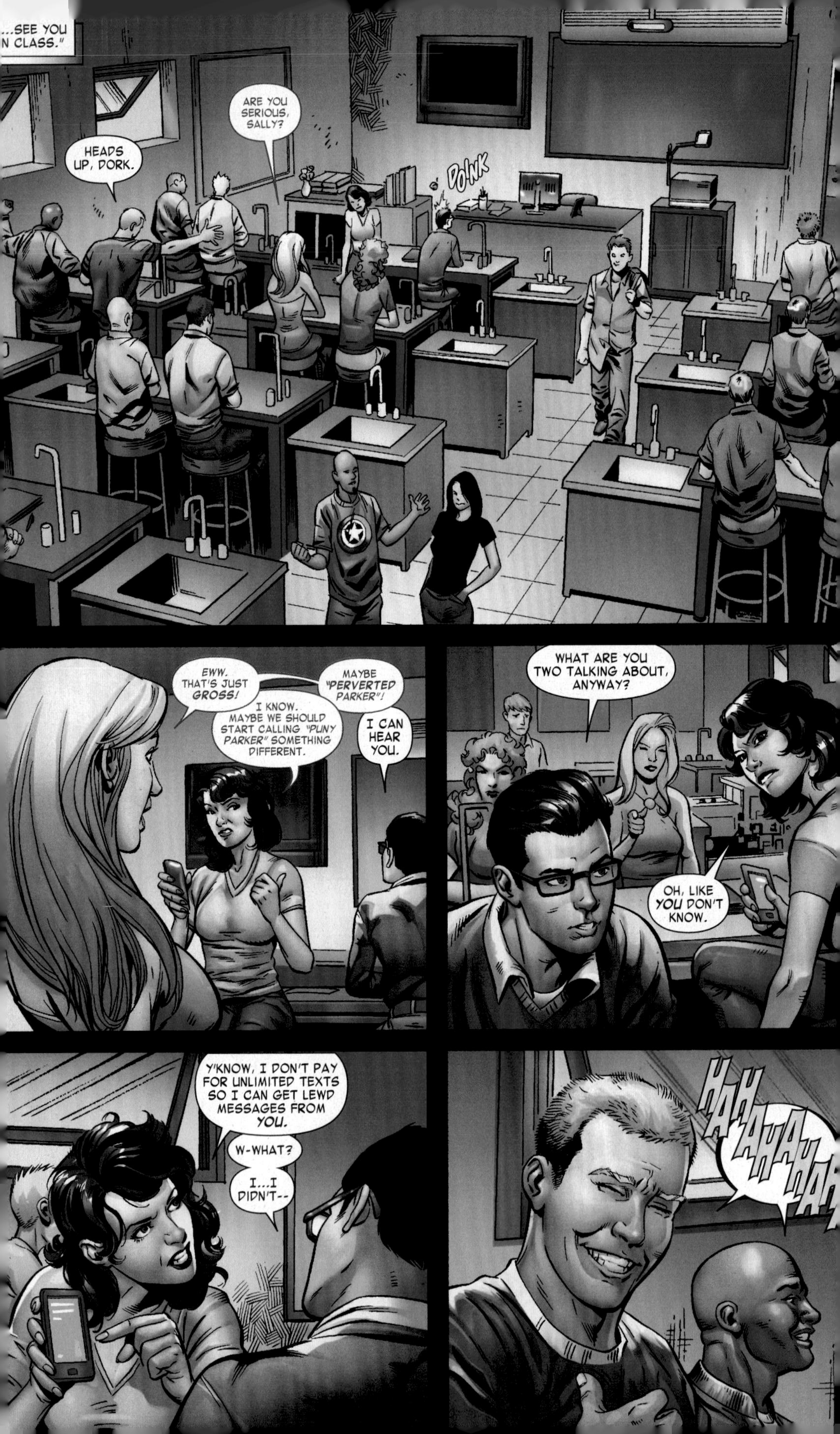
"...SEE YOU
IN CLASS."
HEADS UP, DORK.
ARE YOU SERIOUS, SALLY?
DOINK
EWW. THAT'S JUST GROSS!
MAYBE "PERVERTED PARKER"!
I KNOW. MAYBE WE SHOULD START CALLING "PUNY PARKER" SOMETHING DIFFERENT.
I CAN HEAR YOU.
WHAT ARE YOU TWO TALKING ABOUT, ANYWAY?
OH, LIKE YOU DON'T KNOW.
Y'KNOW, I DON'T PAY FOR UNLIMITED TEXTS SO I CAN GET LEWD MESSAGES FROM YOU.
W-WHAT?
I...I DIDN'T--
HAHAHAHAHA

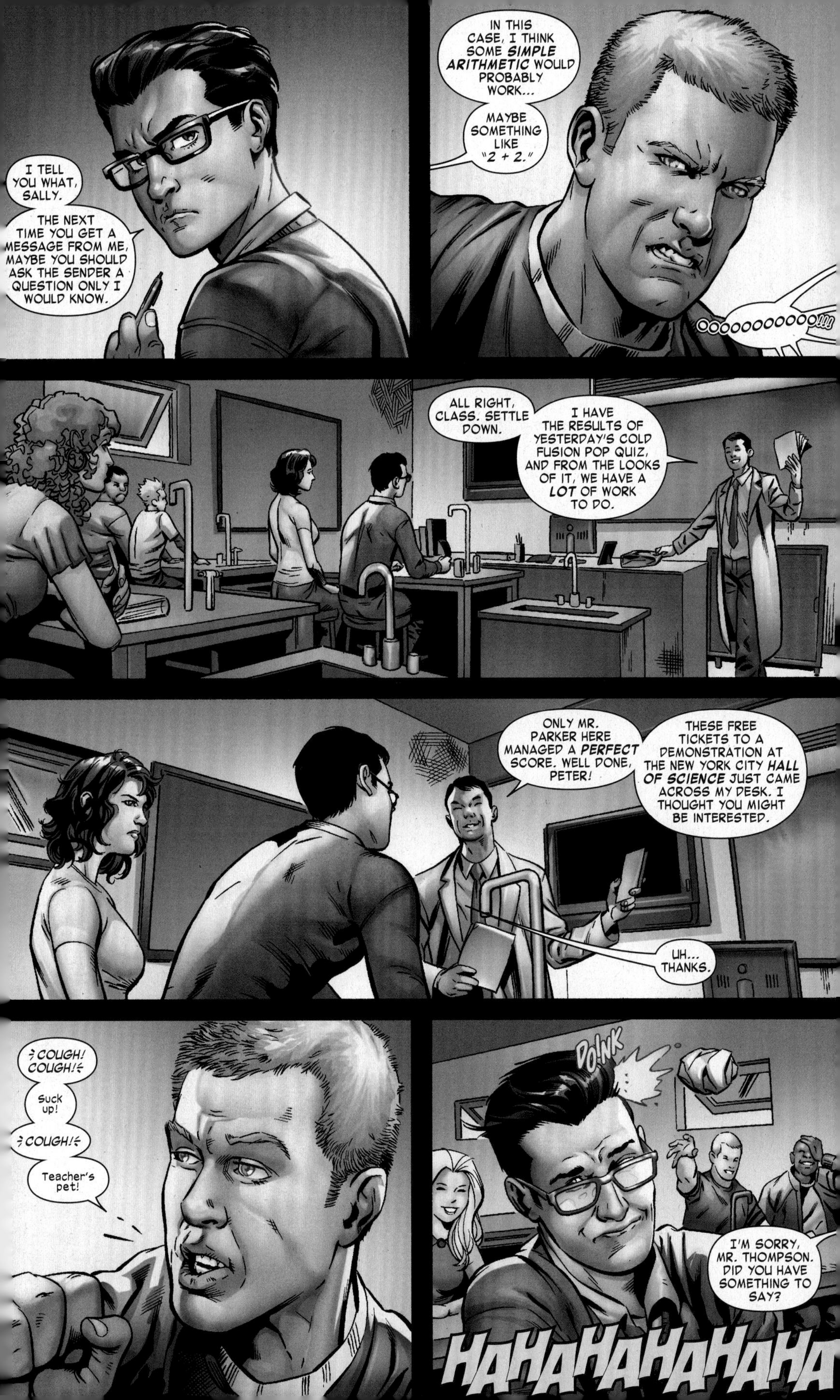

I TELL YOU WHAT, SALLY.
THE NEXT TIME YOU GET A MESSAGE FROM ME, MAYBE YOU SHOULD ASK THE SENDER A QUESTION ONLY I WOULD KNOW.
IN THIS CASE, I THINK SOME SIMPLE ARITHMETIC WOULD PROBABLY WORK...
MAYBE SOMETHING LIKE "2 + 2."
OOOOOOOOOOOO!!!
ALL RIGHT, CLASS. SETTLE DOWN.
I HAVE THE RESULTS OF YESTERDAY'S COLD FUSION POP QUIZ, AND FROM THE LOOKS OF IT, WE HAVE A LOT OF WORK TO DO.
ONLY MR. PARKER HERE MANAGED A PERFECT SCORE. WELL DONE, PETER!
THESE FREE TICKETS TO A DEMONSTRATION AT THE NEW YORK CITY HALL OF SCIENCE JUST CAME ACROSS MY DESK. I THOUGHT YOU MIGHT BE INTERESTED.
UH... THANKS.
COUGH! COUGH!
Suck up!
COUGH!
Teacher's pet!
DOINK
I'M SORRY, MR. THOMPSON. DID YOU HAVE SOMETHING TO SAY?
HAHAHAHAHAHAHA

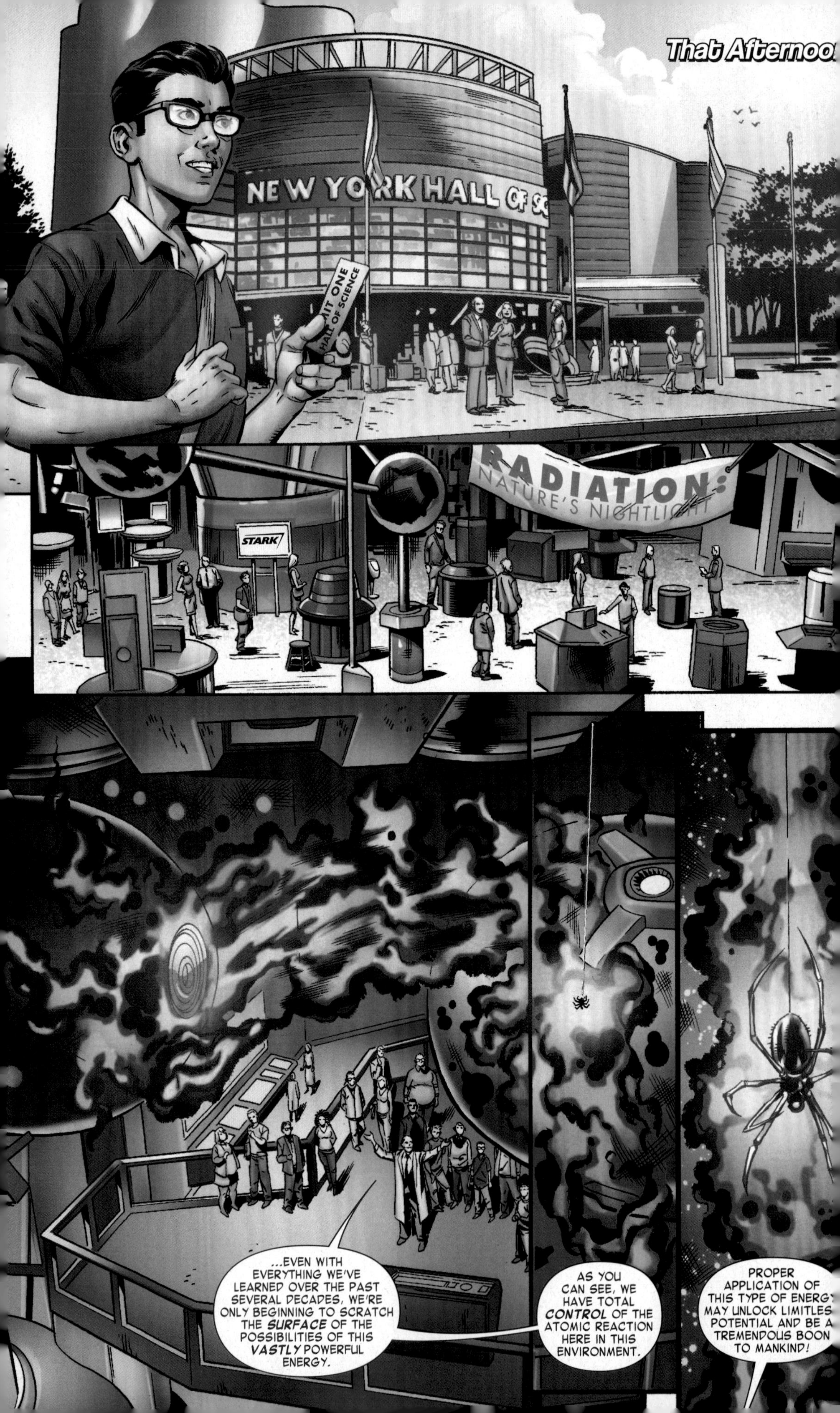
That Afternoo
NEW YORK HALL OF SC
ADMIT ONE HALL OF SCIENCE
RADIATION: NATURE'S NIGHTLIGHT
STARK
...EVEN WITH EVERYTHING WE'VE LEARNED OVER THE PAST SEVERAL DECADES, WE'RE ONLY BEGINNING TO SCRATCH THE SURFACE OF THE POSSIBILITIES OF THIS VASTLY POWERFUL ENERGY.
AS YOU CAN SEE, WE HAVE TOTAL CONTROL OF THE ATOMIC REACTION HERE IN THIS ENVIRONMENT.
PROPER APPLICATION OF THIS TYPE OF ENERGY MAY UNLOCK LIMITLES POTENTIAL AND BE A TREMENDOUS BOON TO MANKIND!

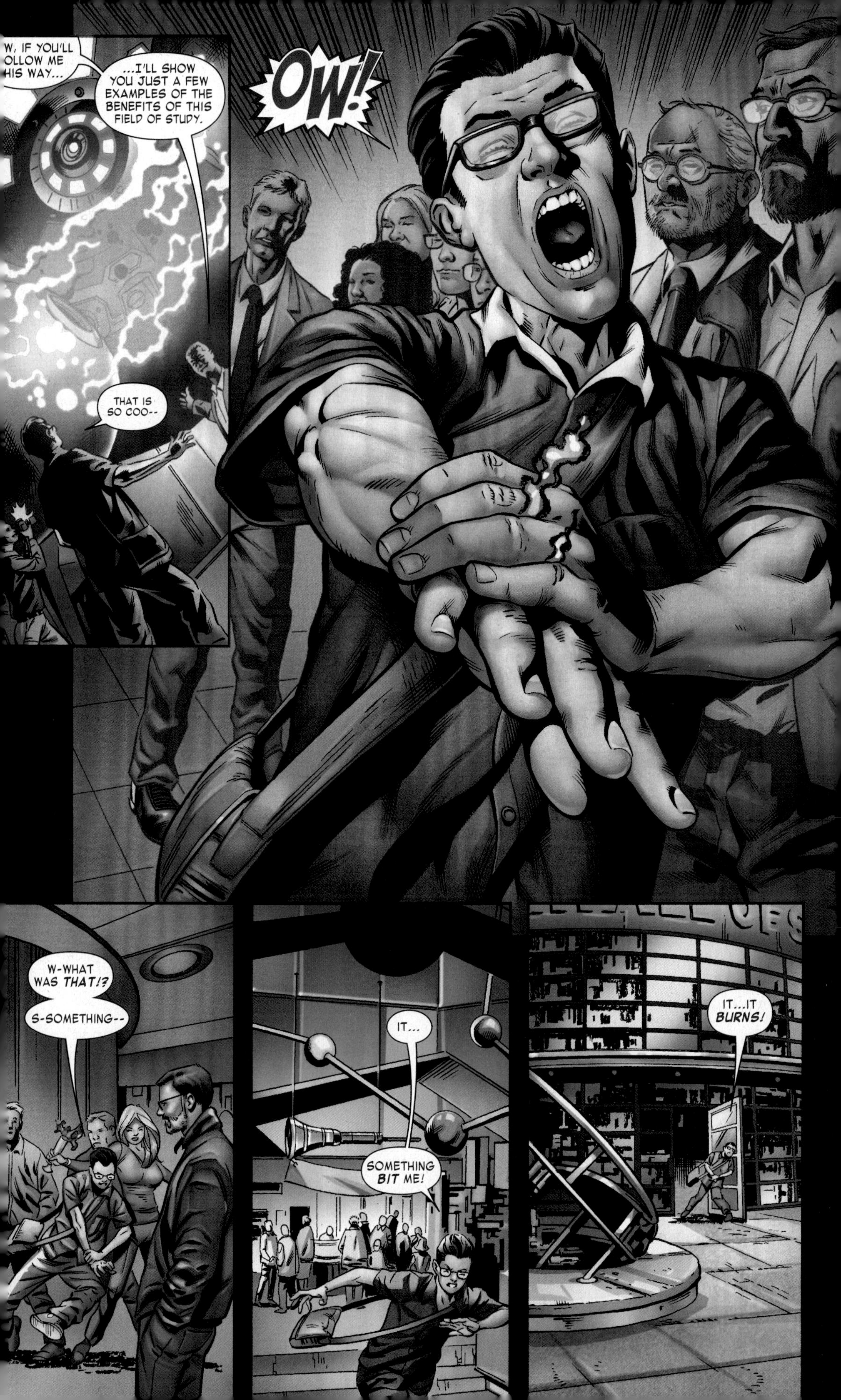

W, IF YOU'LL OLLOW ME HIS WAY...
...I'LL SHOW YOU JUST A FEW EXAMPLES OF THE BENEFITS OF THIS FIELD OF STUDY.
THAT IS SO COO--
OW!
W-WHAT WAS THAT!?
S-SOMETHING--
IT...
SOMETHING BIT ME!
IT...IT BURNS!

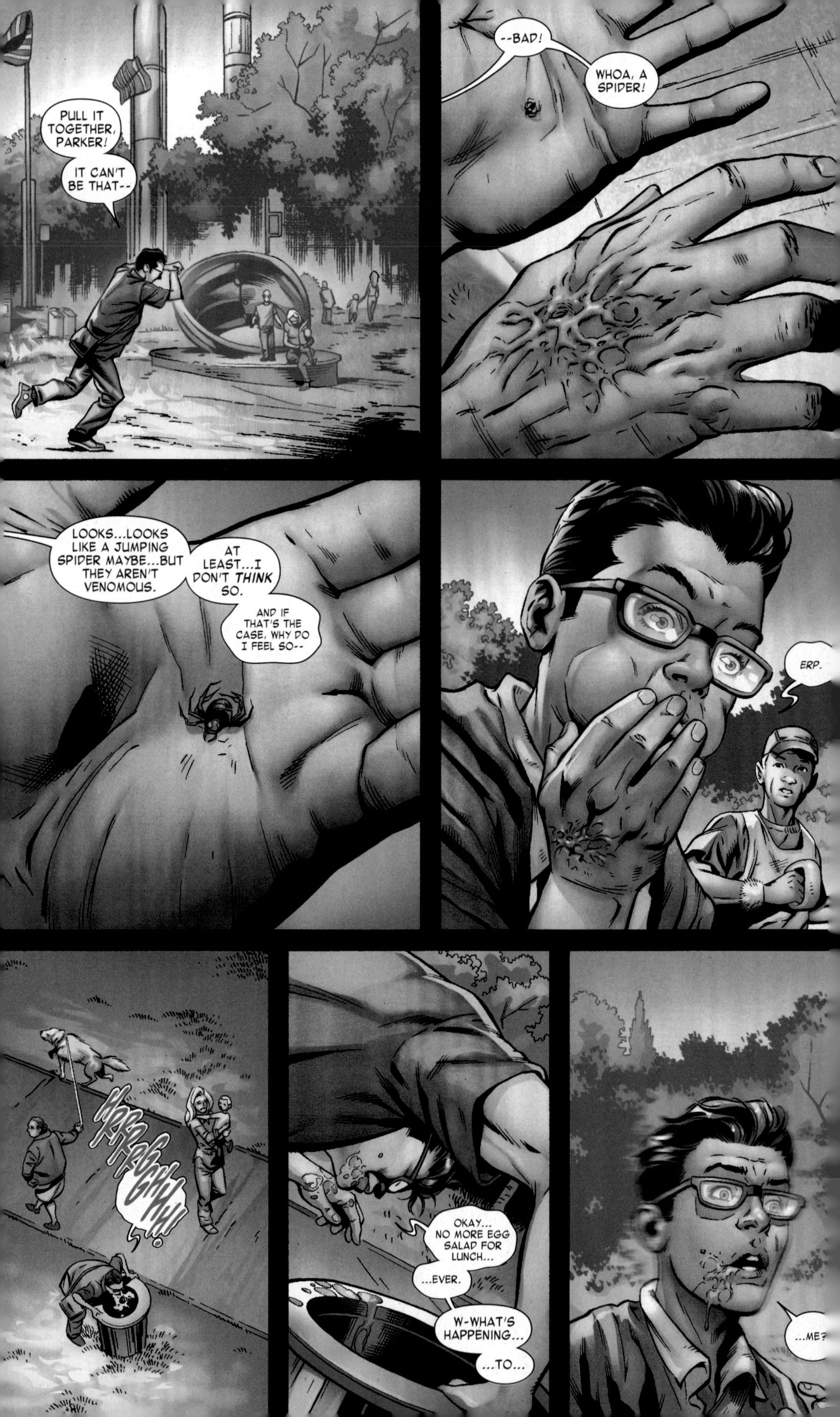
PULL IT TOGETHER, PARKER!
IT CAN'T BE THAT--
--BAD!
WHOA, A SPIDER!
LOOKS...LOOKS LIKE A JUMPING SPIDER MAYBE...BUT THEY AREN'T VENOMOUS.
AT LEAST...I DON'T THINK SO.
AND IF THAT'S THE CASE, WHY DO I FEEL SO--
ERP.
HRRRGHHH!!
OKAY... NO MORE EGG SALAD FOR LUNCH...
...EVER.
W-WHAT'S HAPPENING...
...TO...
...ME?

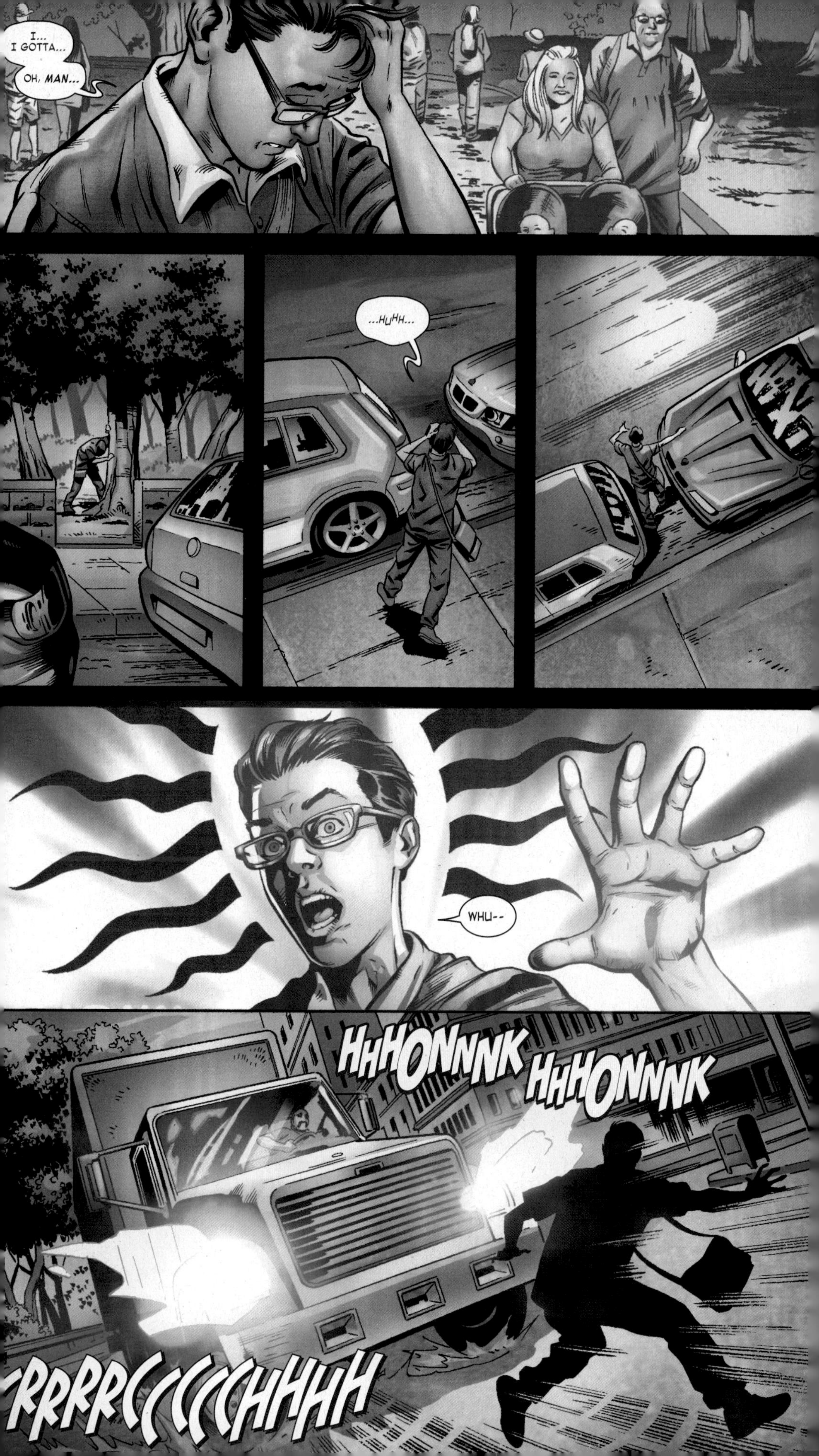
I... I GOTTA...
OH, MAN...
...HUHH...
WHU--
HHHONNNK
HHHONNNK
RRRRCCCCCHHHH

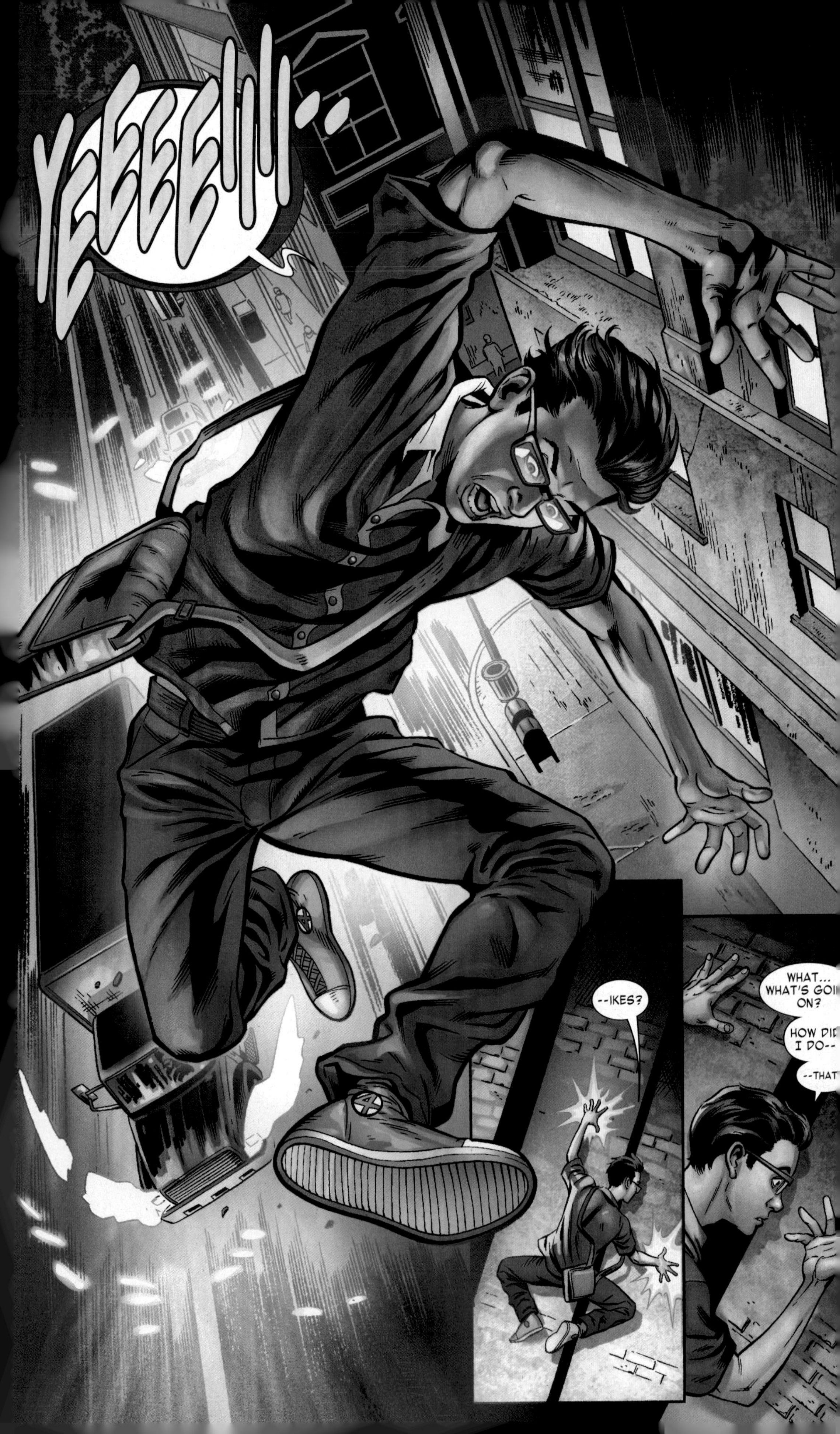
YEEEE!!!..
--IKES?
WHAT... WHAT'S GOI ON?
HOW DID I DO--
--THAT

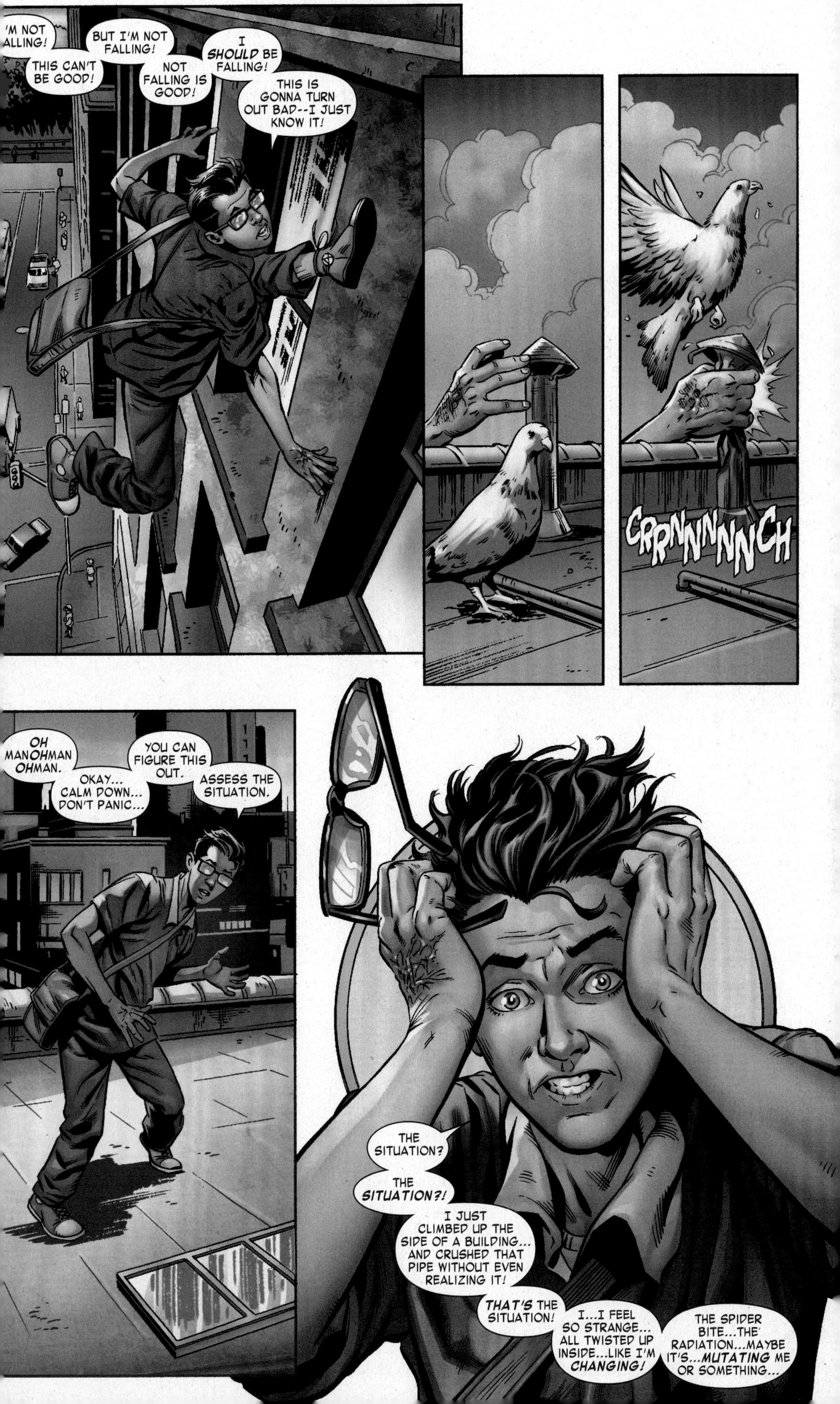
I'M NOT FALLING!
BUT I'M NOT FALLING!
THIS CAN'T BE GOOD!
NOT FALLING IS GOOD!
I SHOULD BE FALLING!
THIS IS GONNA TURN OUT BAD--I JUST KNOW IT!
CRRNNNNNCH
OH MANOHMAN OHMAN.
OKAY... CALM DOWN... DON'T PANIC...
YOU CAN FIGURE THIS OUT.
ASSESS THE SITUATION.
THE SITUATION?
THE SITUATION?!
I JUST CLIMBED UP THE SIDE OF A BUILDING... AND CRUSHED THAT PIPE WITHOUT EVEN REALIZING IT!
THAT'S THE SITUATION!
I...I FEEL SO STRANGE... ALL TWISTED UP INSIDE...LIKE I'M CHANGING!
THE SPIDER BITE...THE RADIATION...MAYBE IT'S...MUTATING ME OR SOMETHING...

MUTATION!

OH... OH, NO...

I...I'M TOO YOUNG TO BE *MUTATED!*

M-MAYBE IT WON'T BE SO BAD. I MEAN, NOBODY EVER *DIED* FROM ONE LITTLE RADIOACTIVE SPIDER BITE.

RIGHT?

"BUT WHAT IF I CONTINUE TO CHANGE INTO SOME SORT OF *MONSTER?*"

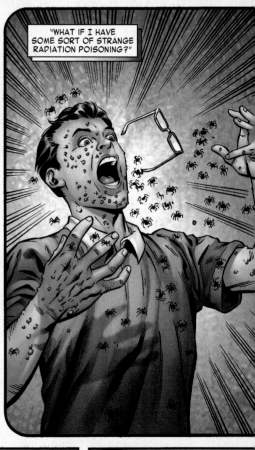

"WHAT IF I HAVE SOME SORT OF STRANGE RADIATION POISONING?"

I DON'T KNOW WHAT'S GOING ON, BUT THIS IS NO PLACE TO FIGURE IT OUT.

I ALWAYS KNEW THAT *SCIENCE* WOULD BE THE DEATH OF ME!

I BETTER GET--

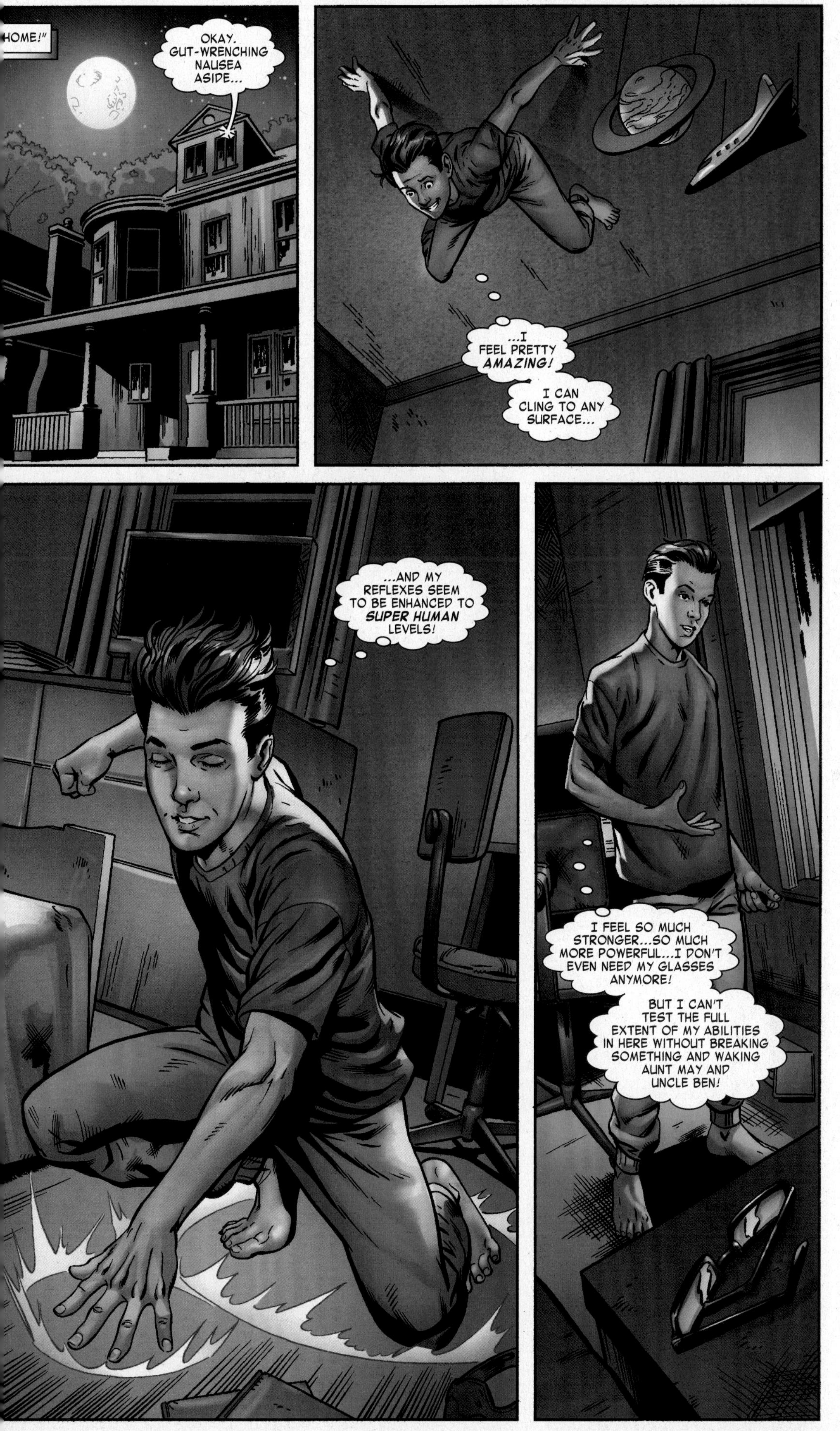
HOME!"
OKAY. GUT-WRENCHING NAUSEA ASIDE...
...I FEEL PRETTY AMAZING!
I CAN CLING TO ANY SURFACE...
...AND MY REFLEXES SEEM TO BE ENHANCED TO SUPER HUMAN LEVELS!
I FEEL SO MUCH STRONGER...SO MUCH MORE POWERFUL...I DON'T EVEN NEED MY GLASSES ANYMORE!
BUT I CAN'T TEST THE FULL EXTENT OF MY ABILITIES IN HERE WITHOUT BREAKING SOMETHING AND WAKING AUNT MAY AND UNCLE BEN!

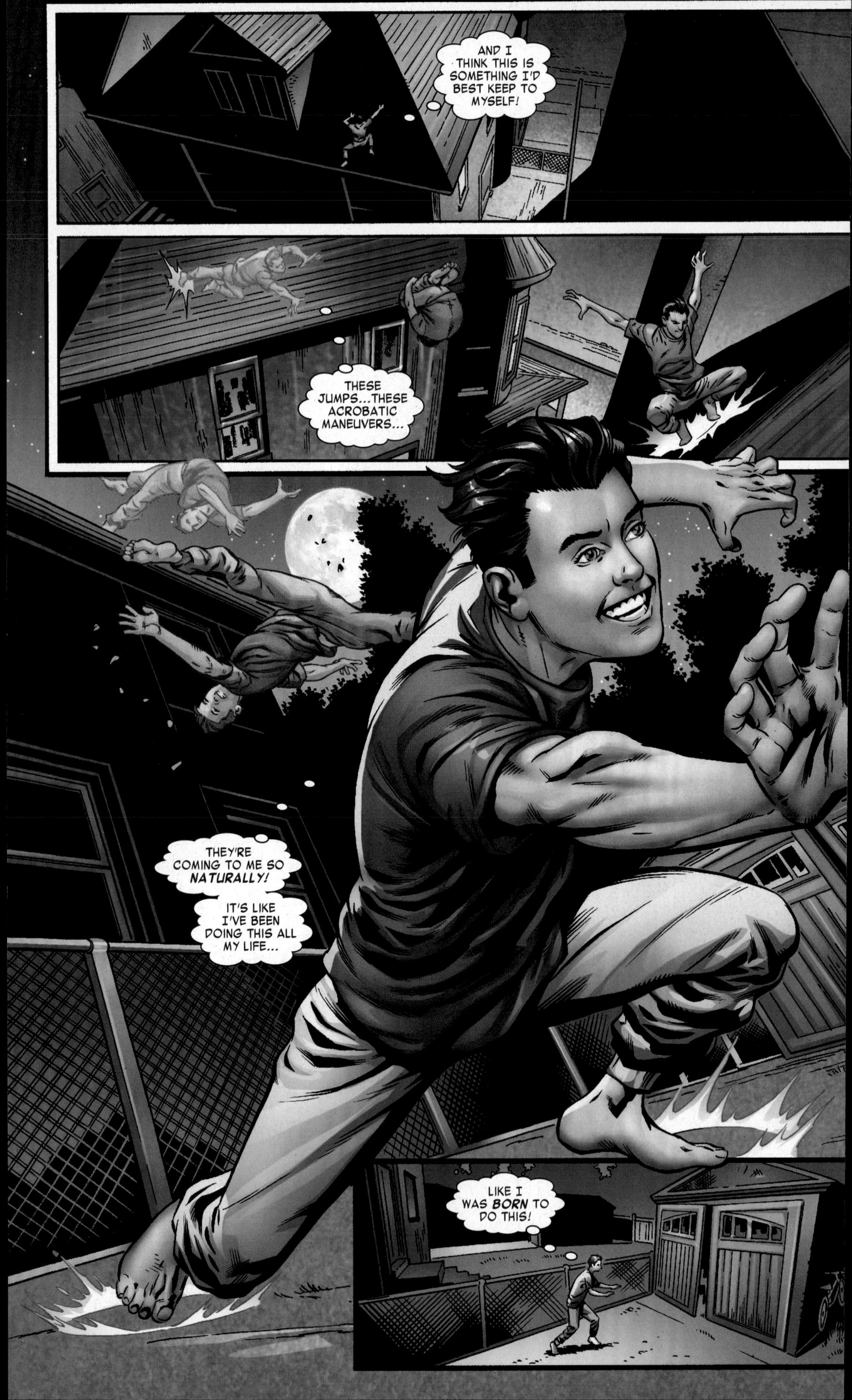
AND I THINK THIS IS SOMETHING I'D BEST KEEP TO MYSELF!
THESE JUMPS...THESE ACROBATIC MANEUVERS...
THEY'RE COMING TO ME SO NATURALLY!
IT'S LIKE I'VE BEEN DOING THIS ALL MY LIFE...
LIKE I WAS BORN TO DO THIS!

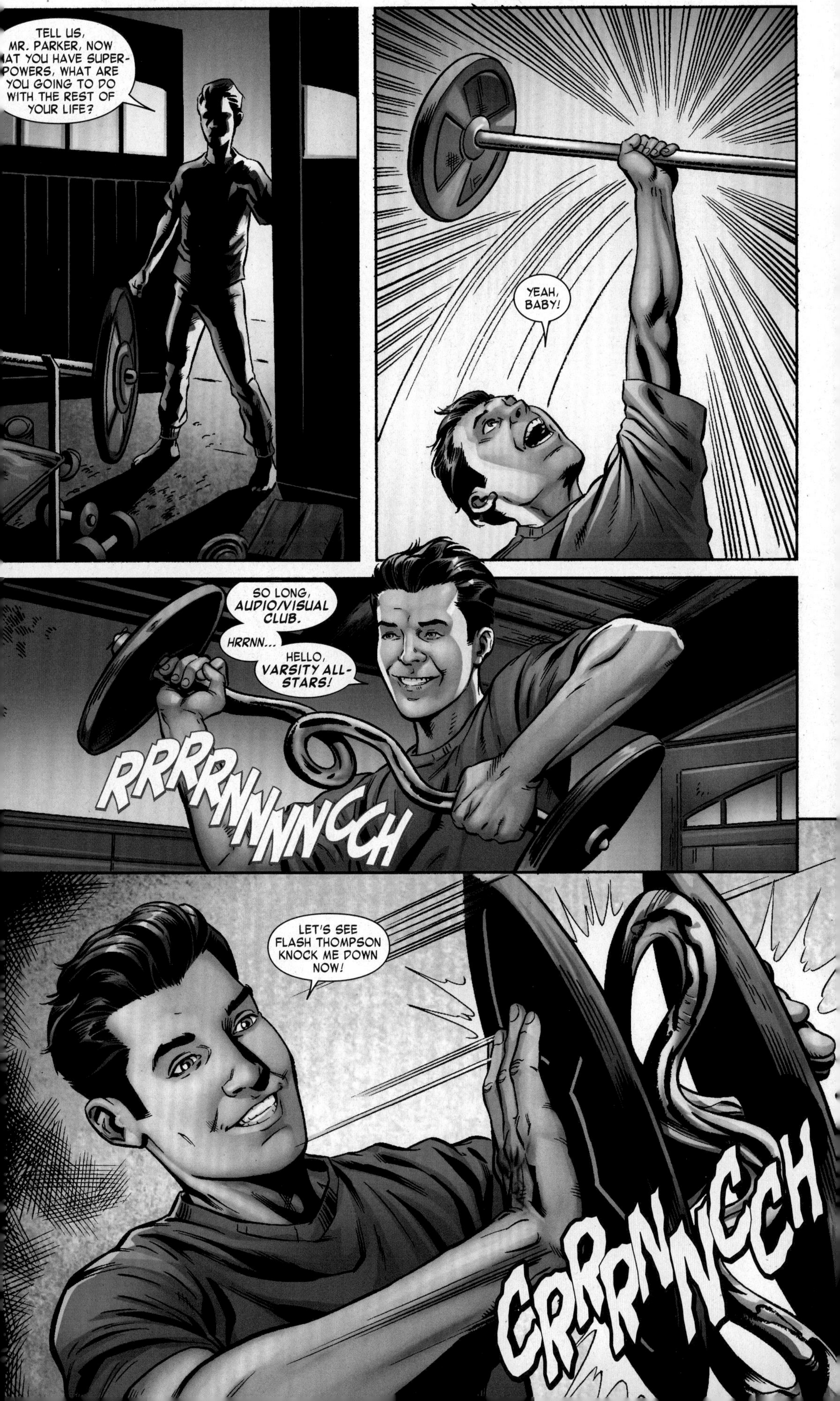
TELL US, MR. PARKER, NOW AT YOU HAVE SUPER-POWERS, WHAT ARE YOU GOING TO DO WITH THE REST OF YOUR LIFE?
YEAH, BABY!
SO LONG, AUDIO/VISUAL CLUB.
HRRNN...
HELLO, VARSITY ALL-STARS!
RRRRNNNNNCCH
LET'S SEE FLASH THOMPSON KNOCK ME DOWN NOW!
CRRRNNCCH

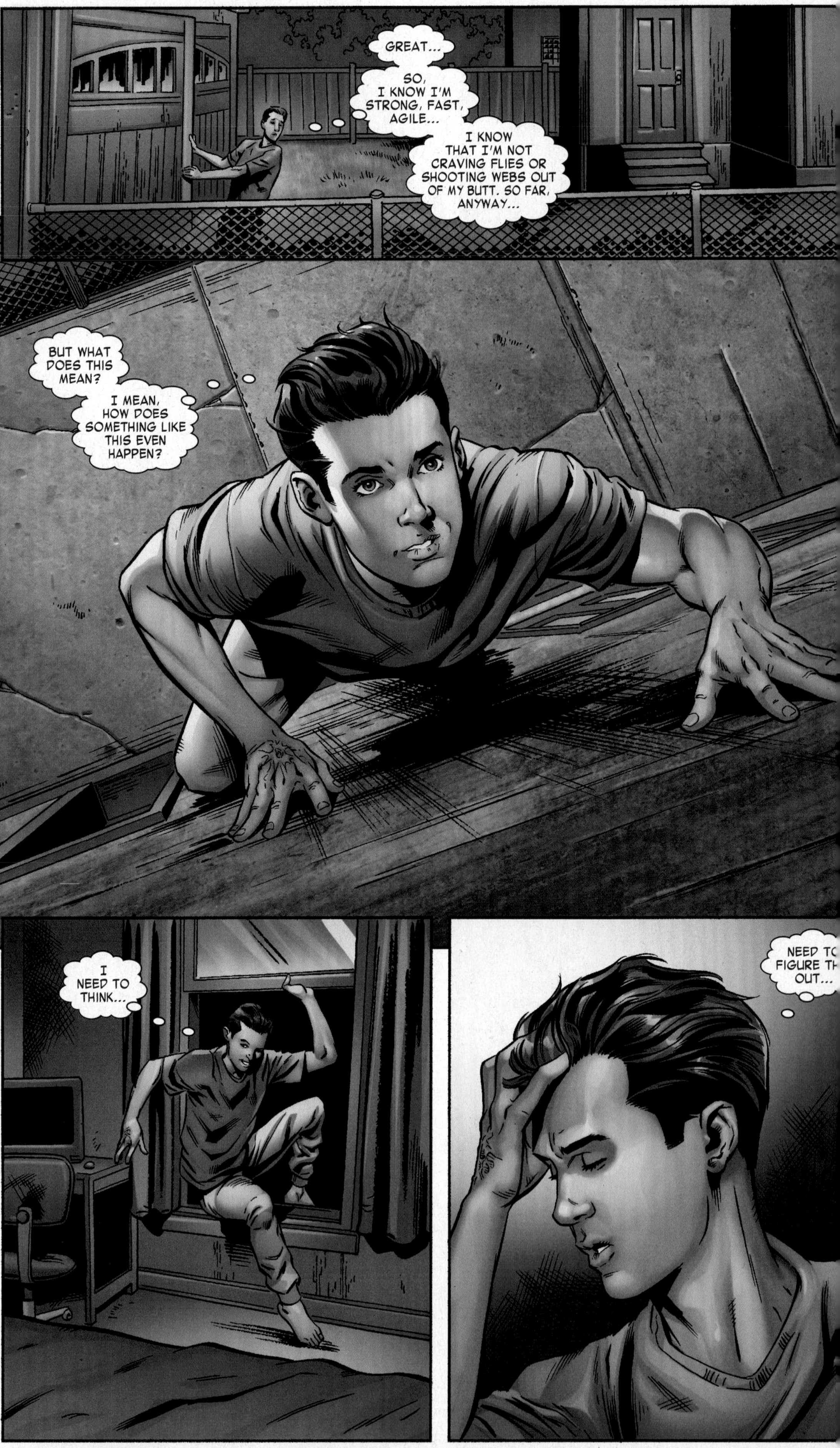
GREAT...
SO, I KNOW I'M STRONG, FAST, AGILE...
I KNOW THAT I'M NOT CRAVING FLIES OR SHOOTING WEBS OUT OF MY BUTT. SO FAR, ANYWAY...
BUT WHAT DOES THIS MEAN?
I MEAN, HOW DOES SOMETHING LIKE THIS EVEN HAPPEN?
I NEED TO THINK...
NEED TO FIGURE TH OUT...

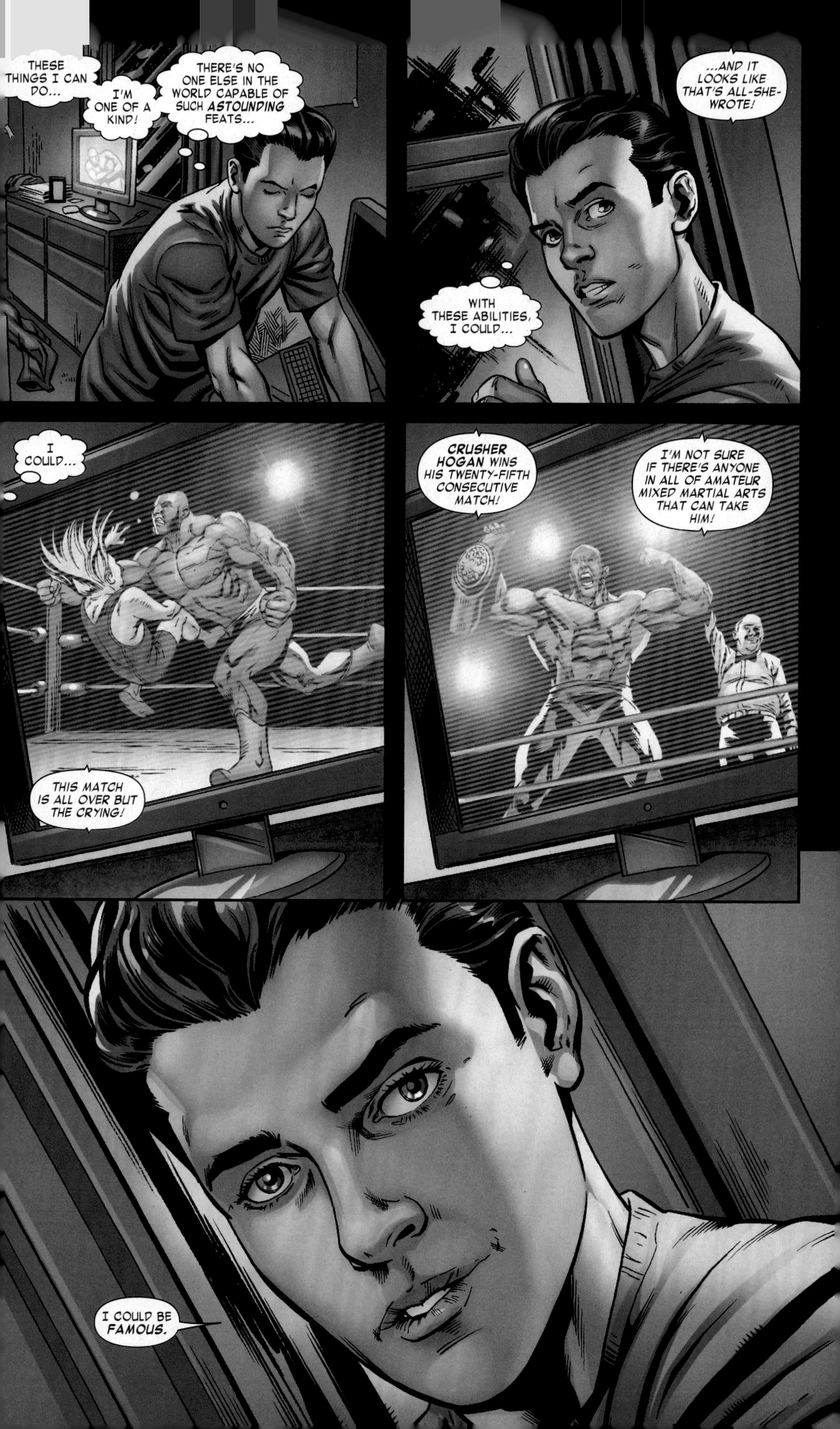
THESE THINGS I CAN DO...
I'M ONE OF A KIND!
THERE'S NO ONE ELSE IN THE WORLD CAPABLE OF SUCH ASTOUNDING FEATS...
...AND IT LOOKS LIKE THAT'S ALL-SHE-WROTE!
WITH THESE ABILITIES, I COULD...
I COULD...
THIS MATCH IS ALL OVER BUT THE CRYING!
CRUSHER HOGAN WINS HIS TWENTY-FIFTH CONSECUTIVE MATCH!
I'M NOT SURE IF THERE'S ANYONE IN ALL OF AMATEUR MIXED MARTIAL ARTS THAT CAN TAKE HIM!
I COULD BE FAMOUS.

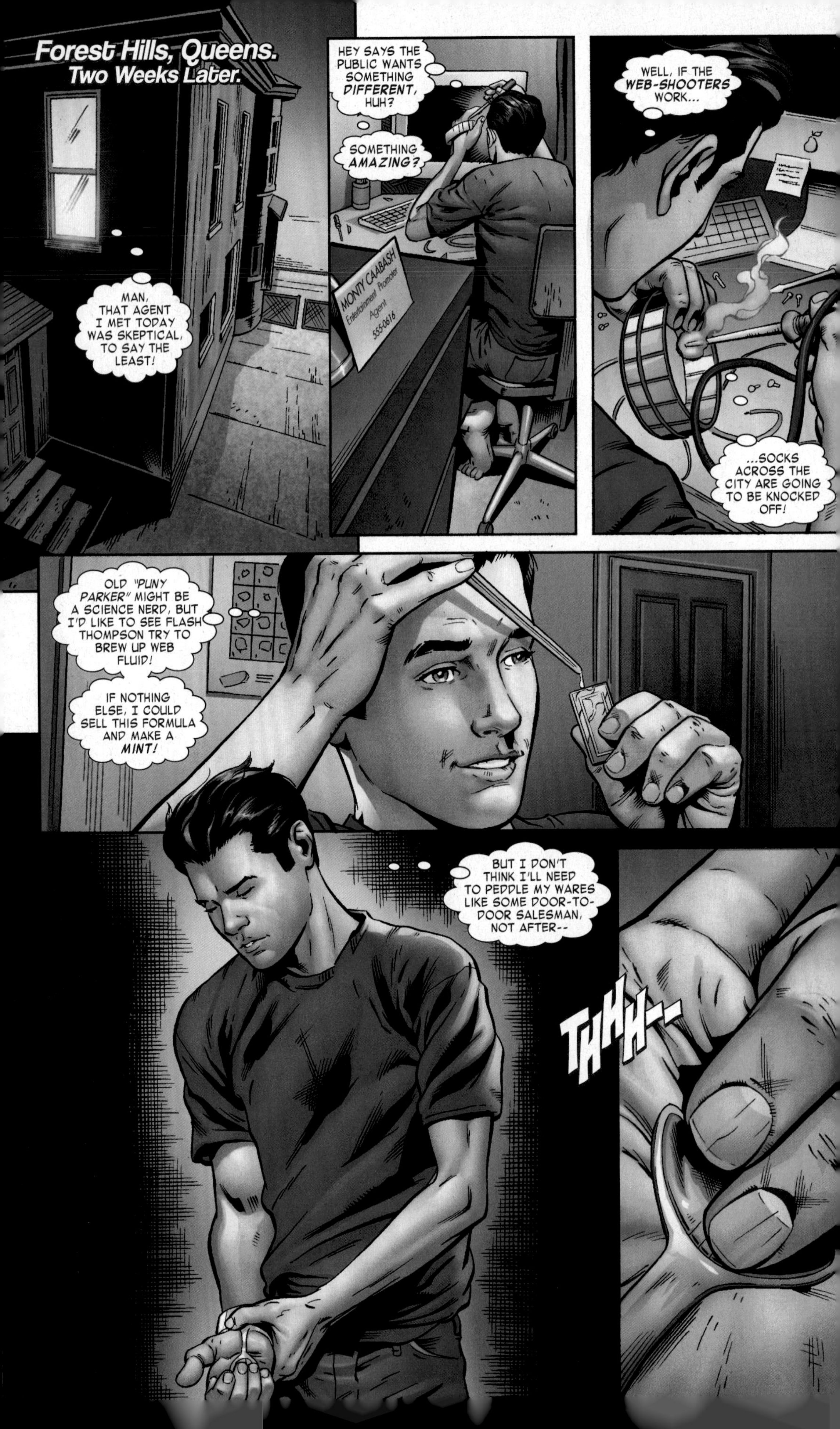
Forest Hills, Queens. Two Weeks Later.
MAN, THAT AGENT I MET TODAY WAS SKEPTICAL, TO SAY THE LEAST!
HEY SAYS THE PUBLIC WANTS SOMETHING DIFFERENT, HUH?
SOMETHING AMAZING?
MONTY CAABASH Entertainment Promoter Agent 555-0616
WELL, IF THE WEB-SHOOTERS WORK...
...SOCKS ACROSS THE CITY ARE GOING TO BE KNOCKED OFF!
OLD "PUNY PARKER" MIGHT BE A SCIENCE NERD, BUT I'D LIKE TO SEE FLASH THOMPSON TRY TO BREW UP WEB FLUID!
IF NOTHING ELSE, I COULD SELL THIS FORMULA AND MAKE A MINT!
BUT I DON'T THINK I'LL NEED TO PEDDLE MY WARES LIKE SOME DOOR-TO-DOOR SALESMAN, NOT AFTER--
THHH--

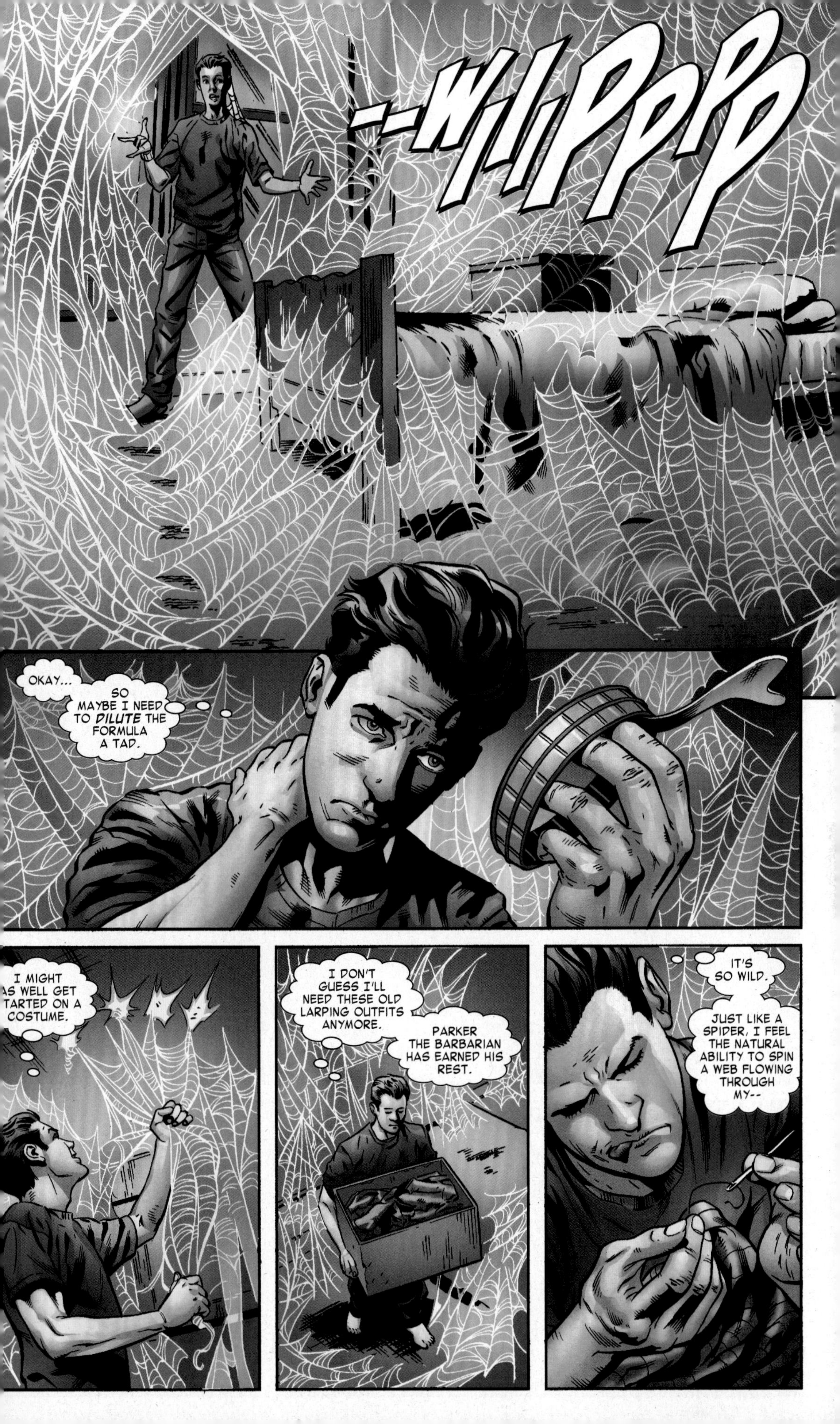
--WHIPPPP
OKAY...
SO MAYBE I NEED TO *DILUTE* THE FORMULA A TAD.
I MIGHT AS WELL GET TARTED ON A COSTUME.
I DON'T GUESS I'LL NEED THESE OLD LARPING OUTFITS ANYMORE.
PARKER THE BARBARIAN HAS EARNED HIS REST.
IT'S SO WILD.
JUST LIKE A SPIDER, I FEEL THE NATURAL ABILITY TO SPIN A WEB FLOWING THROUGH MY--

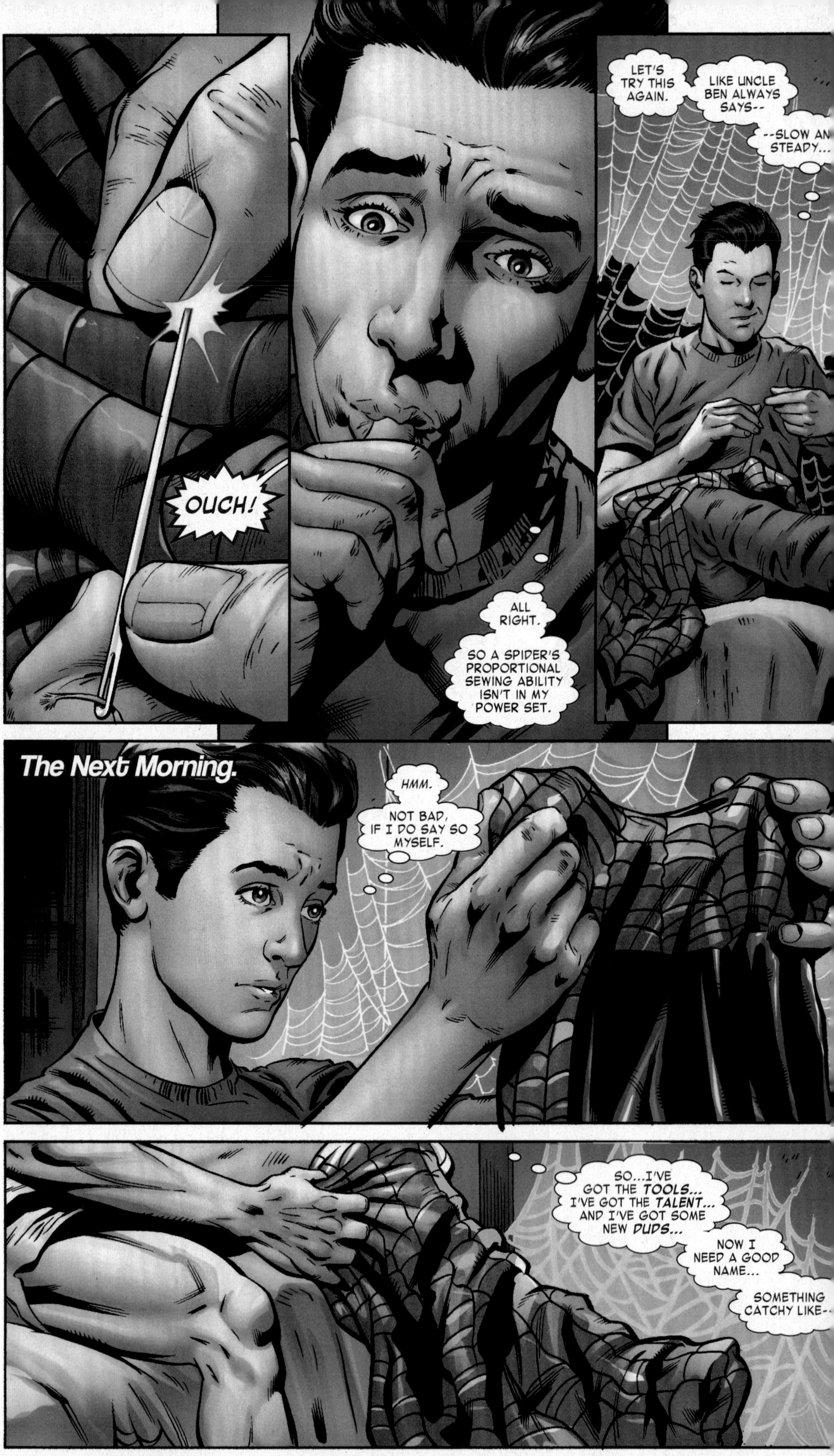
OUCH!
ALL RIGHT.
SO A SPIDER'S PROPORTIONAL SEWING ABILITY ISN'T IN MY POWER SET.
LET'S TRY THIS AGAIN.
LIKE UNCLE BEN ALWAYS SAYS--
--SLOW AN STEADY...
The Next Morning.
HMM.
NOT BAD, IF I DO SAY SO MYSELF.
SO...I'VE GOT THE TOOLS... I'VE GOT THE TALENT... AND I'VE GOT SOME NEW DUDS...
NOW I NEED A GOOD NAME...
SOMETHING CATCHY LIKE--

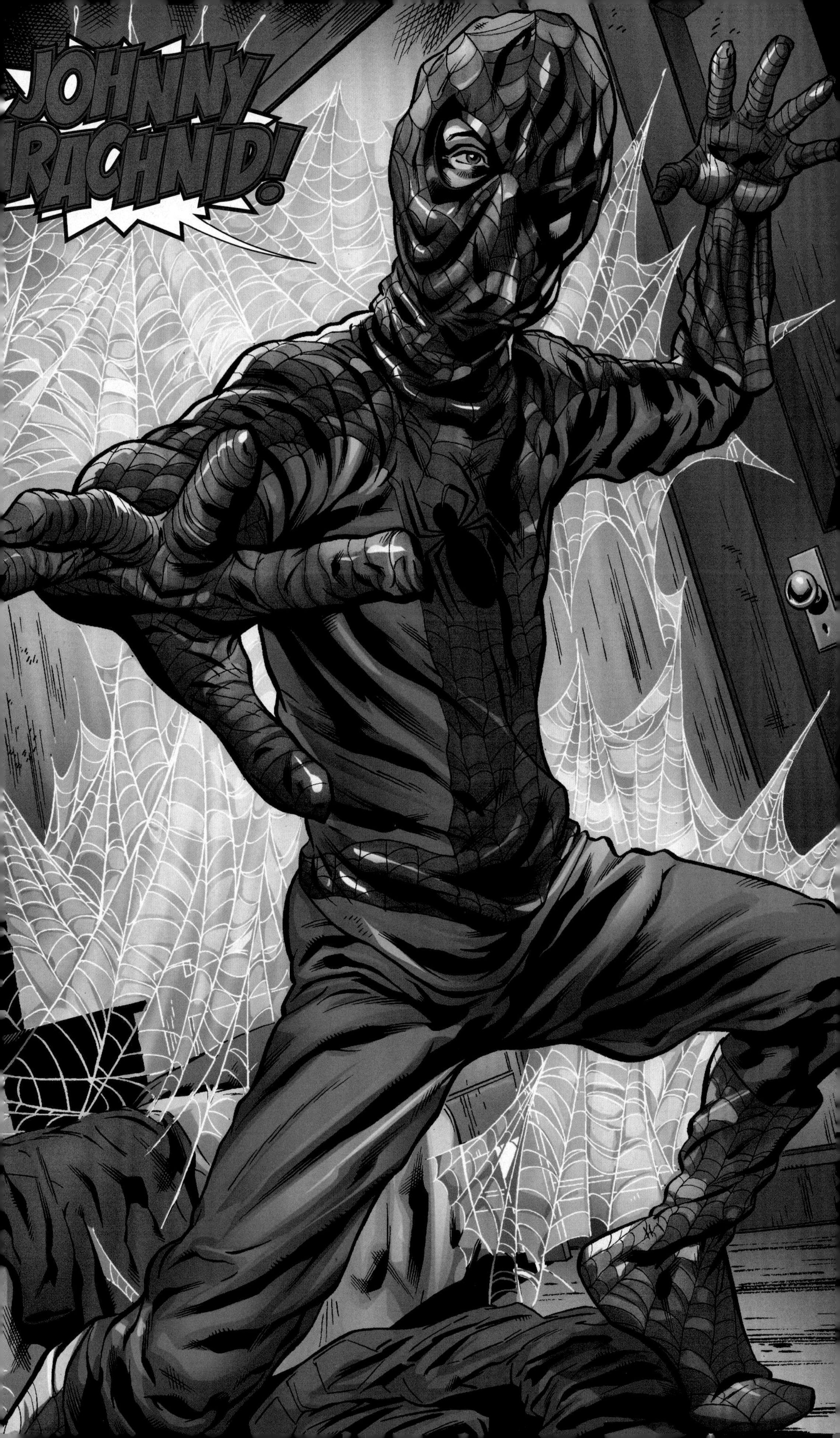
JOHNNY RACHNID!

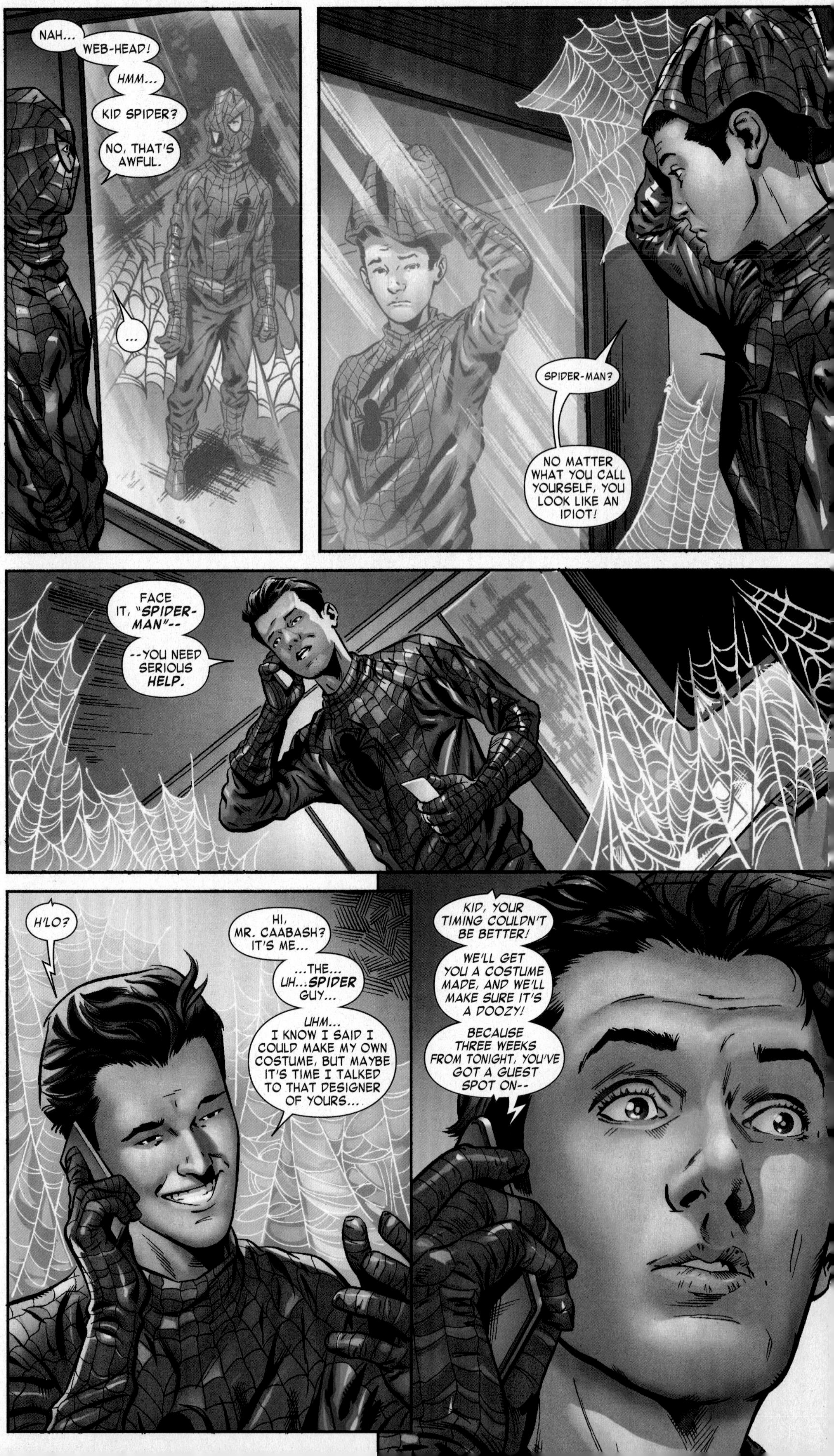
NAH...
WEB-HEAD!
HMM...
KID SPIDER?
NO, THAT'S AWFUL.
...
SPIDER-MAN?
NO MATTER WHAT YOU CALL YOURSELF, YOU LOOK LIKE AN IDIOT!
FACE IT, "SPIDER-MAN"--
--YOU NEED SERIOUS HELP.
H'LO?
HI, MR. CAABASH? IT'S ME...
...THE... UH...SPIDER GUY...
UHM... I KNOW I SAID I COULD MAKE MY OWN COSTUME, BUT MAYBE IT'S TIME I TALKED TO THAT DESIGNER OF YOURS...
KID, YOUR TIMING COULDN'T BE BETTER!
WE'LL GET YOU A COSTUME MADE, AND WE'LL MAKE SURE IT'S A DOOZY!
BECAUSE THREE WEEKS FROM TONIGHT, YOU'VE GOT A GUEST SPOT ON--

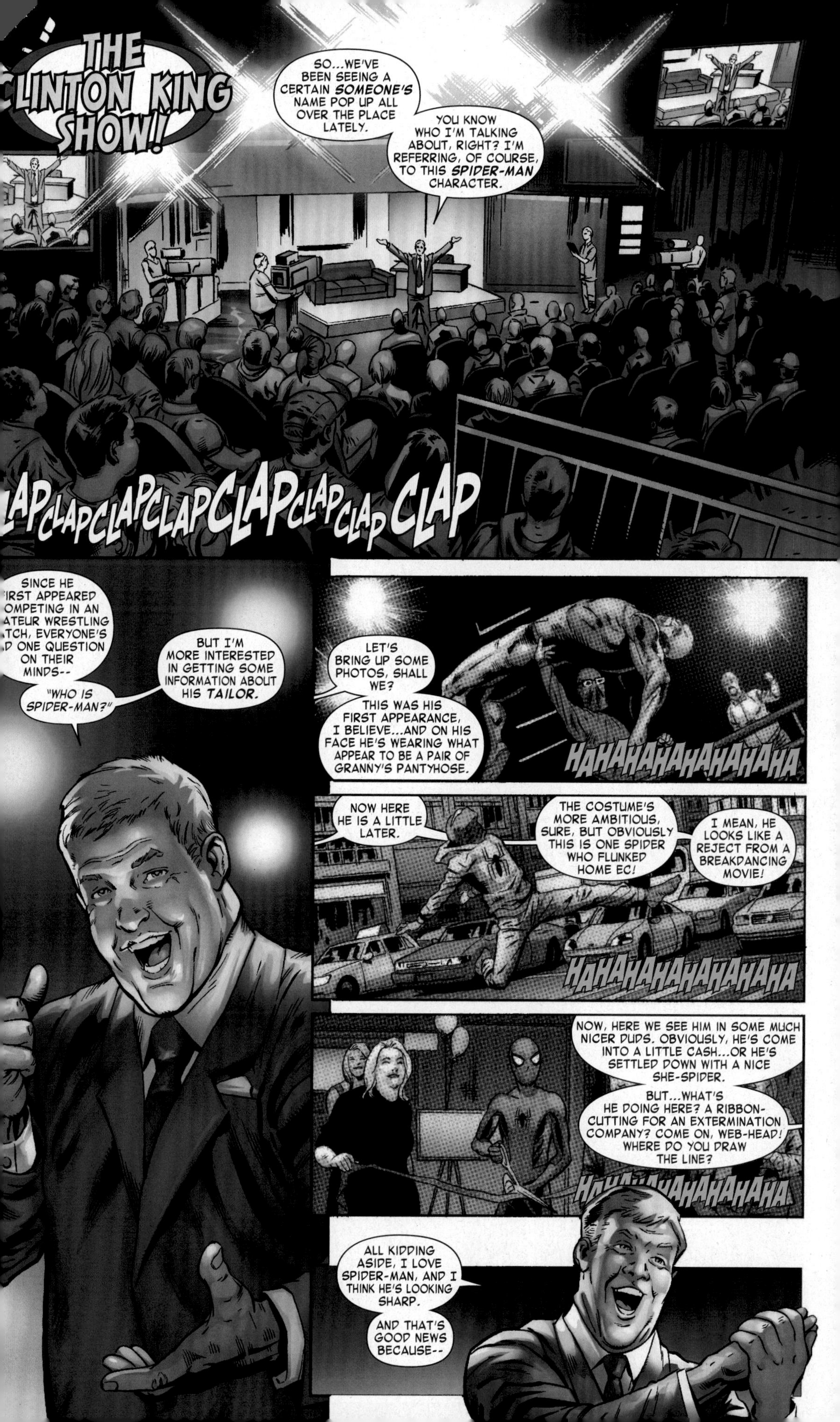
THE CLINTON KING SHOW!!
SO...WE'VE BEEN SEEING A CERTAIN SOMEONE'S NAME POP UP ALL OVER THE PLACE LATELY.
YOU KNOW WHO I'M TALKING ABOUT, RIGHT? I'M REFERRING, OF COURSE, TO THIS SPIDER-MAN CHARACTER.
LAP CLAP CLAP CLAP CLAP CLAP CLAP CLAP
SINCE HE FIRST APPEARED COMPETING IN AN ATEUR WRESTLING TCH, EVERYONE'S D ONE QUESTION ON THEIR MINDS--
"WHO IS SPIDER-MAN?"
BUT I'M MORE INTERESTED IN GETTING SOME INFORMATION ABOUT HIS TAILOR.
LET'S BRING UP SOME PHOTOS, SHALL WE?
THIS WAS HIS FIRST APPEARANCE, I BELIEVE...AND ON HIS FACE HE'S WEARING WHAT APPEAR TO BE A PAIR OF GRANNY'S PANTYHOSE.
HAHAHAHAHAHAHAHA
NOW HERE HE IS A LITTLE LATER.
THE COSTUME'S MORE AMBITIOUS, SURE, BUT OBVIOUSLY THIS IS ONE SPIDER WHO FLUNKED HOME EC!
I MEAN, HE LOOKS LIKE A REJECT FROM A BREAKDANCING MOVIE!
HAHAHAHAHAHAHAHA
NOW, HERE WE SEE HIM IN SOME MUCH NICER DUDS. OBVIOUSLY, HE'S COME INTO A LITTLE CASH...OR HE'S SETTLED DOWN WITH A NICE SHE-SPIDER.
BUT...WHAT'S HE DOING HERE? A RIBBON-CUTTING FOR AN EXTERMINATION COMPANY? COME ON, WEB-HEAD! WHERE DO YOU DRAW THE LINE?
HAHAHAHAHA
ALL KIDDING ASIDE, I LOVE SPIDER-MAN, AND I THINK HE'S LOOKING SHARP.
AND THAT'S GOOD NEWS BECAUSE--

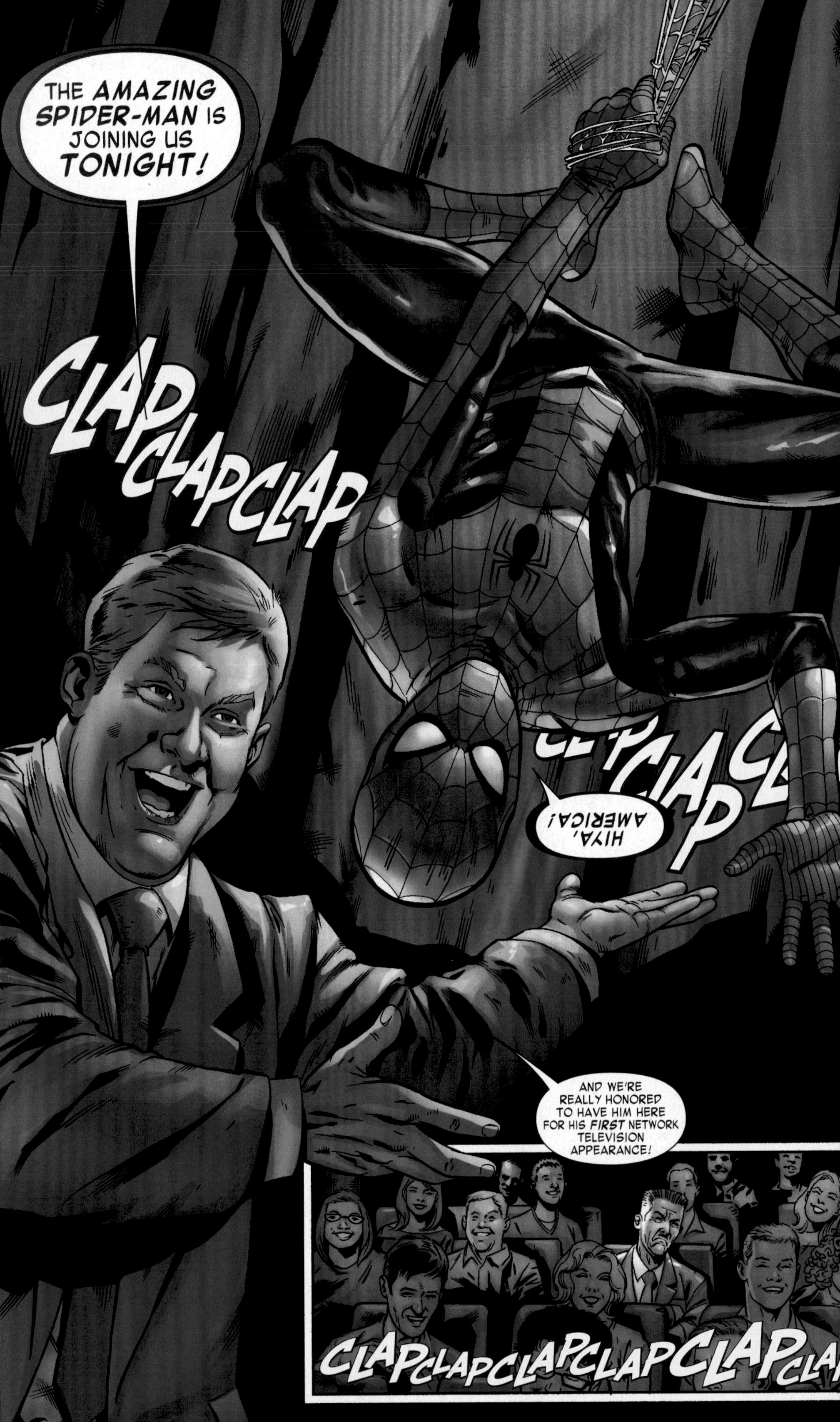
THE AMAZING SPIDER-MAN IS JOINING US TONIGHT!
CLAPCLAPCLAPCLAP
HIYA, AMERICA!
CLAPCLAP
AND WE'RE REALLY HONORED TO HAVE HIM HERE FOR HIS FIRST NETWORK TELEVISION APPEARANCE!
CLAPCLAPCLAPCLAPCLAP

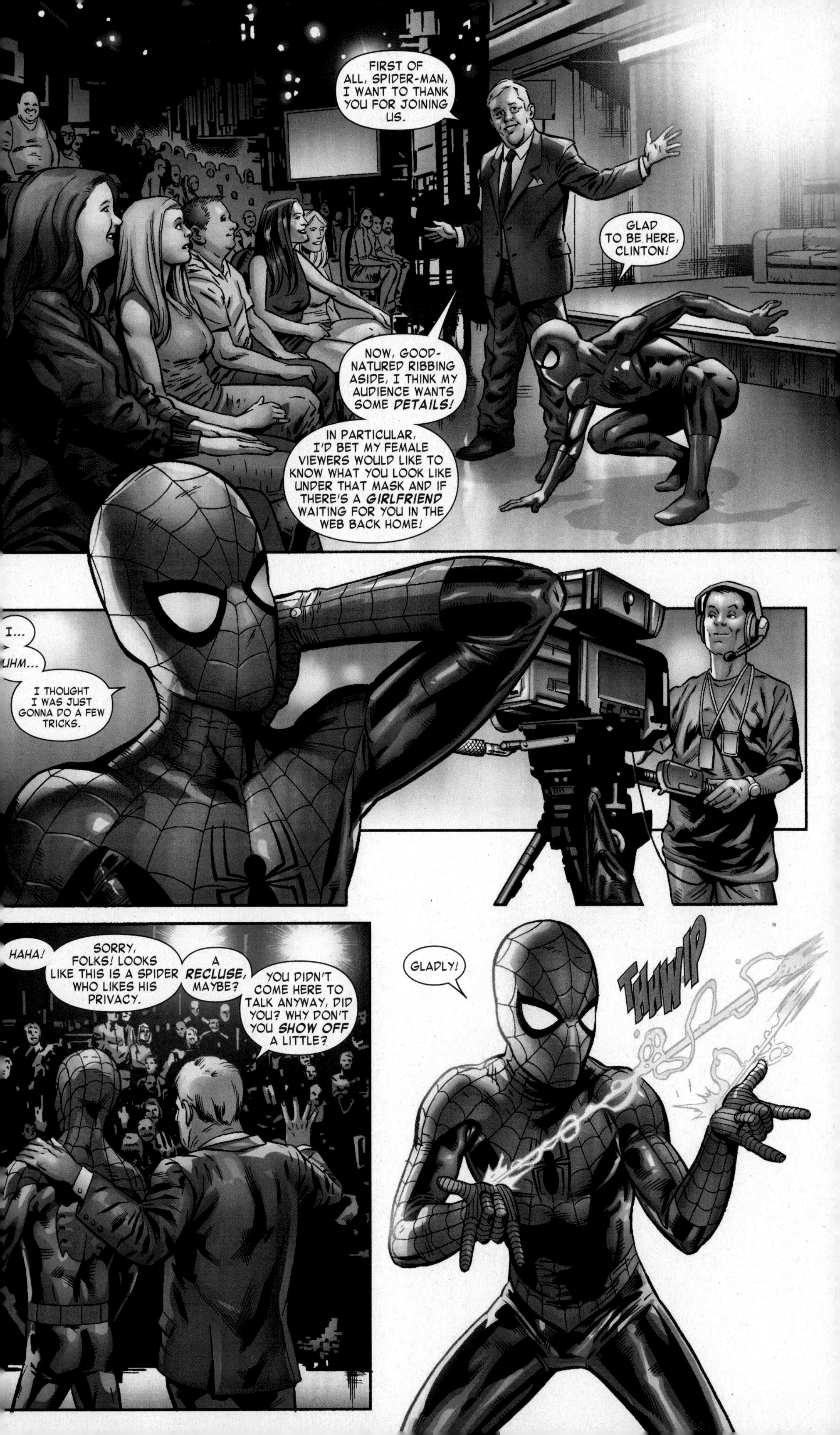
FIRST OF ALL, SPIDER-MAN, I WANT TO THANK YOU FOR JOINING US.
GLAD TO BE HERE, CLINTON!
NOW, GOOD-NATURED RIBBING ASIDE, I THINK MY AUDIENCE WANTS SOME DETAILS!
IN PARTICULAR, I'D BET MY FEMALE VIEWERS WOULD LIKE TO KNOW WHAT YOU LOOK LIKE UNDER THAT MASK AND IF THERE'S A GIRLFRIEND WAITING FOR YOU IN THE WEB BACK HOME!
I...
UHM...
I THOUGHT I WAS JUST GONNA DO A FEW TRICKS.
HAHA!
SORRY, FOLKS! LOOKS LIKE THIS IS A SPIDER WHO LIKES HIS PRIVACY.
A RECLUSE, MAYBE?
YOU DIDN'T COME HERE TO TALK ANYWAY, DID YOU? WHY DON'T YOU SHOW OFF A LITTLE?
GLADLY!
THWIP

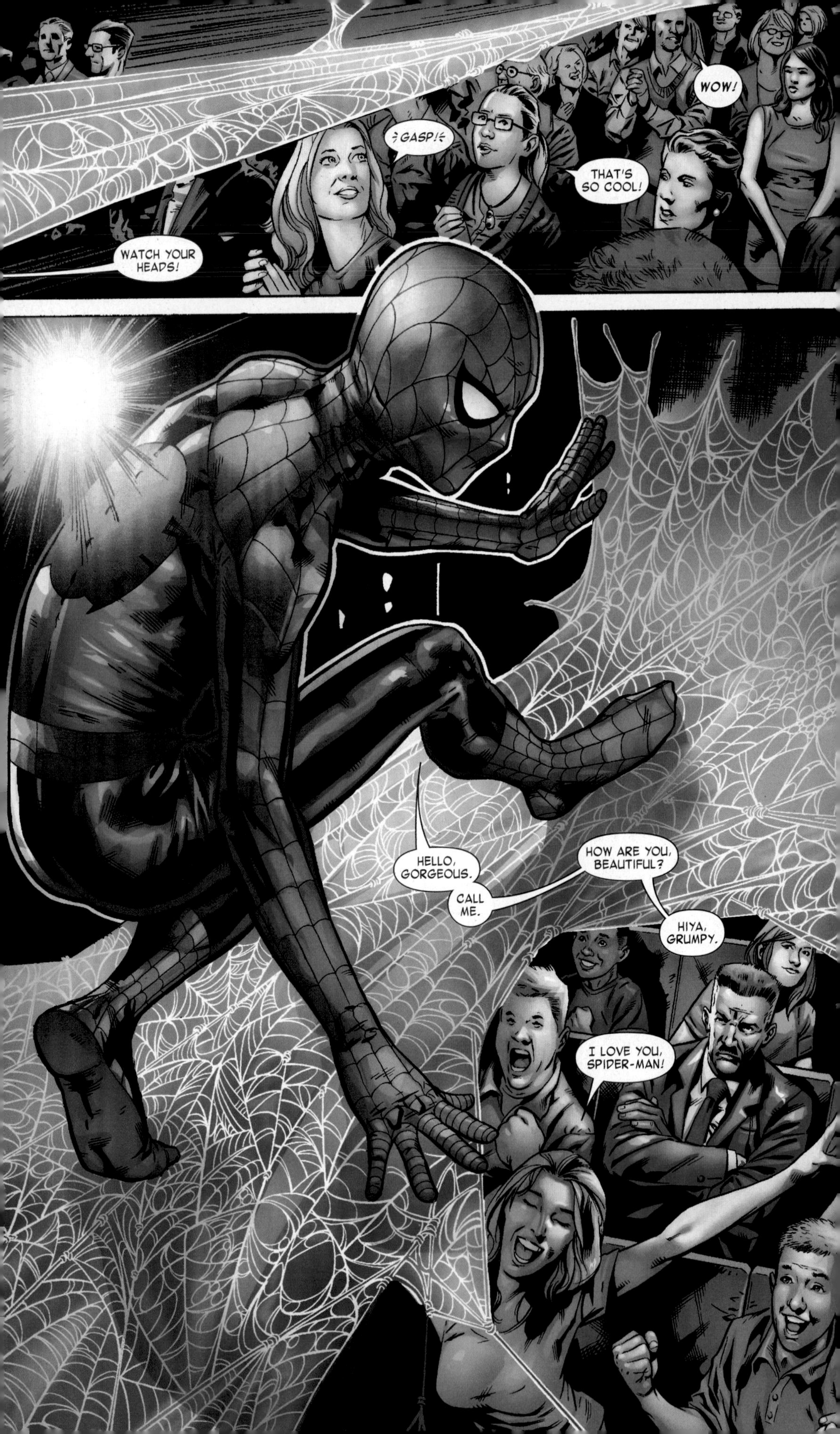

WOW!
GASP!
THAT'S SO COOL!
WATCH YOUR HEADS!
HELLO, GORGEOUS.
CALL ME.
HOW ARE YOU, BEAUTIFUL?
HIYA, GRUMPY.
I LOVE YOU, SPIDER-MAN!

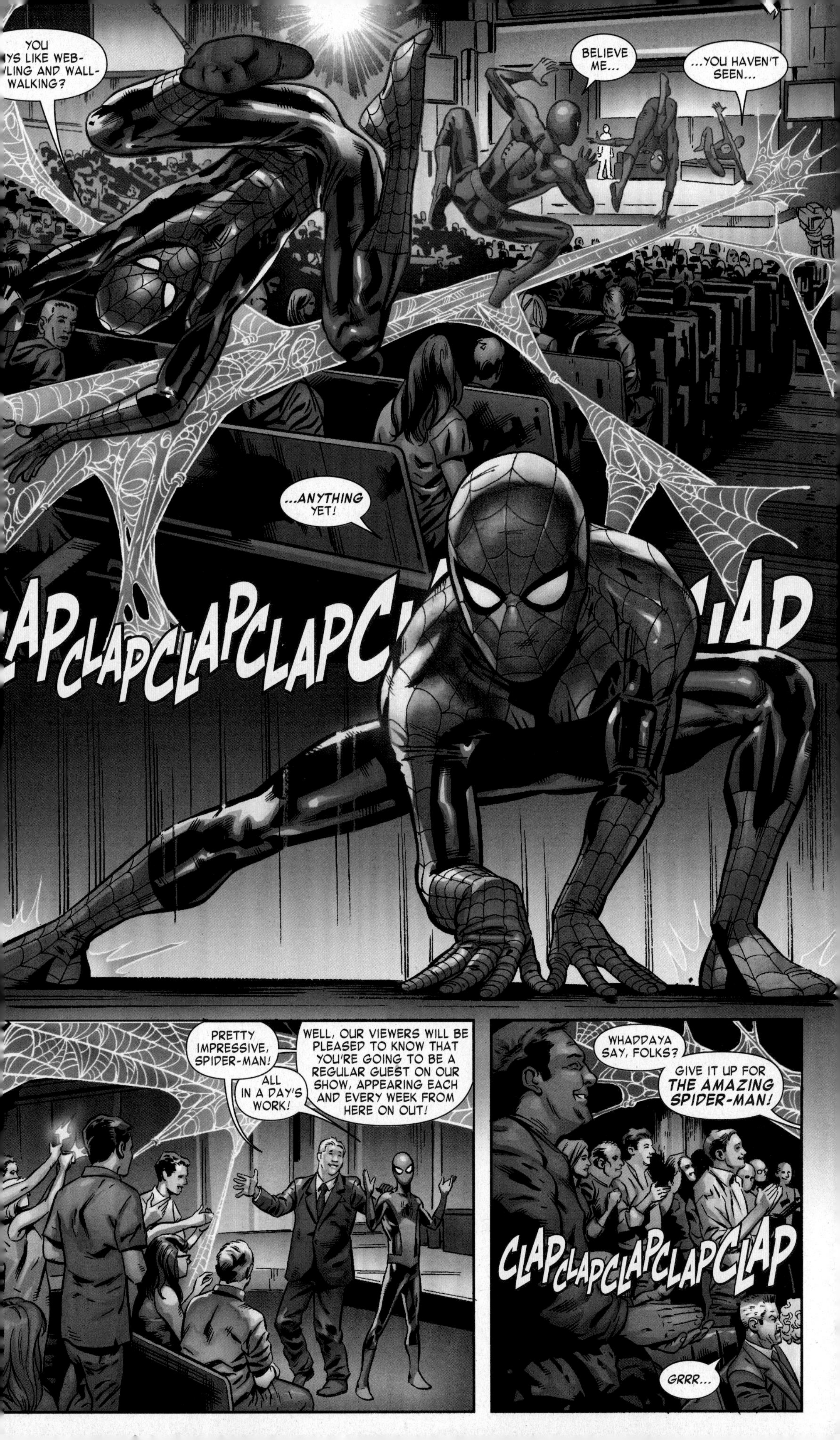
YOU
YS LIKE WEB-
LING AND WALL-
WALKING?
BELIEVE ME...
...YOU HAVEN'T SEEN...
...ANYTHING YET!
CLAPCLAPCLAPCLAPC
AP
PRETTY IMPRESSIVE, SPIDER-MAN!
ALL IN A DAY'S WORK!
WELL, OUR VIEWERS WILL BE PLEASED TO KNOW THAT YOU'RE GOING TO BE A REGULAR GUEST ON OUR SHOW, APPEARING EACH AND EVERY WEEK FROM HERE ON OUT!
WHADDAYA SAY, FOLKS?
GIVE IT UP FOR THE AMAZING SPIDER-MAN!
CLAPCLAPCLAPCLAPCLAP
GRRR...

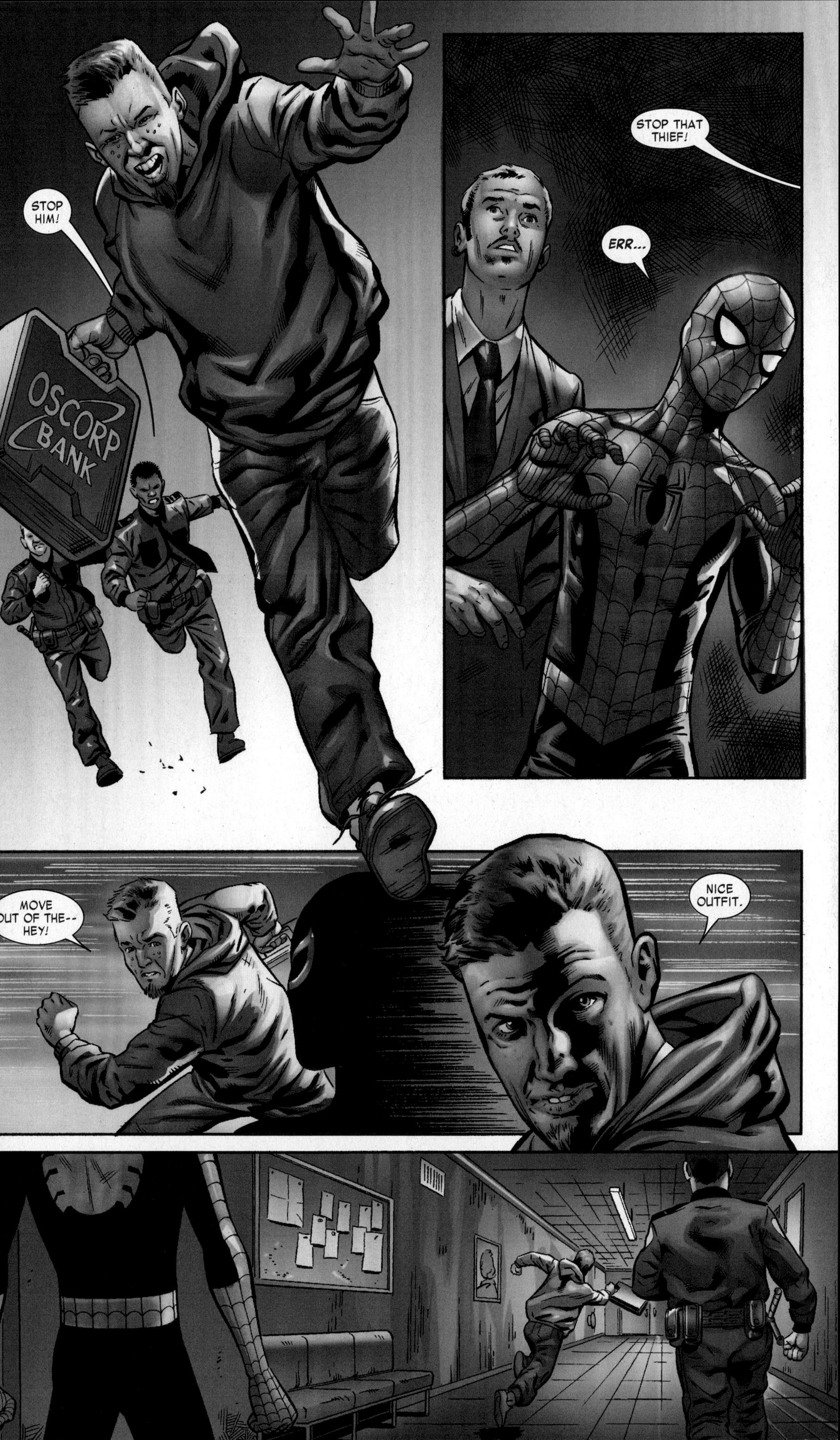

STOP HIM!
OSCORP BANK
STOP THAT THIEF!
ERR...
MOVE OUT OF THE-- HEY!
NICE OUTFIT.

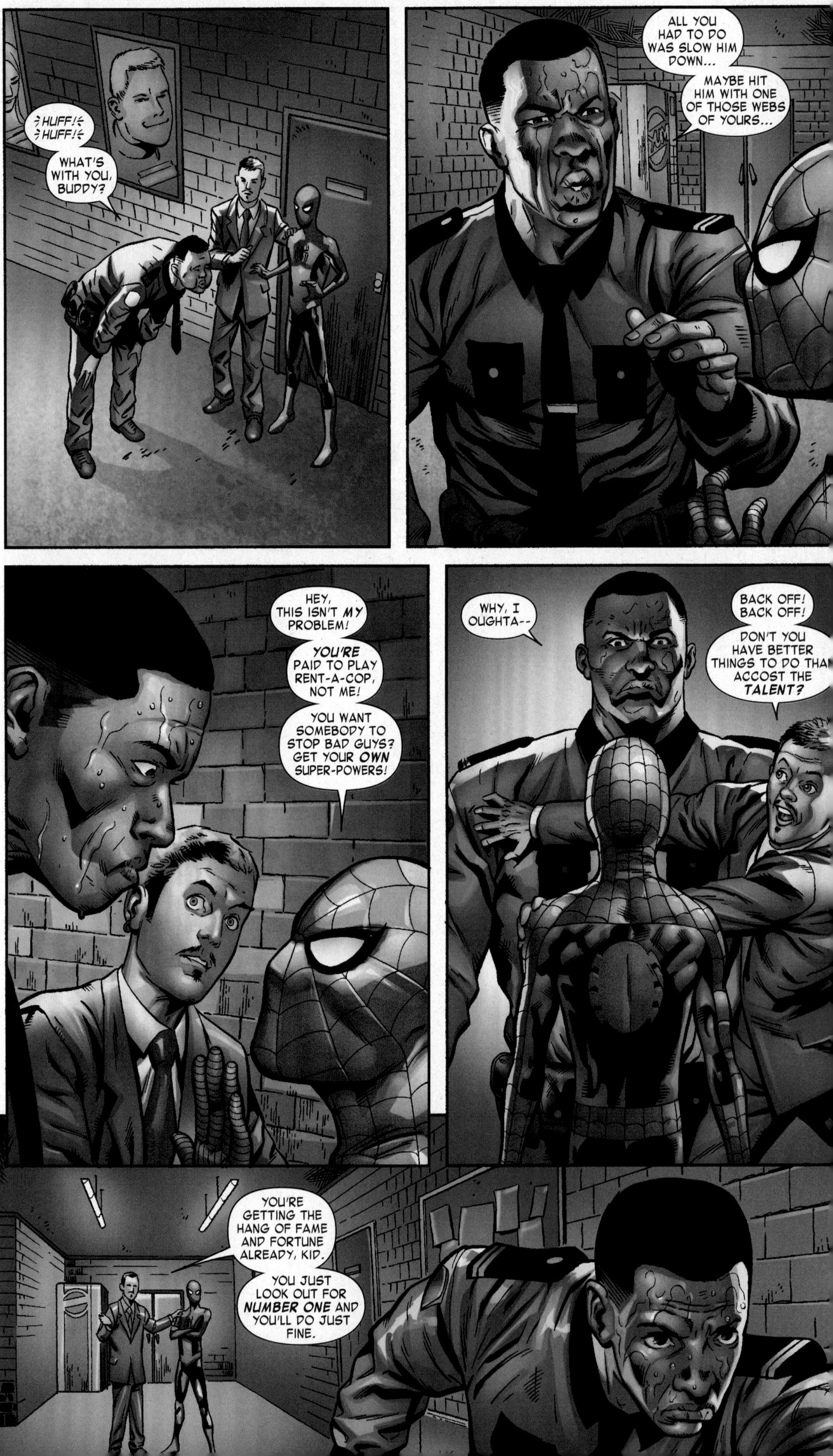
HUFF! HUFF!
WHAT'S WITH YOU, BUDDY?
ALL YOU HAD TO DO WAS SLOW HIM DOWN...
MAYBE HIT HIM WITH ONE OF THOSE WEBS OF YOURS...
HEY, THIS ISN'T MY PROBLEM!
YOU'RE PAID TO PLAY RENT-A-COP, NOT ME!
YOU WANT SOMEBODY TO STOP BAD GUYS? GET YOUR OWN SUPER-POWERS!
WHY, I OUGHTA--
BACK OFF! BACK OFF!
DON'T YOU HAVE BETTER THINGS TO DO THA ACCOST THE TALENT?
YOU'RE GETTING THE HANG OF FAME AND FORTUNE ALREADY, KID.
YOU JUST LOOK OUT FOR NUMBER ONE AND YOU'LL DO JUST FINE.

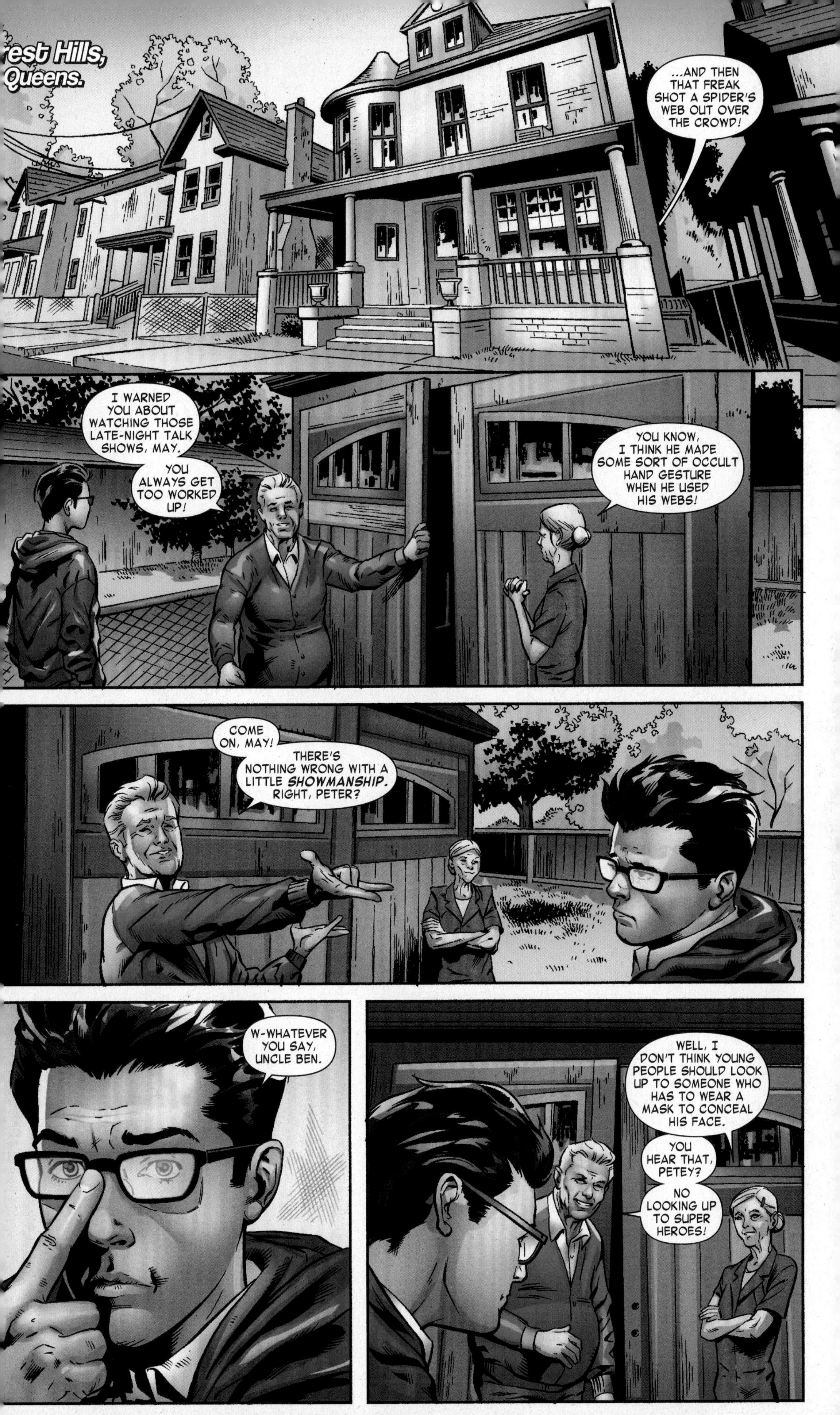
rest Hills,
Queens.
...AND THEN THAT FREAK SHOT A SPIDER'S WEB OUT OVER THE CROWD!
I WARNED YOU ABOUT WATCHING THOSE LATE-NIGHT TALK SHOWS, MAY.
YOU ALWAYS GET TOO WORKED UP!
YOU KNOW, I THINK HE MADE SOME SORT OF OCCULT HAND GESTURE WHEN HE USED HIS WEBS!
COME ON, MAY!
THERE'S NOTHING WRONG WITH A LITTLE SHOWMANSHIP. RIGHT, PETER?
W-WHATEVER YOU SAY, UNCLE BEN.
WELL, I DON'T THINK YOUNG PEOPLE SHOULD LOOK UP TO SOMEONE WHO HAS TO WEAR A MASK TO CONCEAL HIS FACE.
YOU HEAR THAT, PETEY?
NO LOOKING UP TO SUPER HEROES!

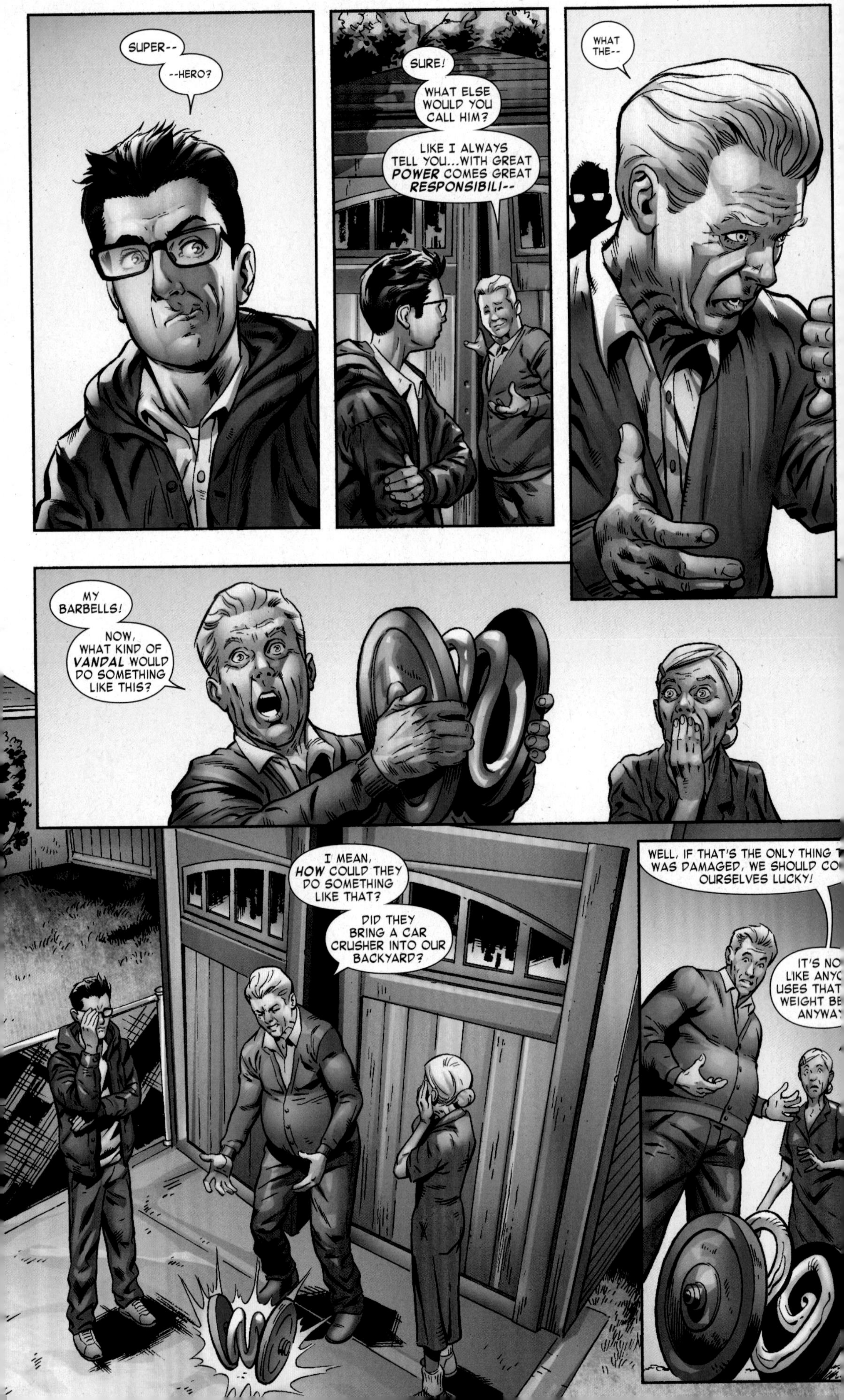
SUPER--
--HERO?
SURE!
WHAT ELSE WOULD YOU CALL HIM?
LIKE I ALWAYS TELL YOU...WITH GREAT POWER COMES GREAT RESPONSIBILI--
WHAT THE--
MY BARBELLS!
NOW, WHAT KIND OF VANDAL WOULD DO SOMETHING LIKE THIS?
I MEAN, HOW COULD THEY DO SOMETHING LIKE THAT?
DID THEY BRING A CAR CRUSHER INTO OUR BACKYARD?
WELL, IF THAT'S THE ONLY THING T
WAS DAMAGED, WE SHOULD CO
OURSELVES LUCKY!
IT'S NO
LIKE ANYO
USES THAT
WEIGHT BE
ANYWAY

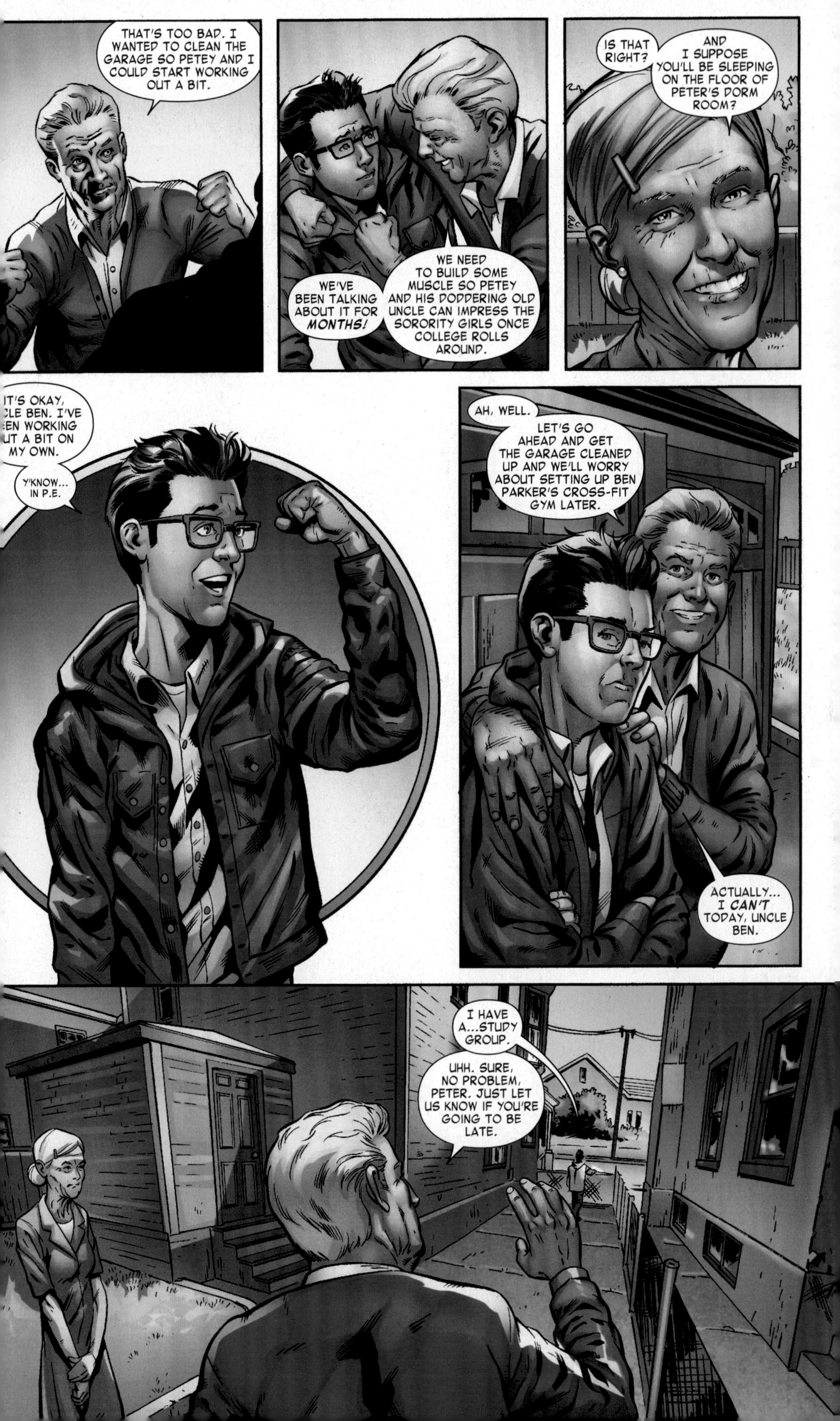
THAT'S TOO BAD. I WANTED TO CLEAN THE GARAGE SO PETEY AND I COULD START WORKING OUT A BIT.
WE'VE BEEN TALKING ABOUT IT FOR *MONTHS!*
WE NEED TO BUILD SOME MUSCLE SO PETEY AND HIS DODDERING OLD UNCLE CAN IMPRESS THE SORORITY GIRLS ONCE COLLEGE ROLLS AROUND.
IS THAT RIGHT?
AND I SUPPOSE YOU'LL BE SLEEPING ON THE FLOOR OF PETER'S DORM ROOM?
IT'S OKAY, CLE BEN. I'VE EEN WORKING UT A BIT ON MY OWN.
Y'KNOW... IN P.E.
AH, WELL.
LET'S GO AHEAD AND GET THE GARAGE CLEANED UP AND WE'LL WORRY ABOUT SETTING UP BEN PARKER'S CROSS-FIT GYM LATER.
ACTUALLY... I *CAN'T* TODAY, UNCLE BEN.
I HAVE A...STUDY GROUP.
UHH. SURE, NO PROBLEM, PETER. JUST LET US KNOW IF YOU'RE GOING TO BE LATE.

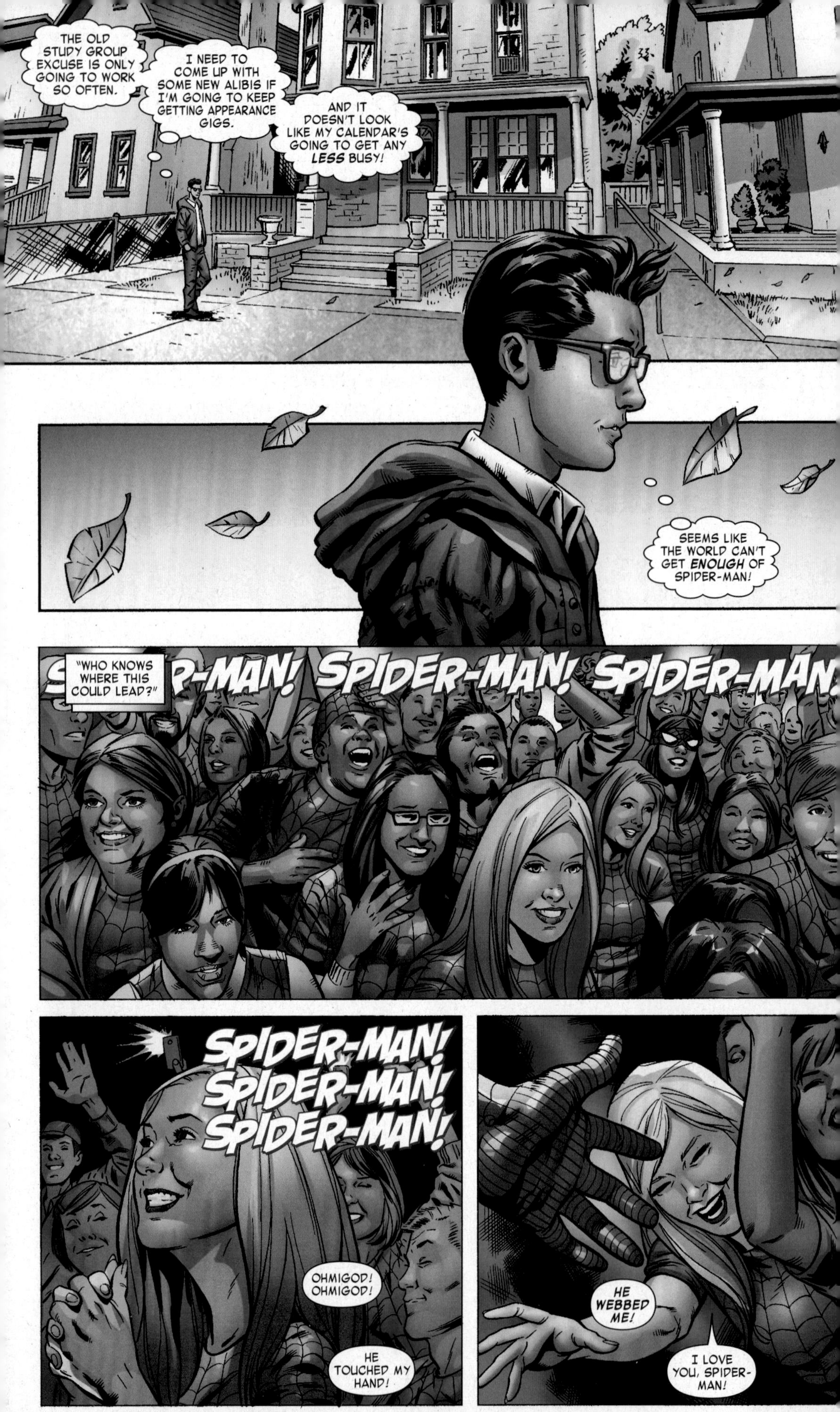

THE OLD STUDY GROUP EXCUSE IS ONLY GOING TO WORK SO OFTEN.
I NEED TO COME UP WITH SOME NEW ALIBIS IF I'M GOING TO KEEP GETTING APPEARANCE GIGS.
AND IT DOESN'T LOOK LIKE MY CALENDAR'S GOING TO GET ANY *LESS* BUSY!
SEEMS LIKE THE WORLD CAN'T GET *ENOUGH* OF SPIDER-MAN!
"WHO KNOWS WHERE THIS COULD LEAD?"
-MAN! SPIDER-MAN! SPIDER-MAN!
SPIDER-MAN! SPIDER-MAN! SPIDER-MAN!
OHMIGOD! OHMIGOD!
HE TOUCHED MY HAND!
HE WEBBED ME!
I LOVE YOU, SPIDER-MAN!

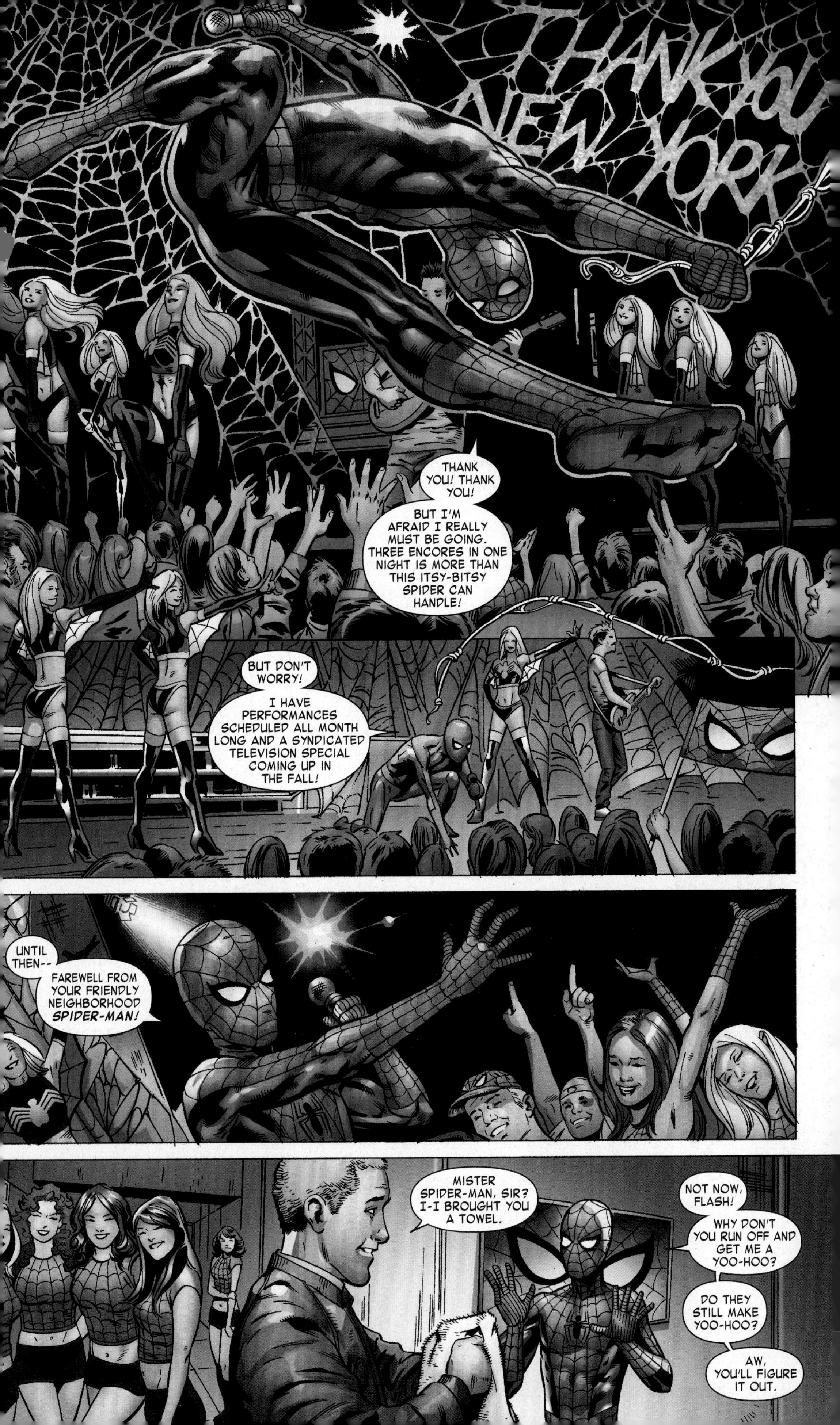
THANK YOU NEW YORK
THANK YOU! THANK YOU!
BUT I'M AFRAID I REALLY MUST BE GOING. THREE ENCORES IN ONE NIGHT IS MORE THAN THIS ITSY-BITSY SPIDER CAN HANDLE!
BUT DON'T WORRY!
I HAVE PERFORMANCES SCHEDULED ALL MONTH LONG AND A SYNDICATED TELEVISION SPECIAL COMING UP IN THE FALL!
UNTIL THEN--
FAREWELL FROM YOUR FRIENDLY NEIGHBORHOOD SPIDER-MAN!
MISTER SPIDER-MAN, SIR? I-I BROUGHT YOU A TOWEL.
NOT NOW, FLASH!
WHY DON'T YOU RUN OFF AND GET ME A YOO-HOO?
DO THEY STILL MAKE YOO-HOO?
AW, YOU'LL FIGURE IT OUT.

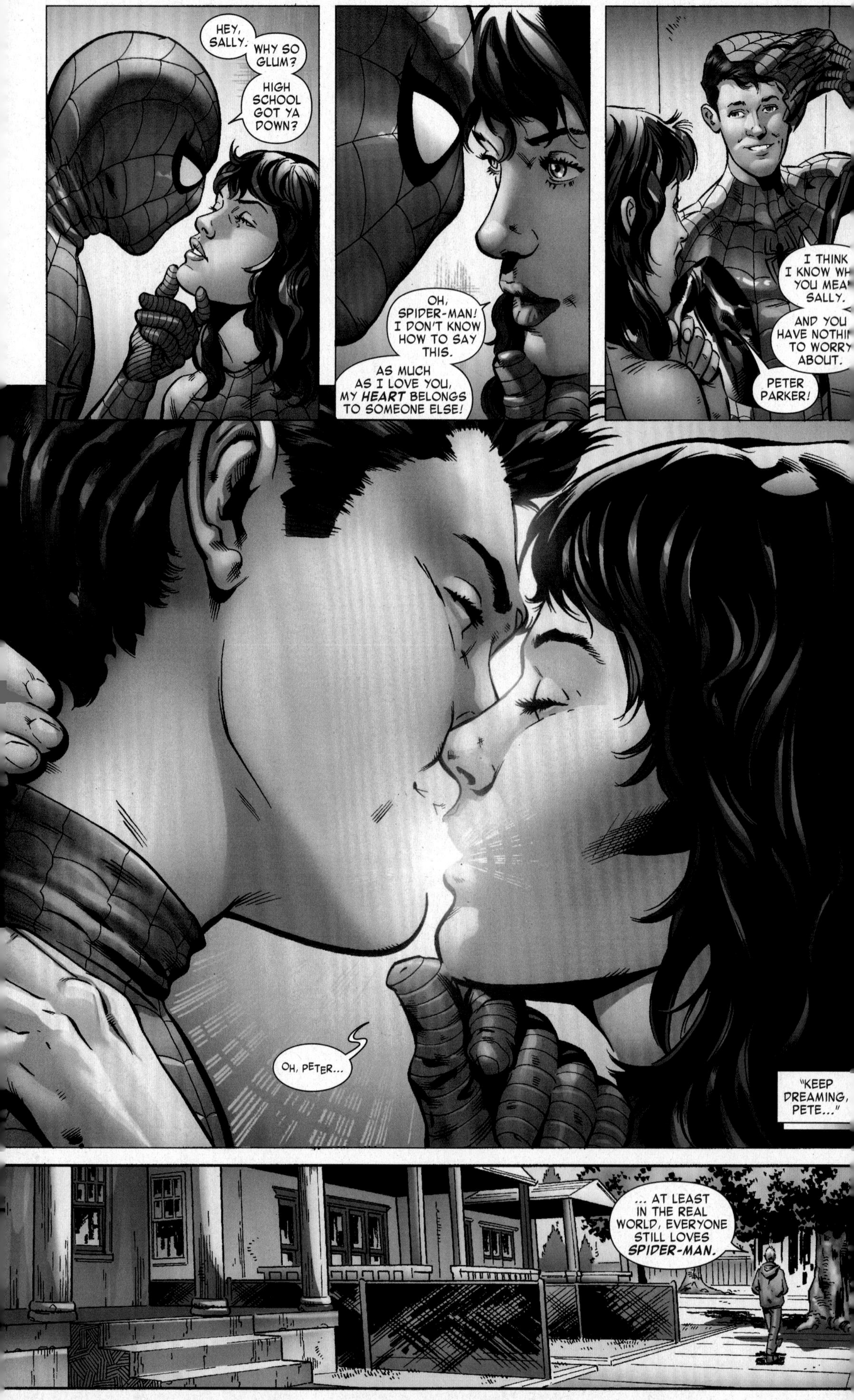

HEY, SALLY.
WHY SO GLUM?
HIGH SCHOOL GOT YA DOWN?
OH, SPIDER-MAN! I DON'T KNOW HOW TO SAY THIS.
AS MUCH AS I LOVE YOU, MY HEART BELONGS TO SOMEONE ELSE!
I THINK I KNOW WH YOU MEA SALLY.
AND YOU HAVE NOTHI TO WORRY ABOUT.
PETER PARKER!
OH, PETER...
"KEEP DREAMING, PETE..."
... AT LEAST IN THE REAL WORLD, EVERYONE STILL LOVES SPIDER-MAN.

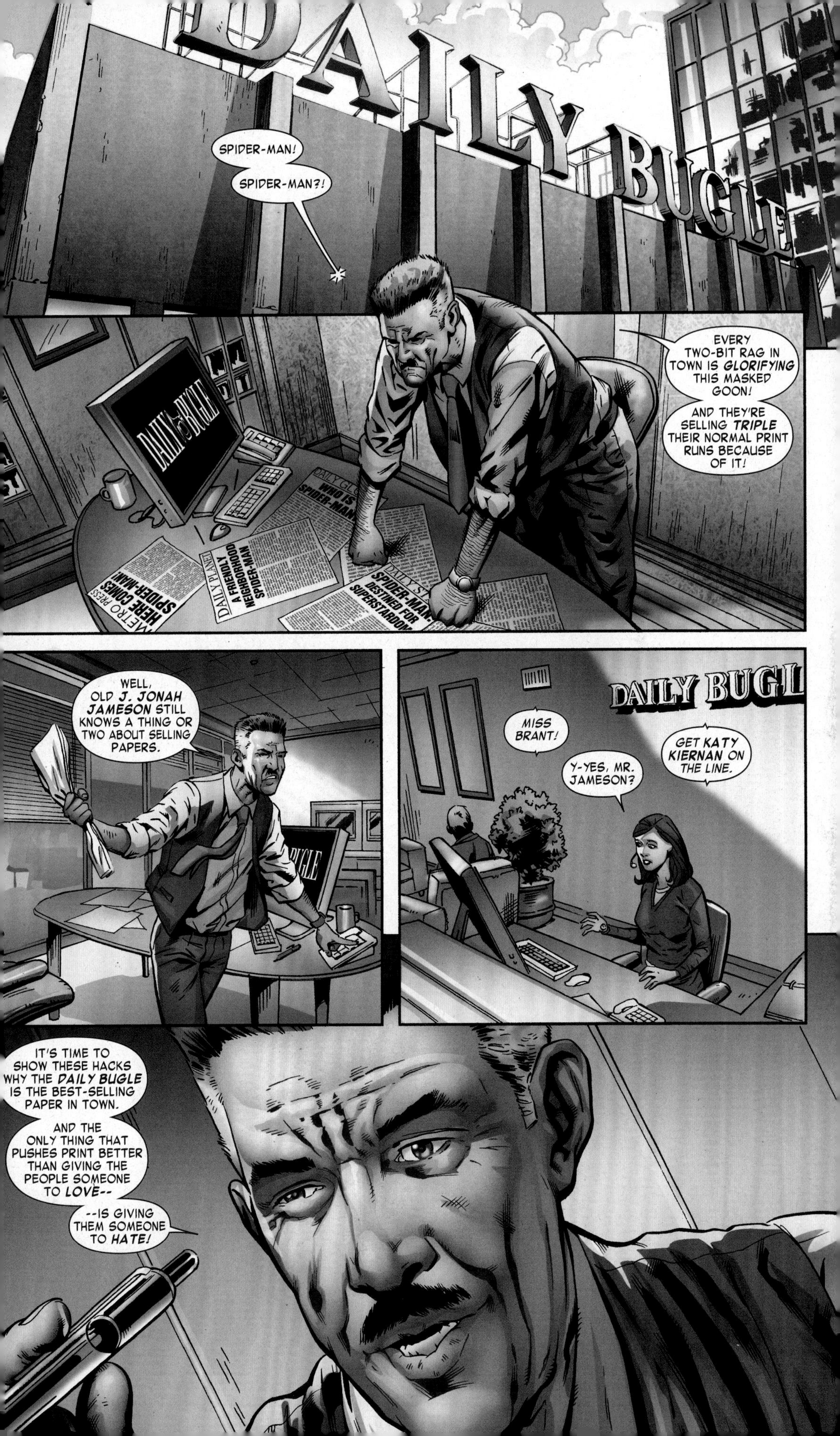
DAILY BUGLE
SPIDER-MAN!
SPIDER-MAN?!
EVERY TWO-BIT RAG IN TOWN IS *GLORIFYING* THIS MASKED GOON!
AND THEY'RE SELLING *TRIPLE* THEIR NORMAL PRINT RUNS BECAUSE OF IT!
DAILY BUGLE
WHO IS SPIDER-MAN
DAILY PLANET
A FRIENDLY NEIGHBORHOOD SPIDER-MAN
HERE COMES SPIDER-MAN
WELL, OLD *J. JONAH JAMESON* STILL KNOWS A THING OR TWO ABOUT SELLING PAPERS.
MISS BRANT!
Y-YES, MR. JAMESON?
GET *KATY KIERNAN* ON THE LINE.
IT'S TIME TO SHOW THESE HACKS WHY THE *DAILY BUGLE* IS THE BEST-SELLING PAPER IN TOWN.
AND THE ONLY THING THAT PUSHES PRINT BETTER THAN GIVING THE PEOPLE SOMEONE TO *LOVE*--
--IS GIVING THEM SOMEONE TO *HATE!*

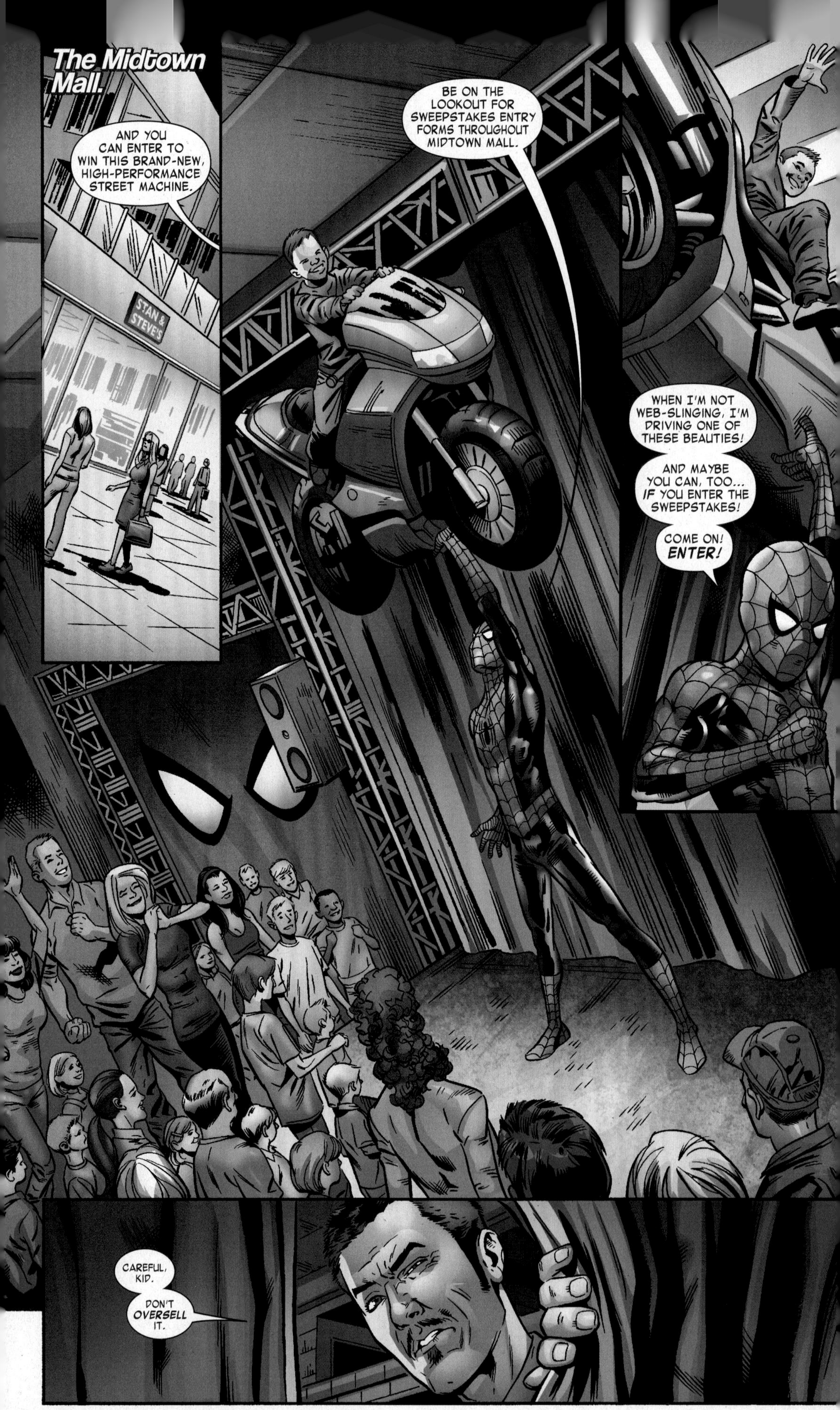

The Midtown Mall.
AND YOU CAN ENTER TO WIN THIS BRAND-NEW, HIGH-PERFORMANCE STREET MACHINE.
STAN & STEVE'S
BE ON THE LOOKOUT FOR SWEEPSTAKES ENTRY FORMS THROUGHOUT MIDTOWN MALL.
WHEN I'M NOT WEB-SLINGING, I'M DRIVING ONE OF THESE BEAUTIES!
AND MAYBE YOU CAN, TOO... IF YOU ENTER THE SWEEPSTAKES!
COME ON! ENTER!
CAREFUL, KID.
DON'T OVERSELL IT.

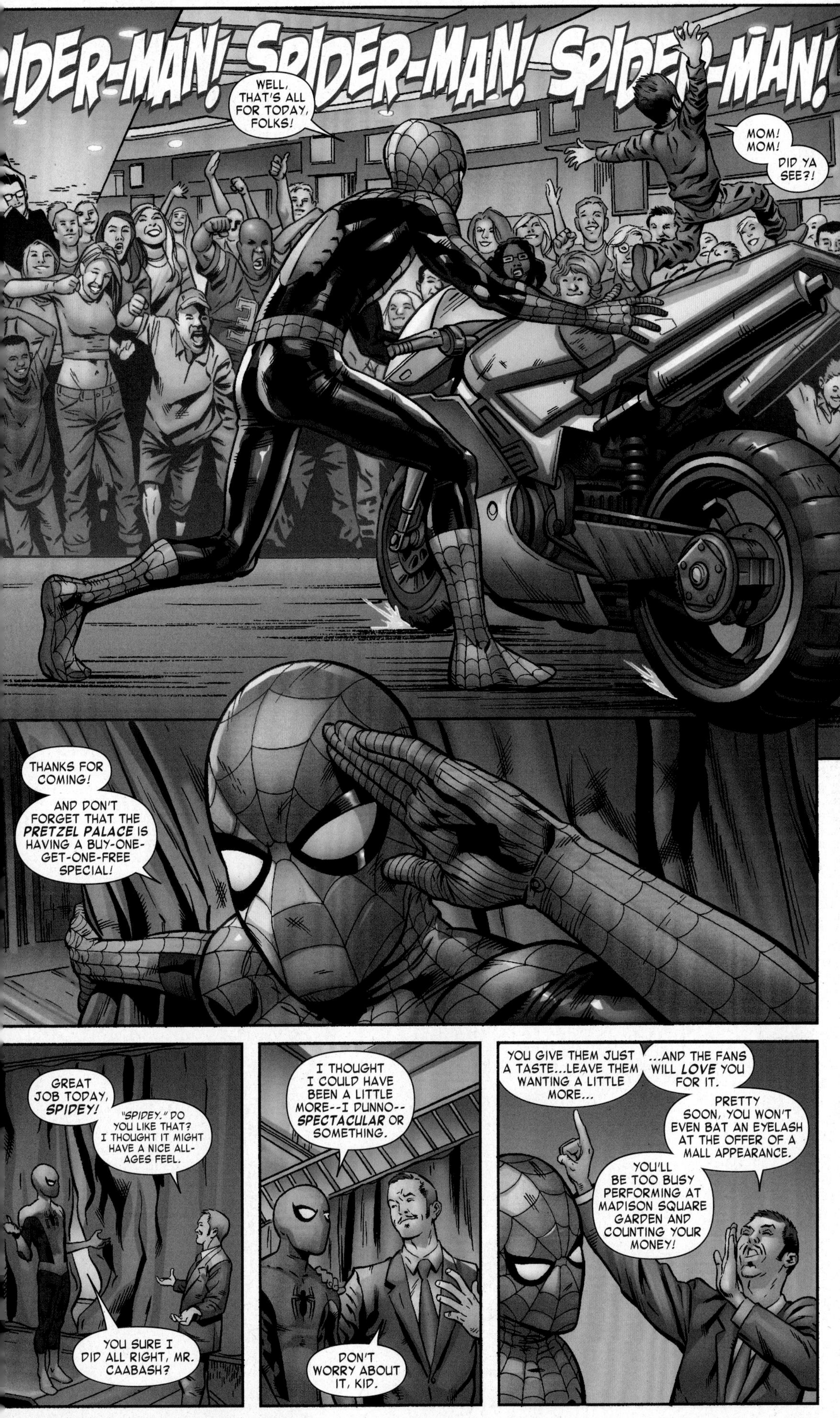
SPIDER-MAN! SPIDER-MAN! SPIDER-MAN!
WELL, THAT'S ALL FOR TODAY, FOLKS!
MOM! MOM!
DID YA SEE?!
THANKS FOR COMING!
AND DON'T FORGET THAT THE PRETZEL PALACE IS HAVING A BUY-ONE-GET-ONE-FREE SPECIAL!
GREAT JOB TODAY, SPIDEY!
"SPIDEY." DO YOU LIKE THAT? I THOUGHT IT MIGHT HAVE A NICE ALL-AGES FEEL.
YOU SURE I DID ALL RIGHT, MR. CAABASH?
I THOUGHT I COULD HAVE BEEN A LITTLE MORE--I DUNNO--SPECTACULAR OR SOMETHING.
DON'T WORRY ABOUT IT, KID.
YOU GIVE THEM JUST A TASTE...LEAVE THEM WANTING A LITTLE MORE...
...AND THE FANS WILL LOVE YOU FOR IT.
PRETTY SOON, YOU WON'T EVEN BAT AN EYELASH AT THE OFFER OF A MALL APPEARANCE.
YOU'LL BE TOO BUSY PERFORMING AT MADISON SQUARE GARDEN AND COUNTING YOUR MONEY!

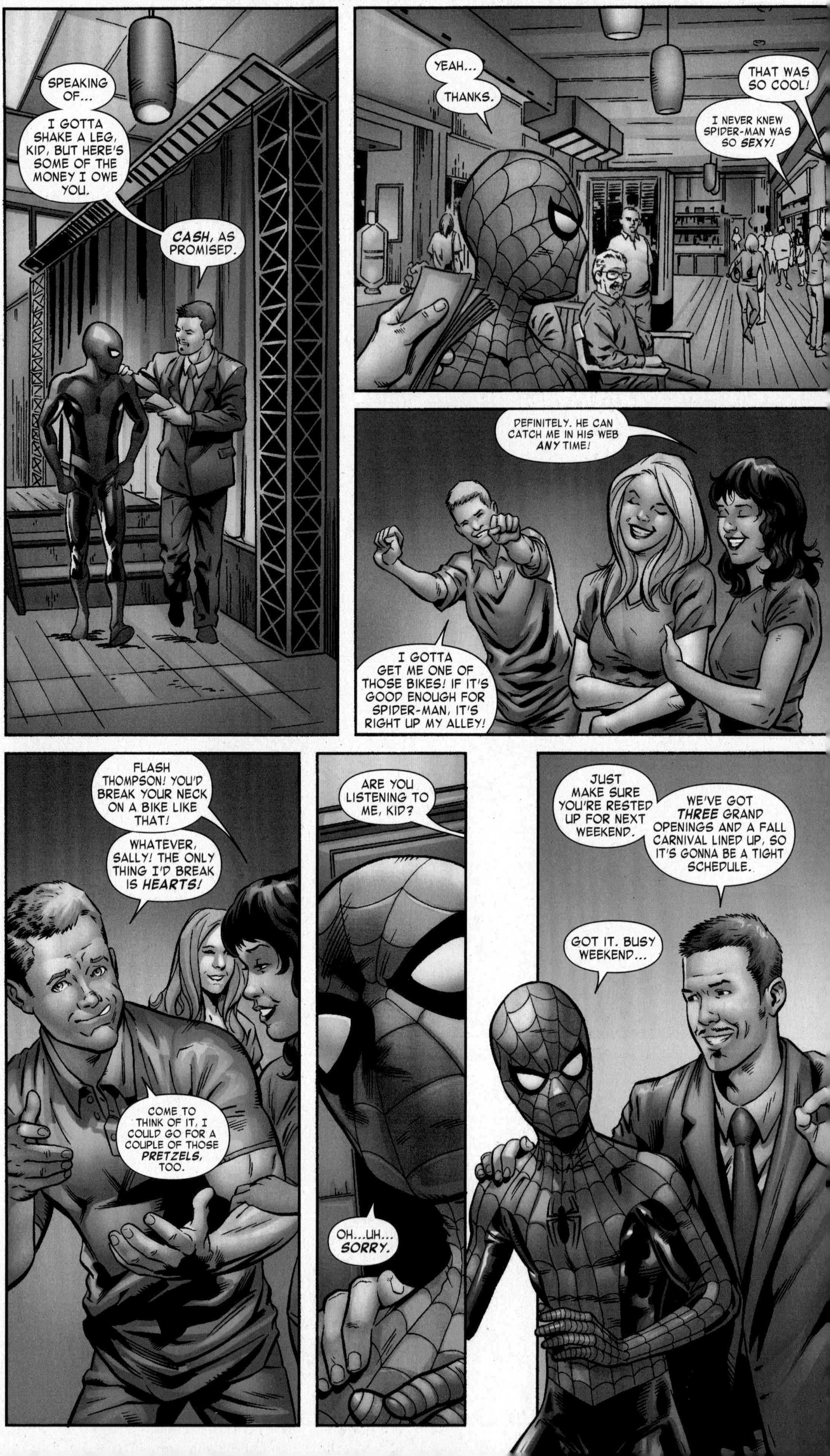
SPEAKING OF...
I GOTTA SHAKE A LEG, KID, BUT HERE'S SOME OF THE MONEY I OWE YOU.
CASH, AS PROMISED.
YEAH...
THANKS.
THAT WAS SO COOL!
I NEVER KNEW SPIDER-MAN WAS SO SEXY!
DEFINITELY. HE CAN CATCH ME IN HIS WEB ANY TIME!
I GOTTA GET ME ONE OF THOSE BIKES! IF IT'S GOOD ENOUGH FOR SPIDER-MAN, IT'S RIGHT UP MY ALLEY!
FLASH THOMPSON! YOU'D BREAK YOUR NECK ON A BIKE LIKE THAT!
WHATEVER, SALLY! THE ONLY THING I'D BREAK IS HEARTS!
COME TO THINK OF IT, I COULD GO FOR A COUPLE OF THOSE PRETZELS, TOO.
ARE YOU LISTENING TO ME, KID?
OH...UH... SORRY.
JUST MAKE SURE YOU'RE RESTED UP FOR NEXT WEEKEND.
WE'VE GOT THREE GRAND OPENINGS AND A FALL CARNIVAL LINED UP, SO IT'S GONNA BE A TIGHT SCHEDULE.
GOT IT. BUSY WEEKEND...

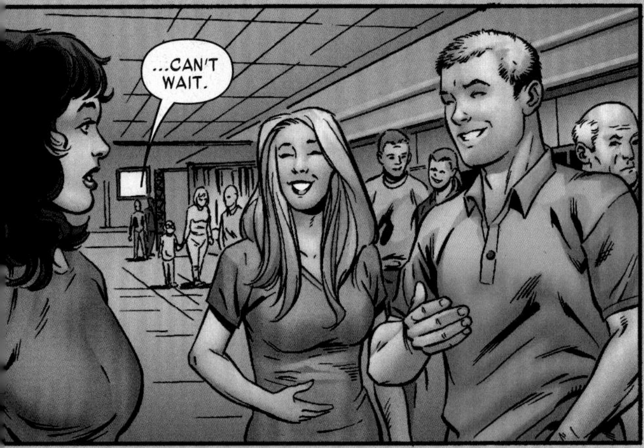
...CAN'T WAIT.

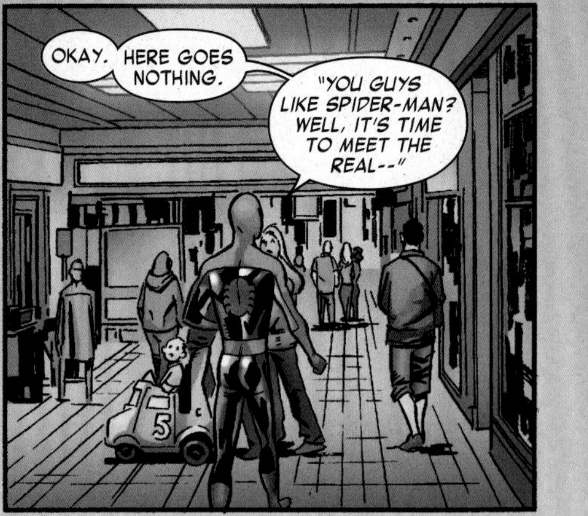
OKAY.
HERE GOES NOTHING.
"YOU GUYS LIKE SPIDER-MAN? WELL, IT'S TIME TO MEET THE REAL--"

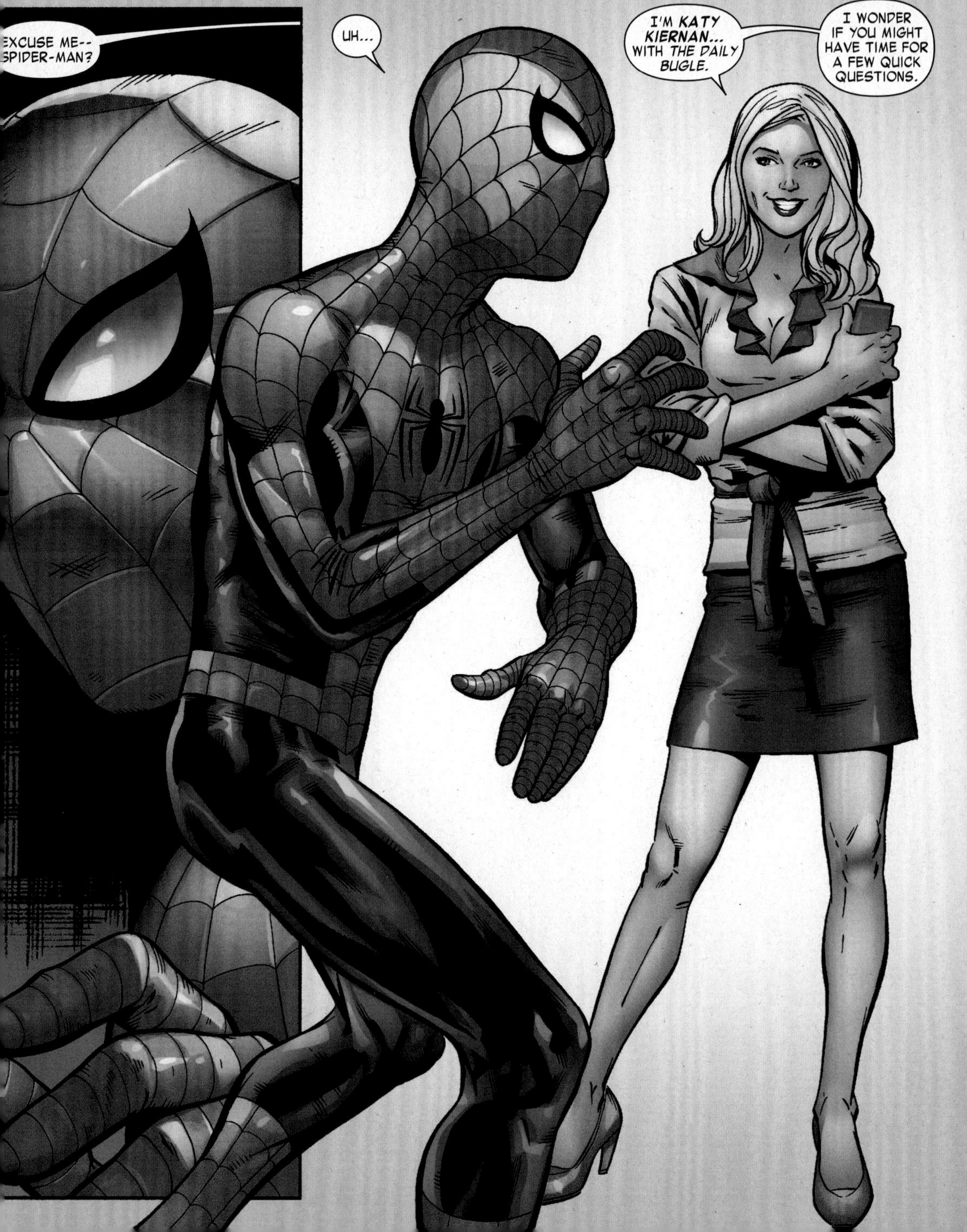
EXCUSE ME-- SPIDER-MAN?
UH...
I'M KATY KIERNAN... WITH THE DAILY BUGLE.
I WONDER IF YOU MIGHT HAVE TIME FOR A FEW QUICK QUESTIONS.

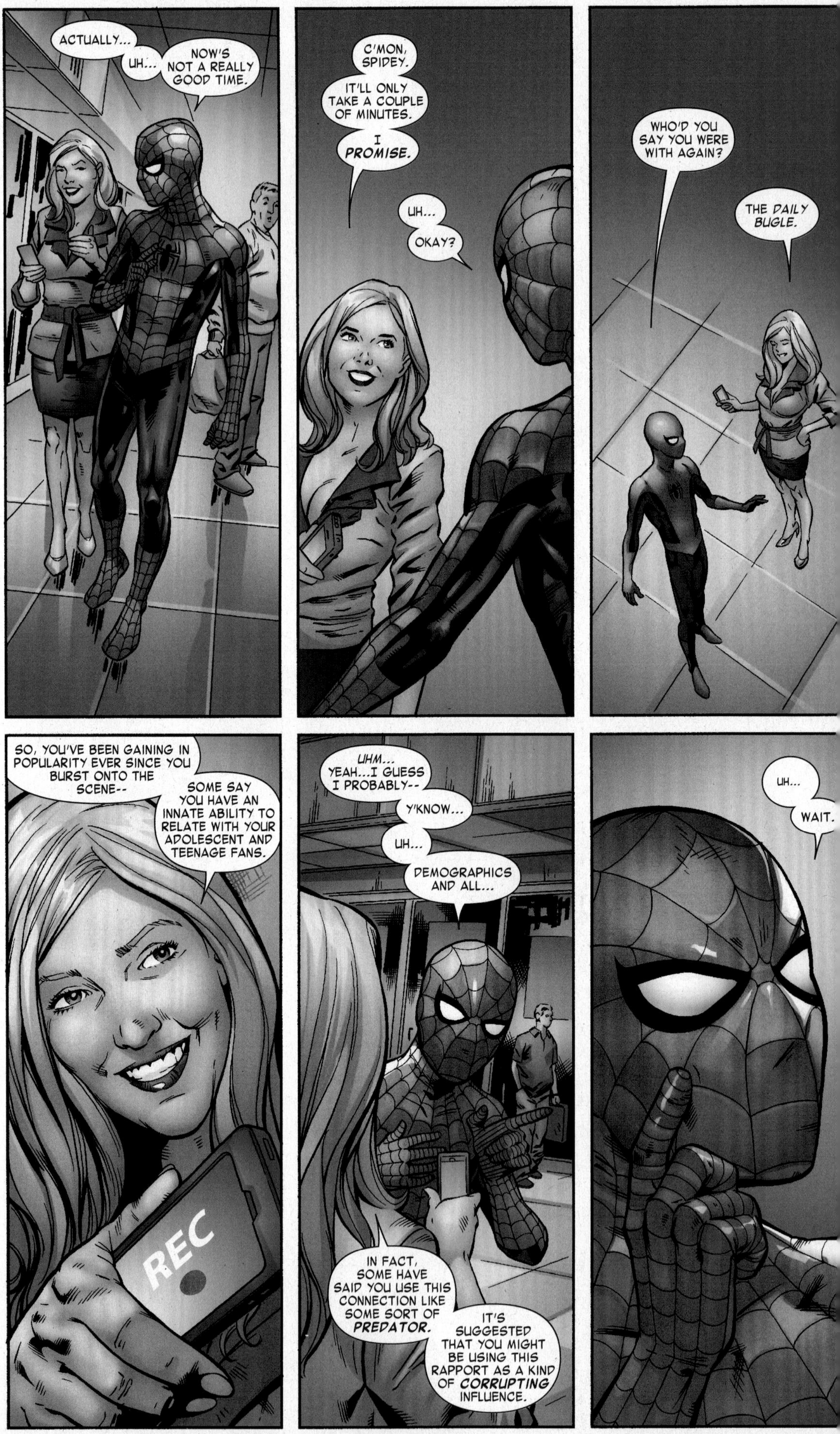

ACTUALLY...
UH...
NOW'S NOT A REALLY GOOD TIME.
C'MON, SPIDEY.
IT'LL ONLY TAKE A COUPLE OF MINUTES.
I PROMISE.
UH...
OKAY?
WHO'D YOU SAY YOU WERE WITH AGAIN?
THE DAILY BUGLE.
SO, YOU'VE BEEN GAINING IN POPULARITY EVER SINCE YOU BURST ONTO THE SCENE--
SOME SAY YOU HAVE AN INNATE ABILITY TO RELATE WITH YOUR ADOLESCENT AND TEENAGE FANS.
REC
UHM... YEAH...I GUESS I PROBABLY--
Y'KNOW...
UH...
DEMOGRAPHICS AND ALL...
IN FACT, SOME HAVE SAID YOU USE THIS CONNECTION LIKE SOME SORT OF PREDATOR.
IT'S SUGGESTED THAT YOU MIGHT BE USING THIS RAPPORT AS A KIND OF CORRUPTING INFLUENCE.
UH...
WAIT.

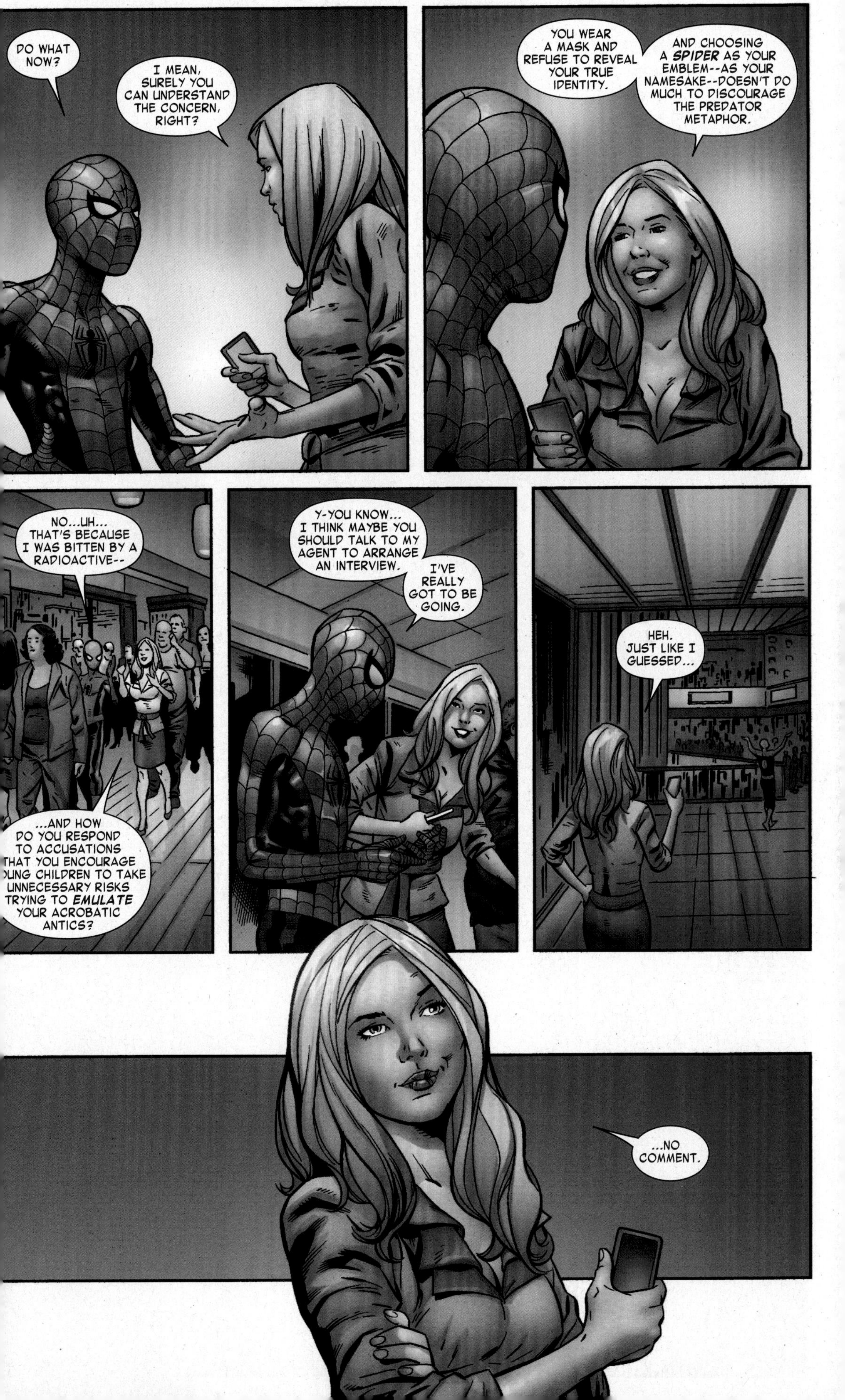
DO WHAT NOW?
I MEAN, SURELY YOU CAN UNDERSTAND THE CONCERN, RIGHT?
YOU WEAR A MASK AND REFUSE TO REVEAL YOUR TRUE IDENTITY.
AND CHOOSING A SPIDER AS YOUR EMBLEM--AS YOUR NAMESAKE--DOESN'T DO MUCH TO DISCOURAGE THE PREDATOR METAPHOR.
NO...UH... THAT'S BECAUSE I WAS BITTEN BY A RADIOACTIVE--
...AND HOW DO YOU RESPOND TO ACCUSATIONS THAT YOU ENCOURAGE YOUNG CHILDREN TO TAKE UNNECESSARY RISKS TRYING TO EMULATE YOUR ACROBATIC ANTICS?
Y-YOU KNOW... I THINK MAYBE YOU SHOULD TALK TO MY AGENT TO ARRANGE AN INTERVIEW.
I'VE REALLY GOT TO BE GOING.
HEH. JUST LIKE I GUESSED...
...NO COMMENT.

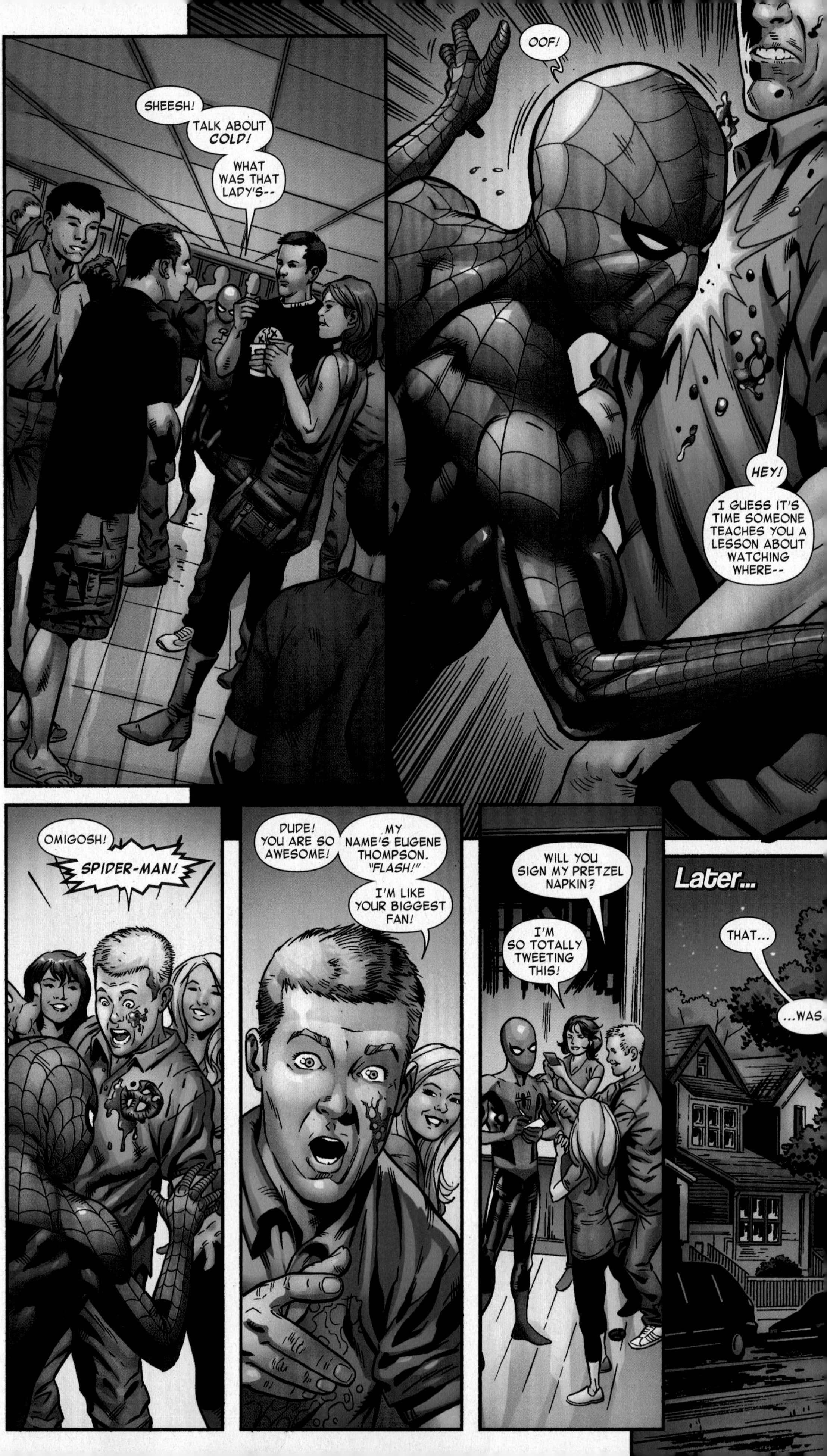
SHEESH!
TALK ABOUT COLD!
WHAT WAS THAT LADY'S--
OOF!
HEY!
I GUESS IT'S TIME SOMEONE TEACHES YOU A LESSON ABOUT WATCHING WHERE--
OMIGOSH!
SPIDER-MAN!
DUDE! YOU ARE SO AWESOME!
...MY NAME'S EUGENE THOMPSON. "FLASH!"
I'M LIKE YOUR BIGGEST FAN!
WILL YOU SIGN MY PRETZEL NAPKIN?
I'M SO TOTALLY TWEETING THIS!
Later...
THAT...
...WAS

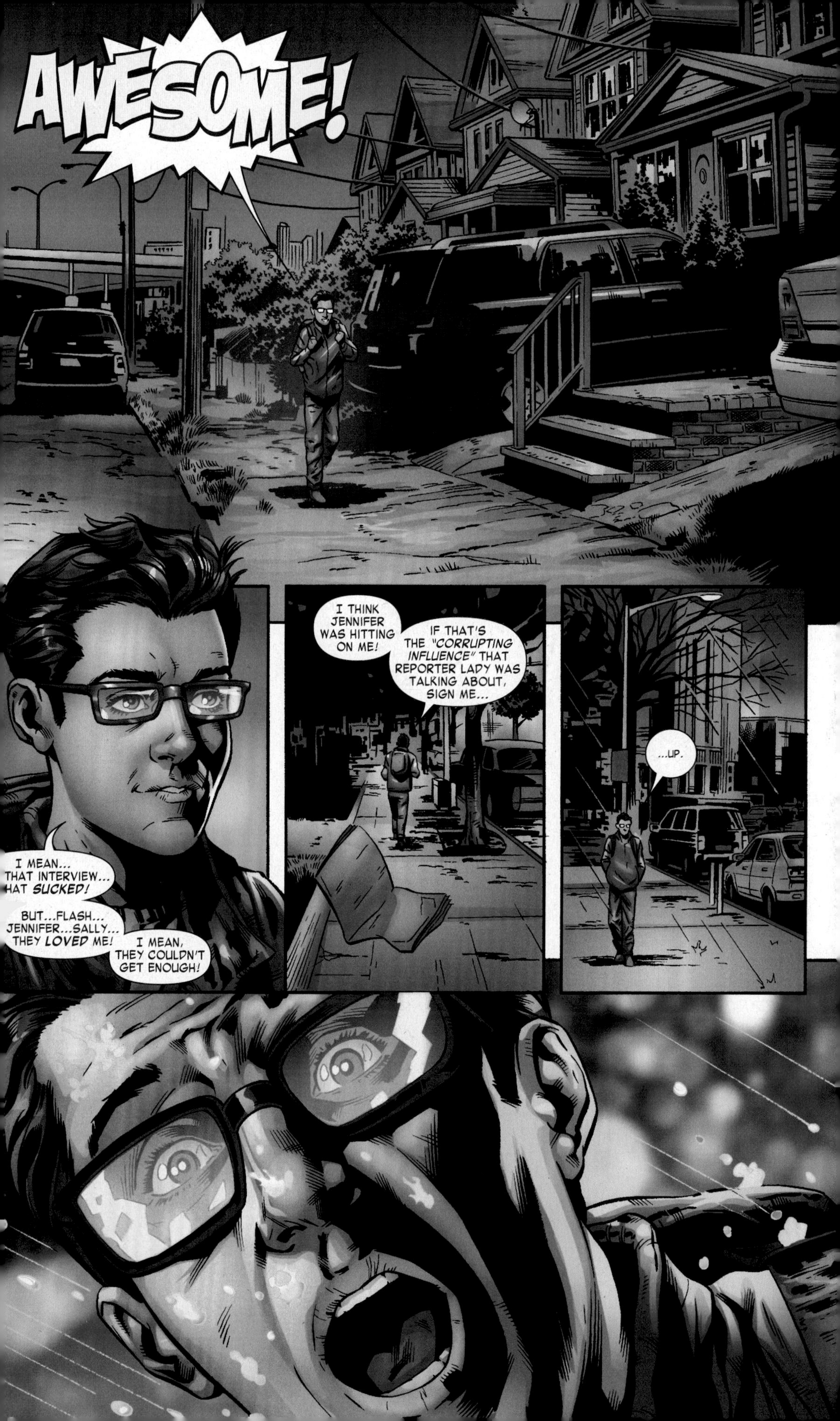
AWESOME!
I MEAN... THAT INTERVIEW... HAT SUCKED!
BUT...FLASH... JENNIFER...SALLY... THEY LOVED ME!
I MEAN, THEY COULDN'T GET ENOUGH!
I THINK JENNIFER WAS HITTING ON ME!
IF THAT'S THE "CORRUPTING INFLUENCE" THAT REPORTER LADY WAS TALKING ABOUT, SIGN ME...
...UP.

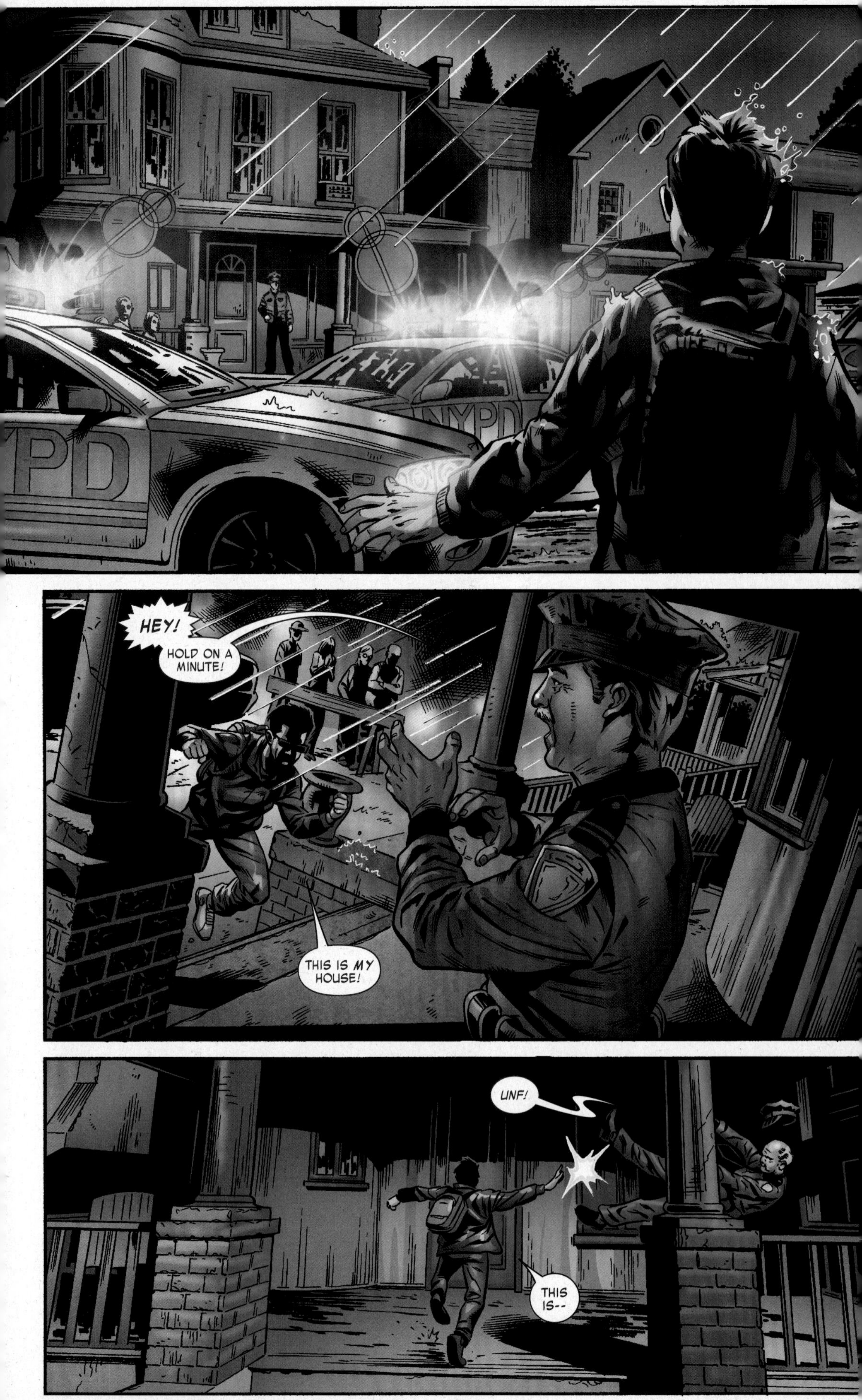
NYPD
NYPD
HEY!
HOLD ON A MINUTE!
THIS IS MY HOUSE!
UNF!
THIS IS--

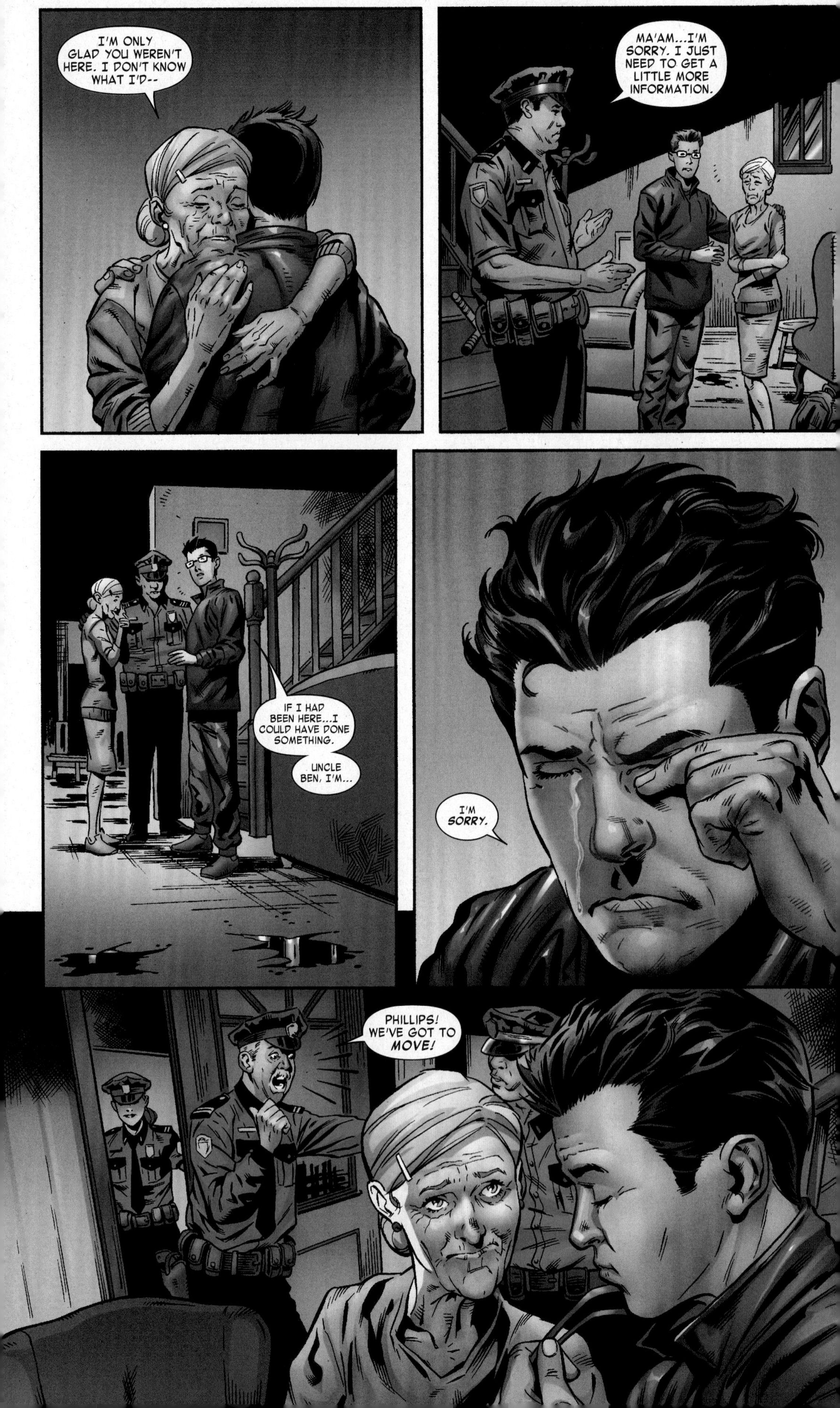
I'M ONLY GLAD YOU WEREN'T HERE. I DON'T KNOW WHAT I'D--
MA'AM...I'M SORRY. I JUST NEED TO GET A LITTLE MORE INFORMATION.
IF I HAD BEEN HERE...I COULD HAVE DONE SOMETHING.
UNCLE BEN, I'M...
I'M *SORRY.*
PHILLIPS! WE'VE GOT TO *MOVE!*

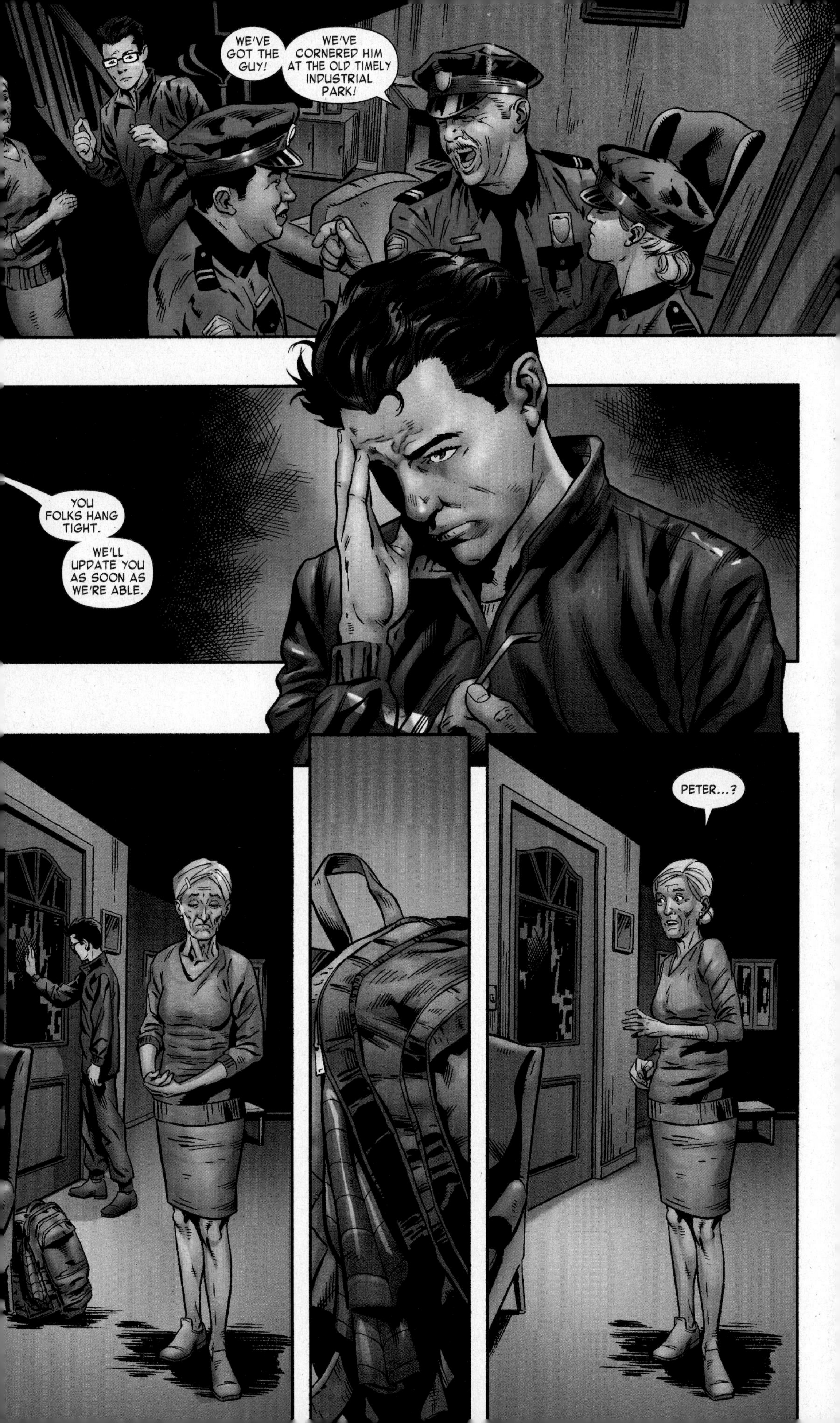
WE'VE GOT THE GUY!
WE'VE CORNERED HIM AT THE OLD TIMELY INDUSTRIAL PARK!
YOU FOLKS HANG TIGHT.
WE'LL UPDATE YOU AS SOON AS WE'RE ABLE.
PETER...?

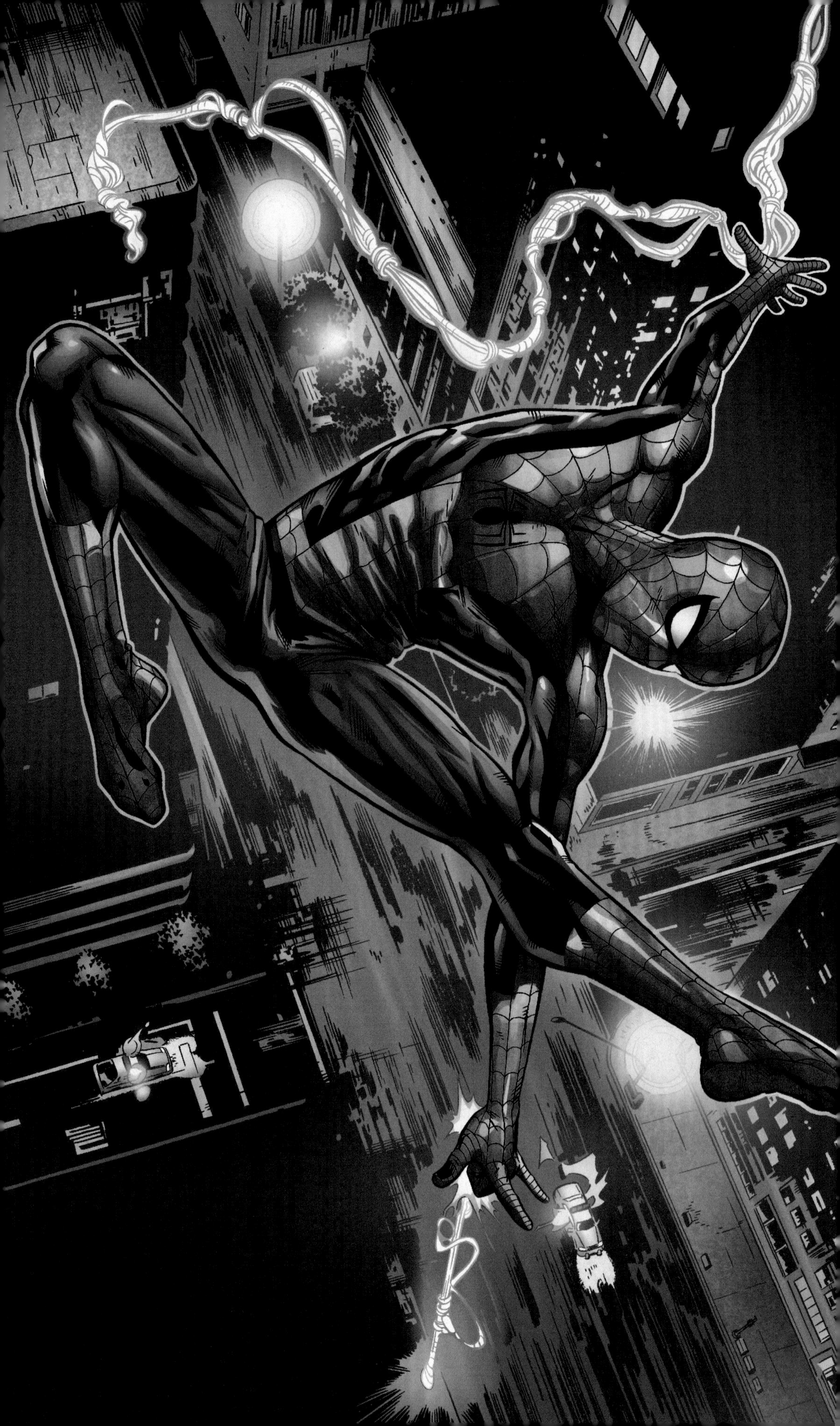

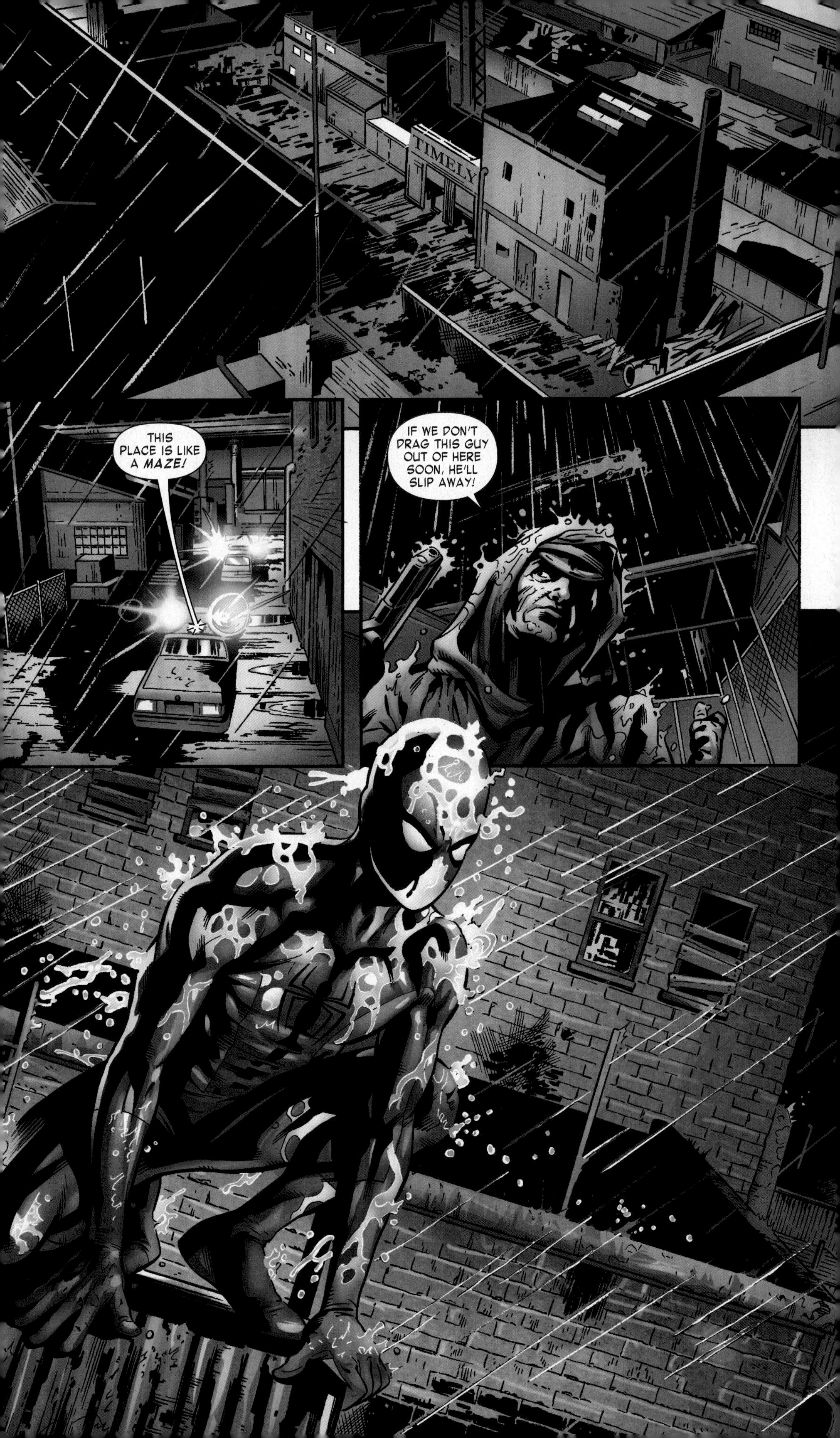
TIMELY
THIS PLACE IS LIKE A MAZE!
IF WE DON'T DRAG THIS GUY OUT OF HERE SOON, HE'LL SLIP AWAY!

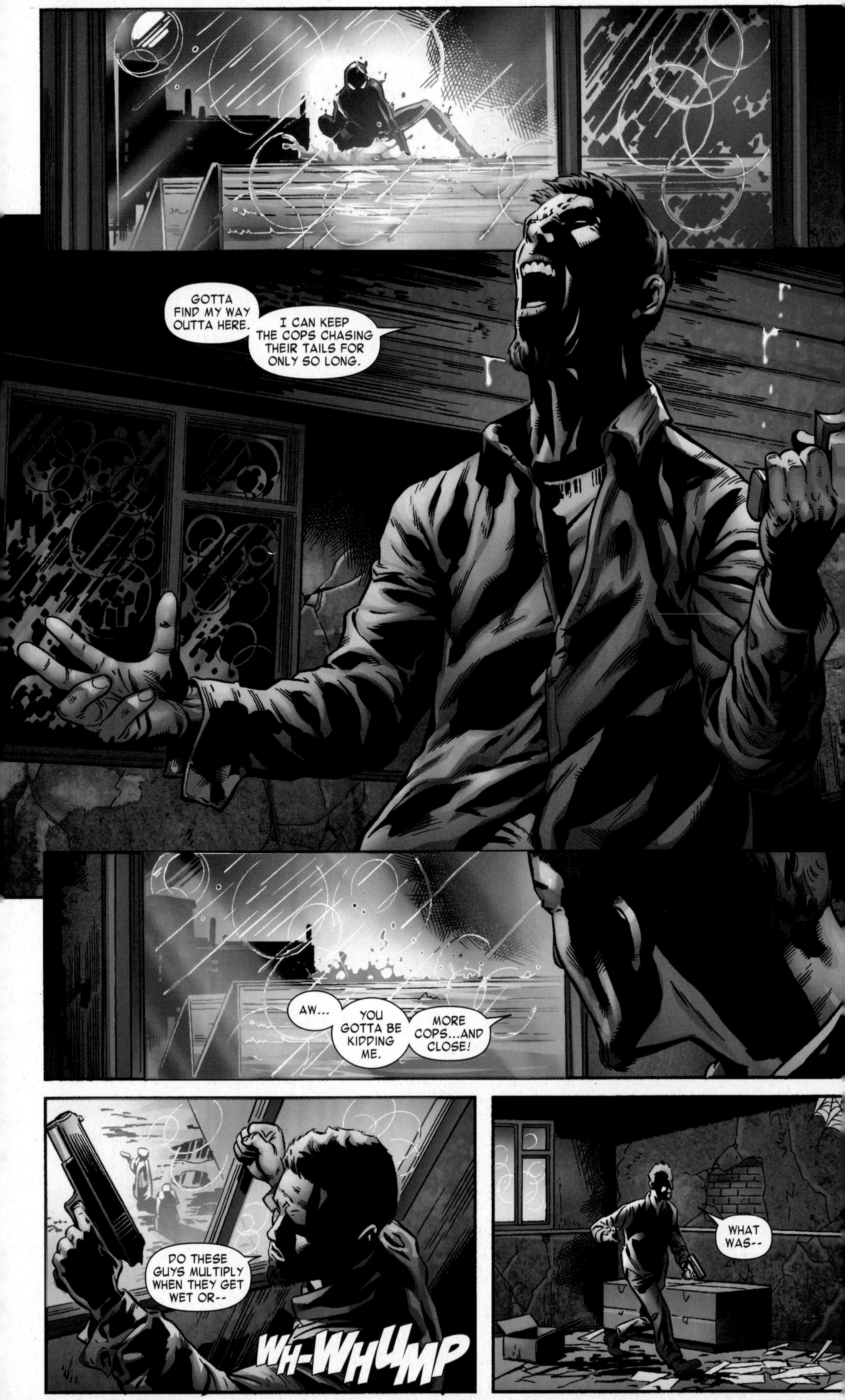
GOTTA FIND MY WAY OUTTA HERE.
I CAN KEEP THE COPS CHASING THEIR TAILS FOR ONLY SO LONG.
AW...
YOU GOTTA BE KIDDING ME.
MORE COPS...AND CLOSE!
DO THESE GUYS MULTIPLY WHEN THEY GET WET OR--
WH-WHUMP
WHAT WAS--

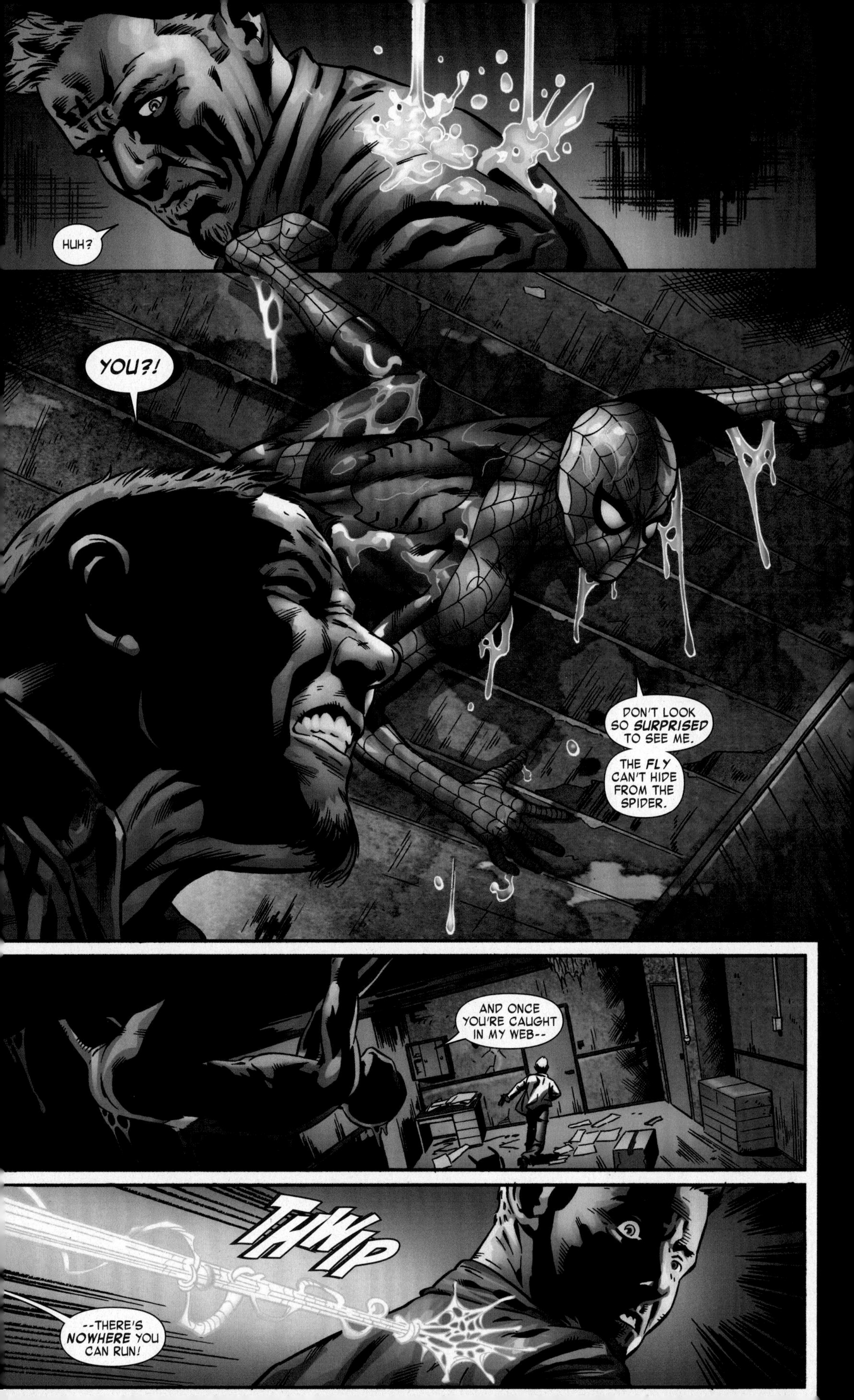
HUH?
YOU?!
DON'T LOOK SO SURPRISED TO SEE ME.
THE FLY CAN'T HIDE FROM THE SPIDER.
AND ONCE YOU'RE CAUGHT IN MY WEB--
THWIP
--THERE'S NOWHERE YOU CAN RUN!

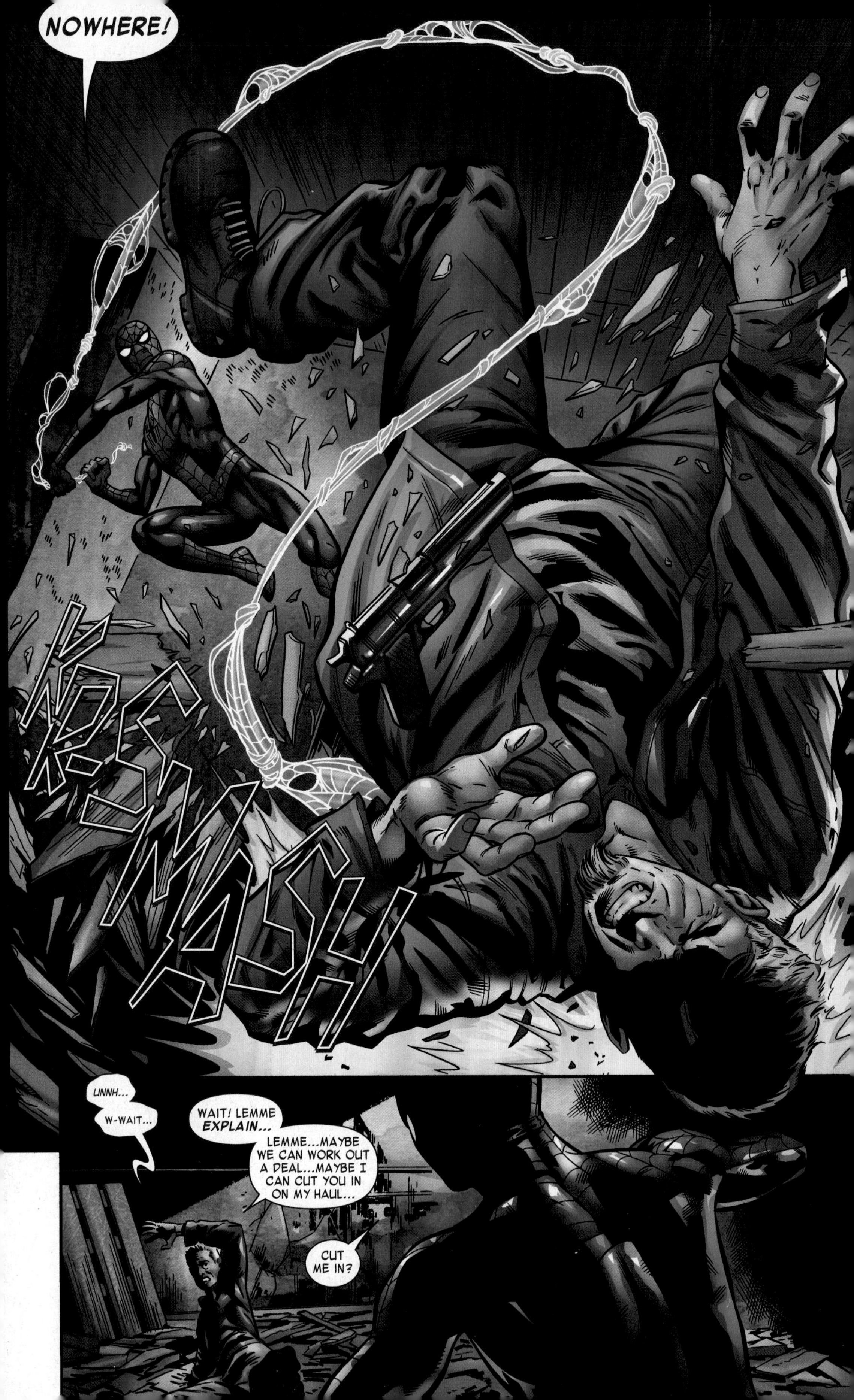
NOWHERE!
KRESMASH!
UNNH...
W-WAIT...
WAIT! LEMME EXPLAIN...
LEMME...MAYBE WE CAN WORK OUT A DEAL...MAYBE I CAN CUT YOU IN ON MY HAUL...
CUT ME IN?

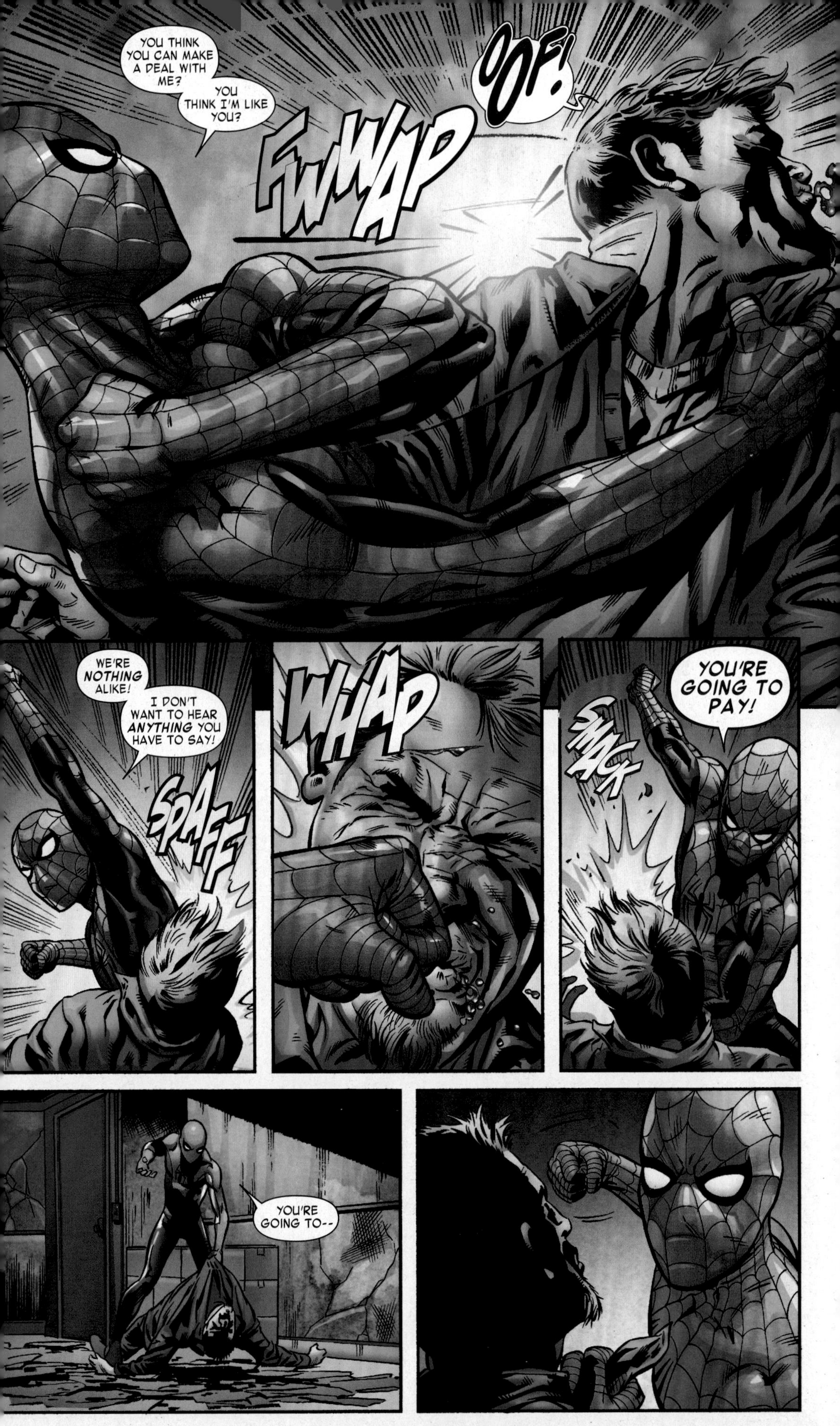
YOU THINK YOU CAN MAKE A DEAL WITH ME?
YOU THINK I'M LIKE YOU?
FWWAP
OOF!
WE'RE *NOTHING* ALIKE!
I DON'T WANT TO HEAR *ANYTHING* YOU HAVE TO SAY!
SPAFF
WHAP
SMACK
YOU'RE GOING TO PAY!
YOU'RE GOING TO--

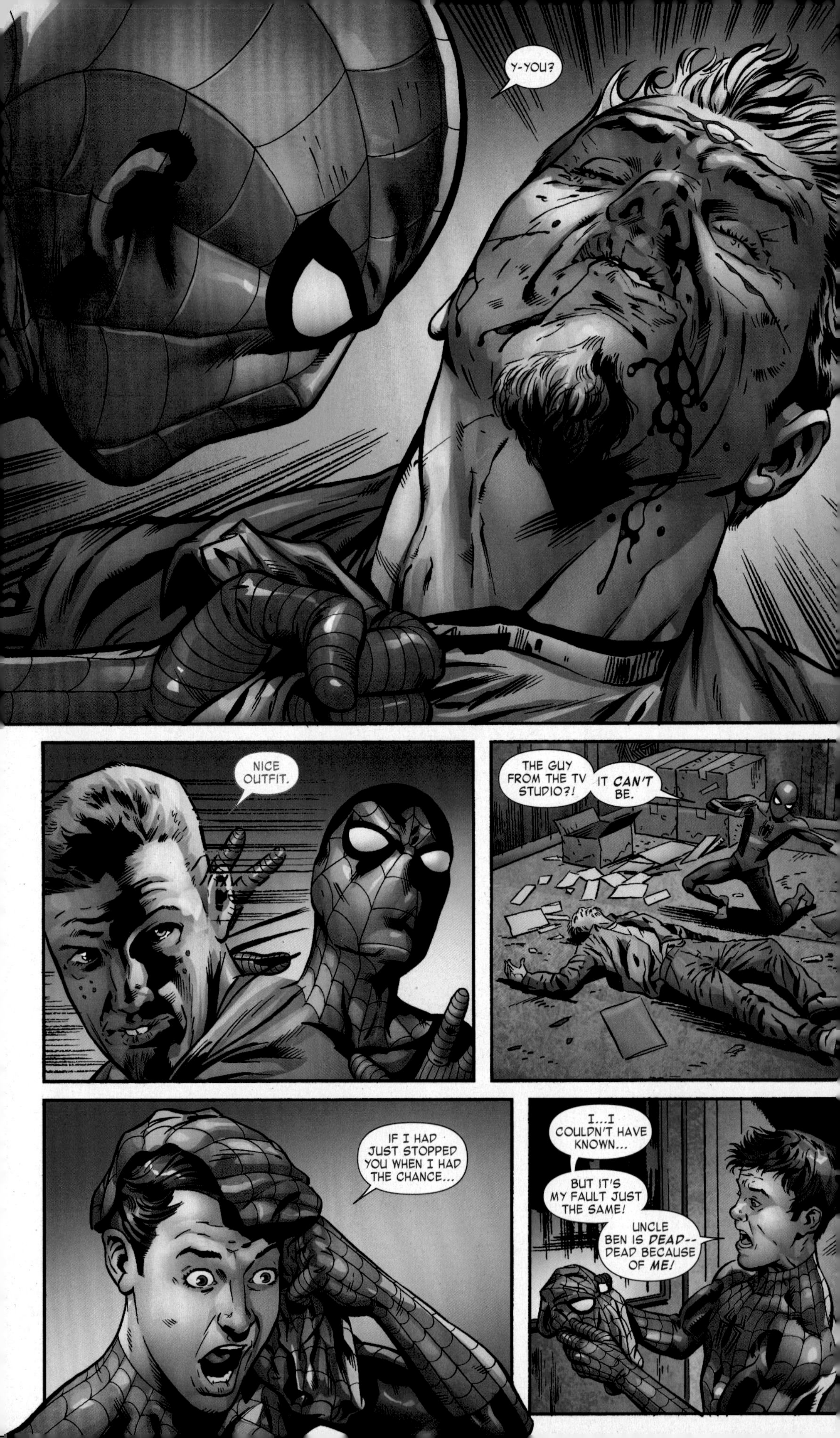
Y-YOU?
NICE OUTFIT.
THE GUY FROM THE TV STUDIO?!
IT CAN'T BE.
IF I HAD JUST STOPPED YOU WHEN I HAD THE CHANCE...
I...I COULDN'T HAVE KNOWN...
BUT IT'S MY FAULT JUST THE SAME!
UNCLE BEN IS DEAD-- DEAD BECAUSE OF ME!

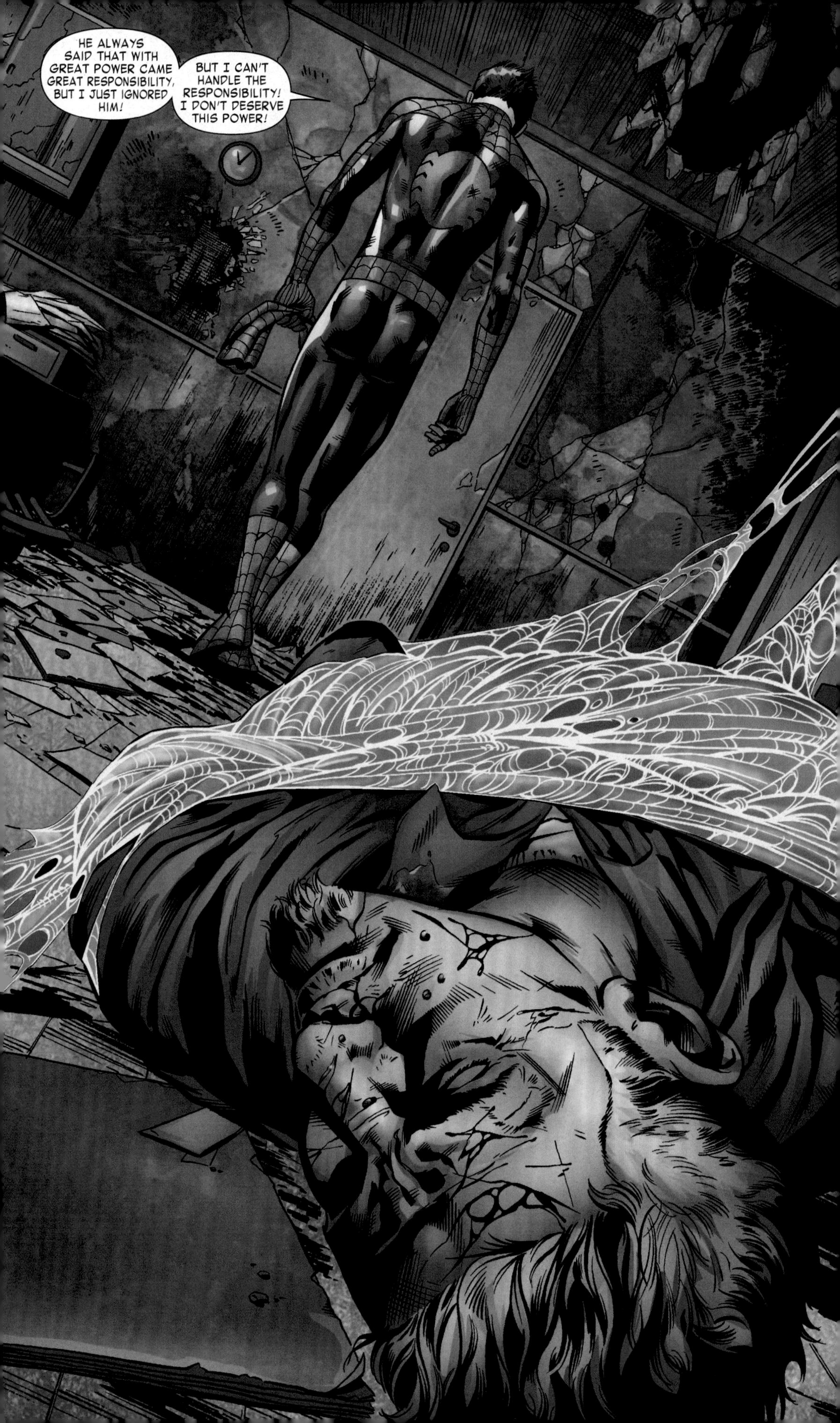
HE ALWAYS SAID THAT WITH GREAT POWER CAME GREAT RESPONSIBILITY, BUT I JUST IGNORED HIM!
BUT I CAN'T HANDLE THE RESPONSIBILITY! I DON'T DESERVE THIS POWER!

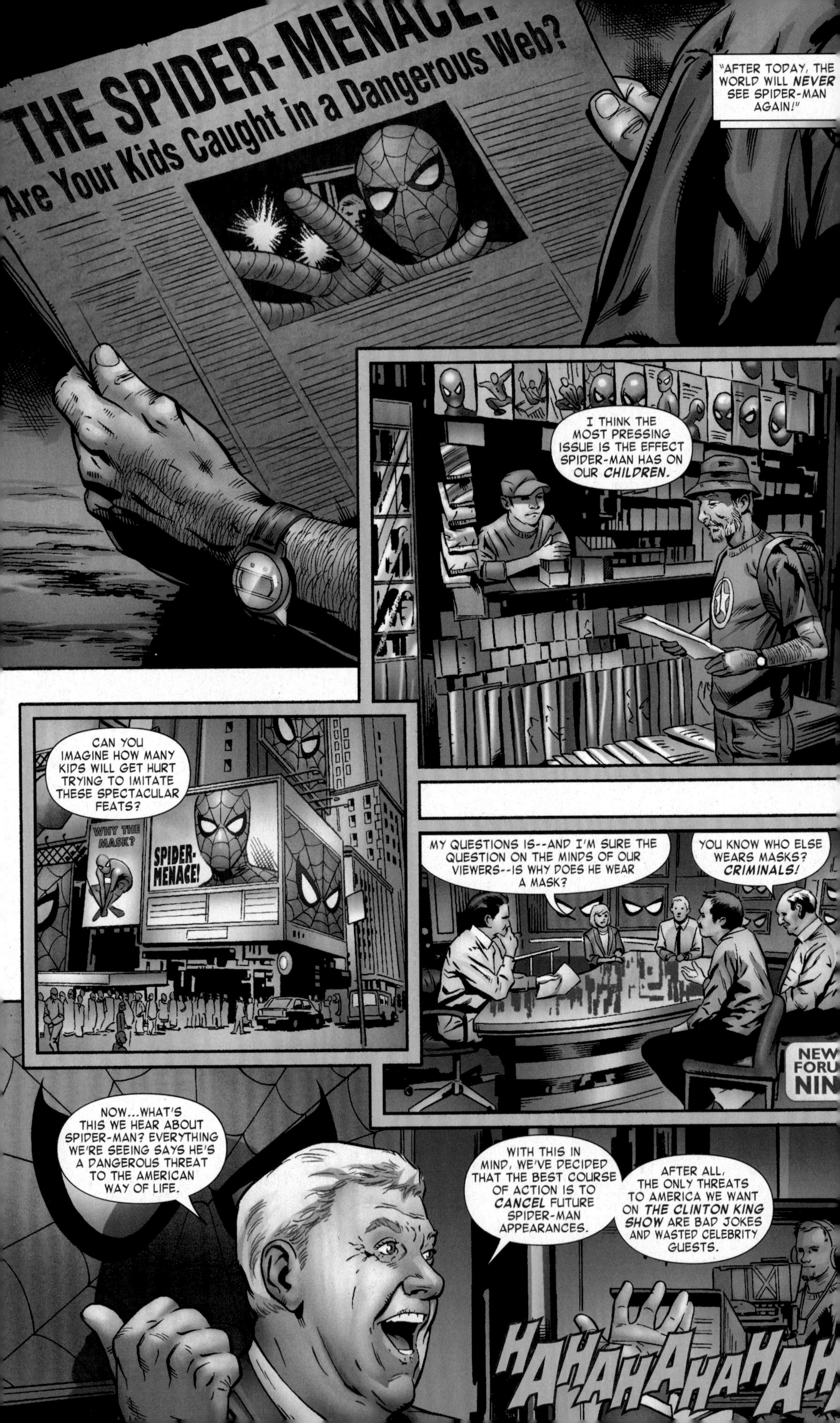
THE SPIDER-MENACE!
Are Your Kids Caught in a Dangerous Web?
"AFTER TODAY, THE WORLD WILL NEVER SEE SPIDER-MAN AGAIN!"
I THINK THE MOST PRESSING ISSUE IS THE EFFECT SPIDER-MAN HAS ON OUR CHILDREN.
CAN YOU IMAGINE HOW MANY KIDS WILL GET HURT TRYING TO IMITATE THESE SPECTACULAR FEATS?
WHY THE MASK?
SPIDER-MENACE!
MY QUESTIONS IS--AND I'M SURE THE QUESTION ON THE MINDS OF OUR VIEWERS--IS WHY DOES HE WEAR A MASK?
YOU KNOW WHO ELSE WEARS MASKS? CRIMINALS!
NOW...WHAT'S THIS WE HEAR ABOUT SPIDER-MAN? EVERYTHING WE'RE SEEING SAYS HE'S A DANGEROUS THREAT TO THE AMERICAN WAY OF LIFE.
WITH THIS IN MIND, WE'VE DECIDED THAT THE BEST COURSE OF ACTION IS TO CANCEL FUTURE SPIDER-MAN APPEARANCES.
AFTER ALL, THE ONLY THREATS TO AMERICA WE WANT ON THE CLINTON KING SHOW ARE BAD JOKES AND WASTED CELEBRITY GUESTS.
HAHAHAHAHAHAHAH

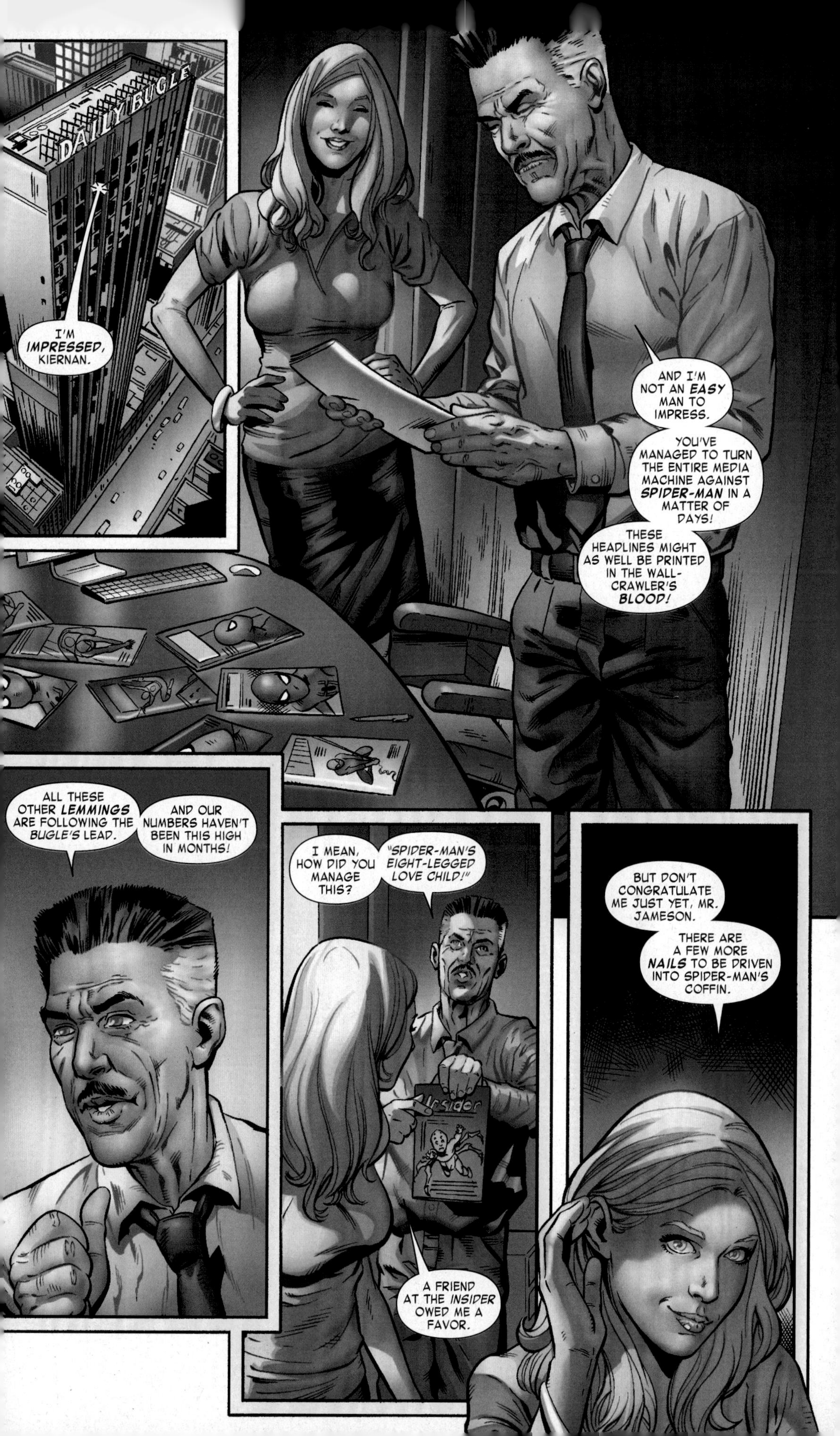
DAILY BUGLE
I'M IMPRESSED, KIERNAN.
AND I'M NOT AN EASY MAN TO IMPRESS.
YOU'VE MANAGED TO TURN THE ENTIRE MEDIA MACHINE AGAINST SPIDER-MAN IN A MATTER OF DAYS!
THESE HEADLINES MIGHT AS WELL BE PRINTED IN THE WALL-CRAWLER'S BLOOD!
ALL THESE OTHER LEMMINGS ARE FOLLOWING THE BUGLE'S LEAD.
AND OUR NUMBERS HAVEN'T BEEN THIS HIGH IN MONTHS!
I MEAN, HOW DID YOU MANAGE THIS?
"SPIDER-MAN'S EIGHT-LEGGED LOVE CHILD!"
A FRIEND AT THE INSIDER OWED ME A FAVOR.
BUT DON'T CONGRATULATE ME JUST YET, MR. JAMESON.
THERE ARE A FEW MORE NAILS TO BE DRIVEN INTO SPIDER-MAN'S COFFIN.

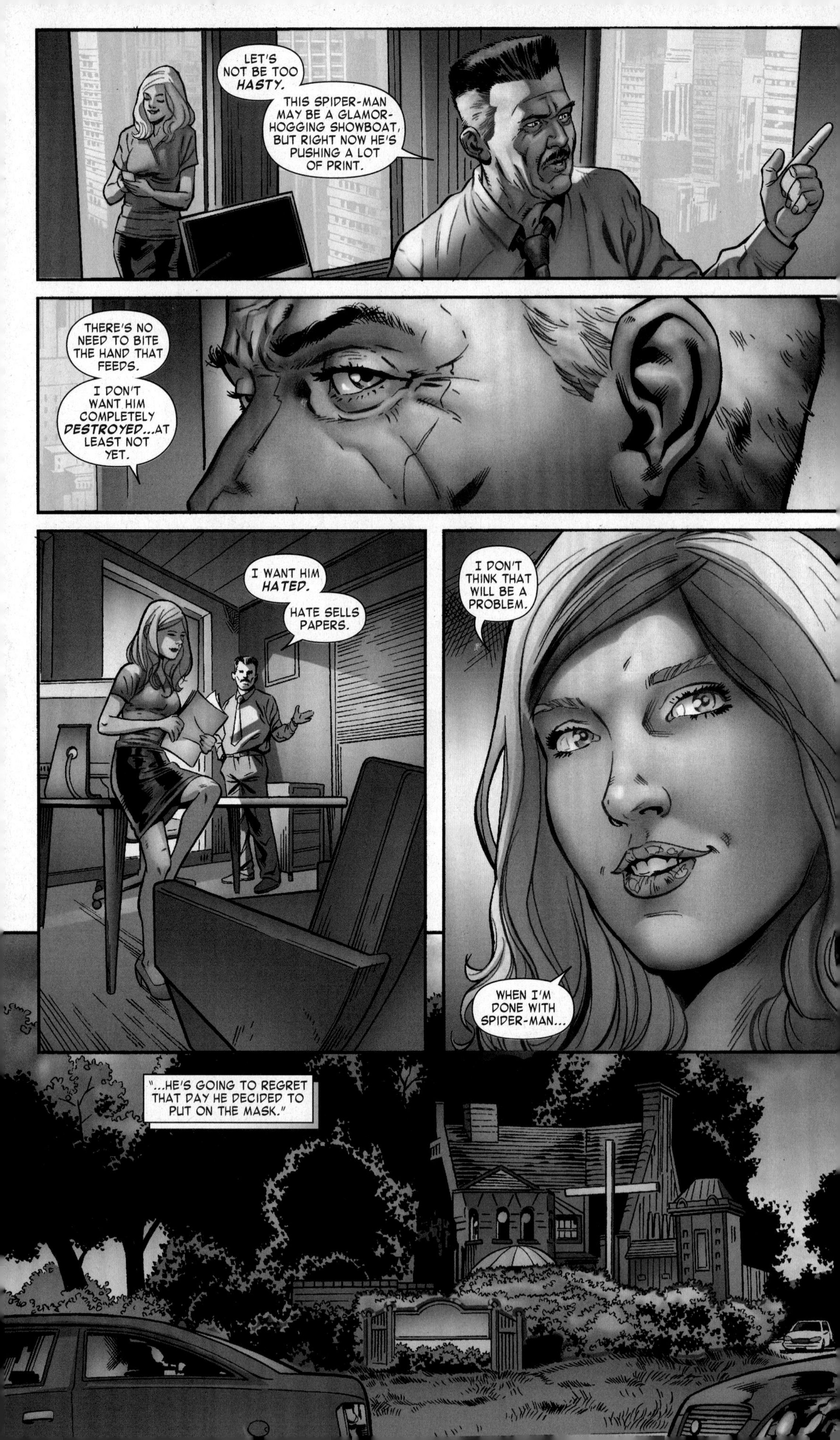

LET'S NOT BE TOO HASTY.
THIS SPIDER-MAN MAY BE A GLAMOR-HOGGING SHOWBOAT, BUT RIGHT NOW HE'S PUSHING A LOT OF PRINT.
THERE'S NO NEED TO BITE THE HAND THAT FEEDS.
I DON'T WANT HIM COMPLETELY DESTROYED...AT LEAST NOT YET.
I WANT HIM HATED.
HATE SELLS PAPERS.
I DON'T THINK THAT WILL BE A PROBLEM.
WHEN I'M DONE WITH SPIDER-MAN...
"...HE'S GOING TO REGRET THAT DAY HE DECIDED TO PUT ON THE MASK."

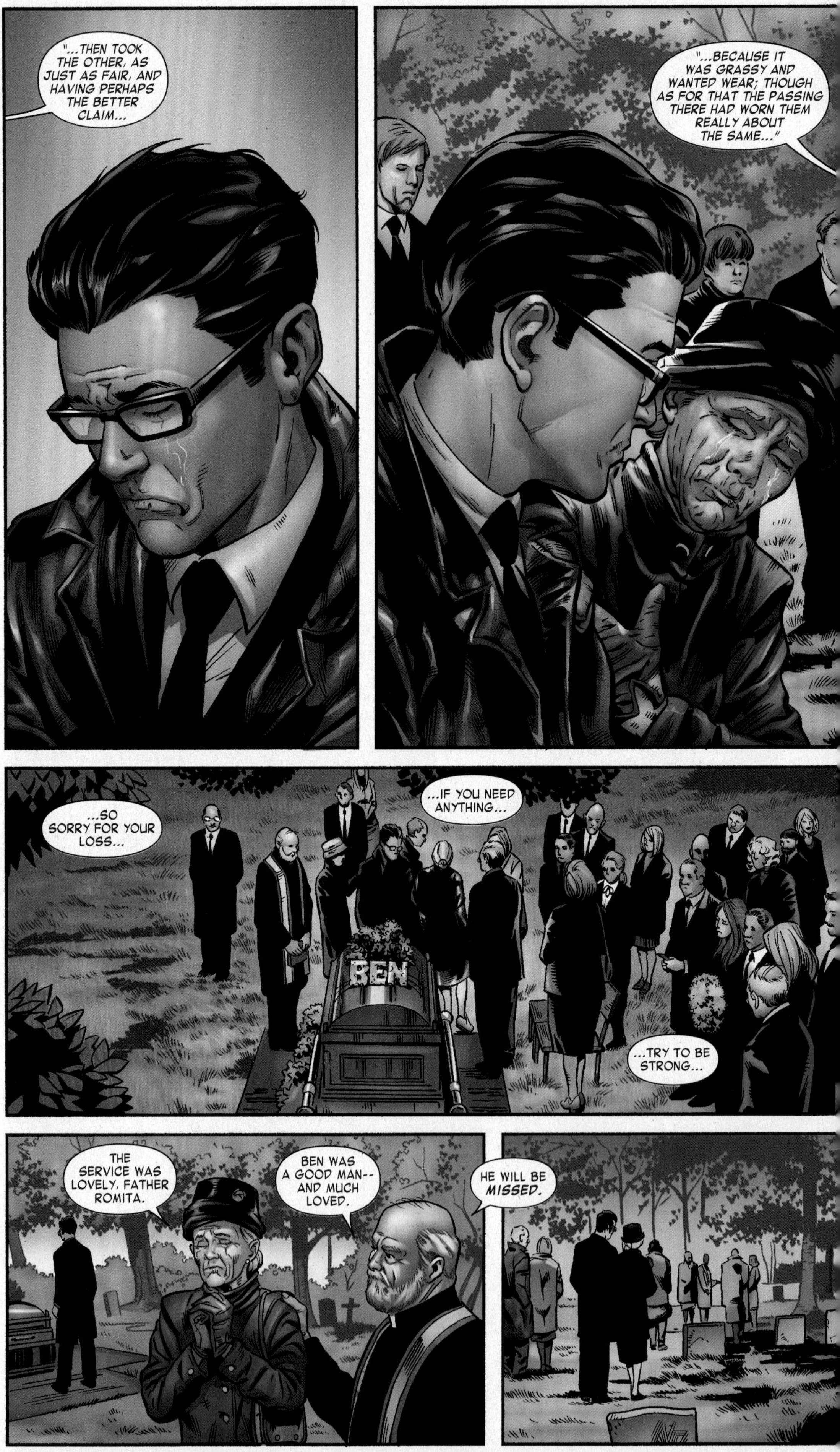
"...THEN TOOK THE OTHER, AS JUST AS FAIR, AND HAVING PERHAPS THE BETTER CLAIM...
"...BECAUSE IT WAS GRASSY AND WANTED WEAR; THOUGH AS FOR THAT THE PASSING THERE HAD WORN THEM REALLY ABOUT THE SAME..."
...SO SORRY FOR YOUR LOSS...
...IF YOU NEED ANYTHING...
...TRY TO BE STRONG...
THE SERVICE WAS LOVELY, FATHER ROMITA.
BEN WAS A GOOD MAN-- AND MUCH LOVED.
HE WILL BE *MISSED*.

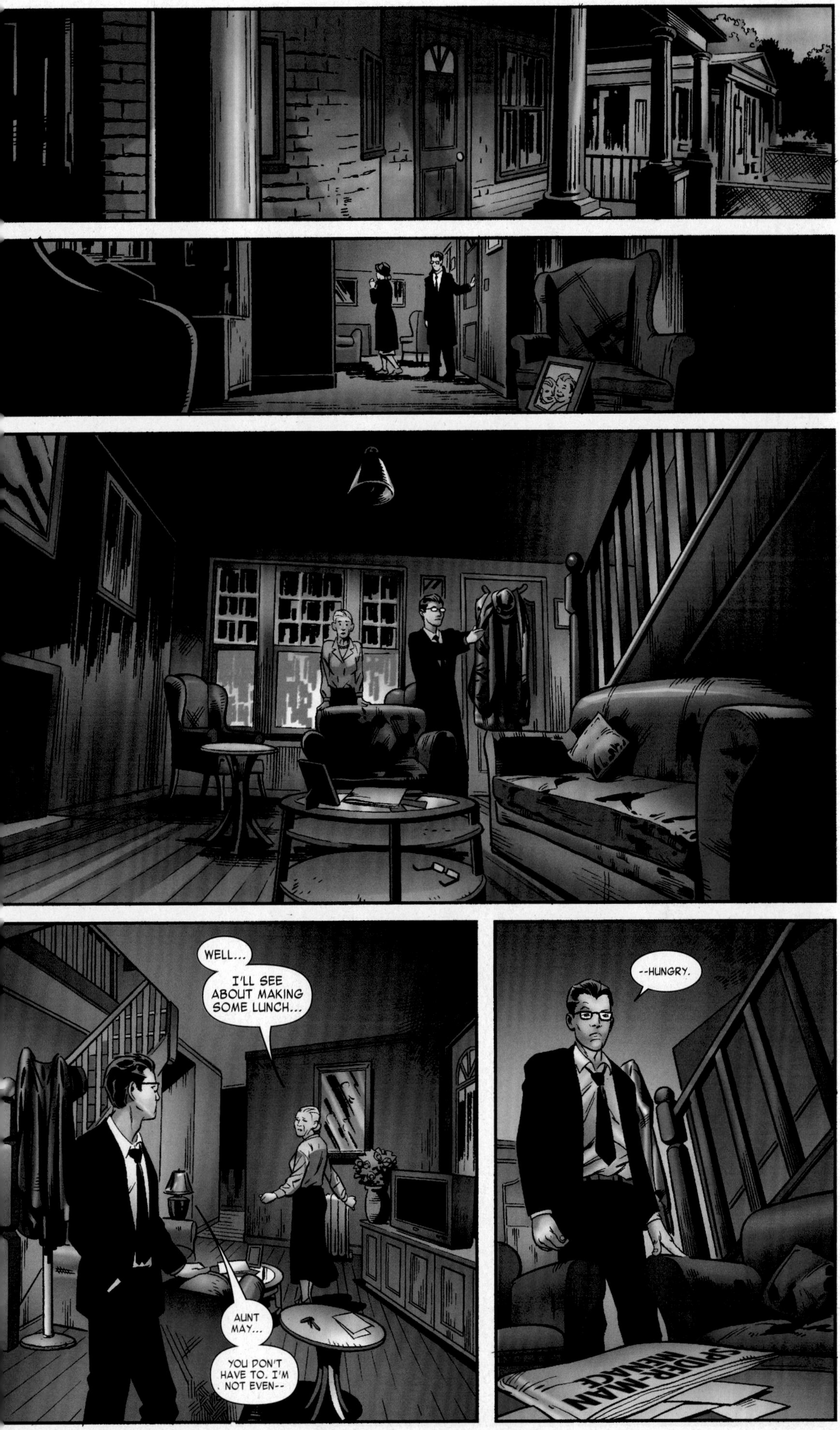
WELL...
I'LL SEE ABOUT MAKING SOME LUNCH...
AUNT MAY...
YOU DON'T HAVE TO. I'M NOT EVEN--
--HUNGRY.
SPIDER-MAN MENACE

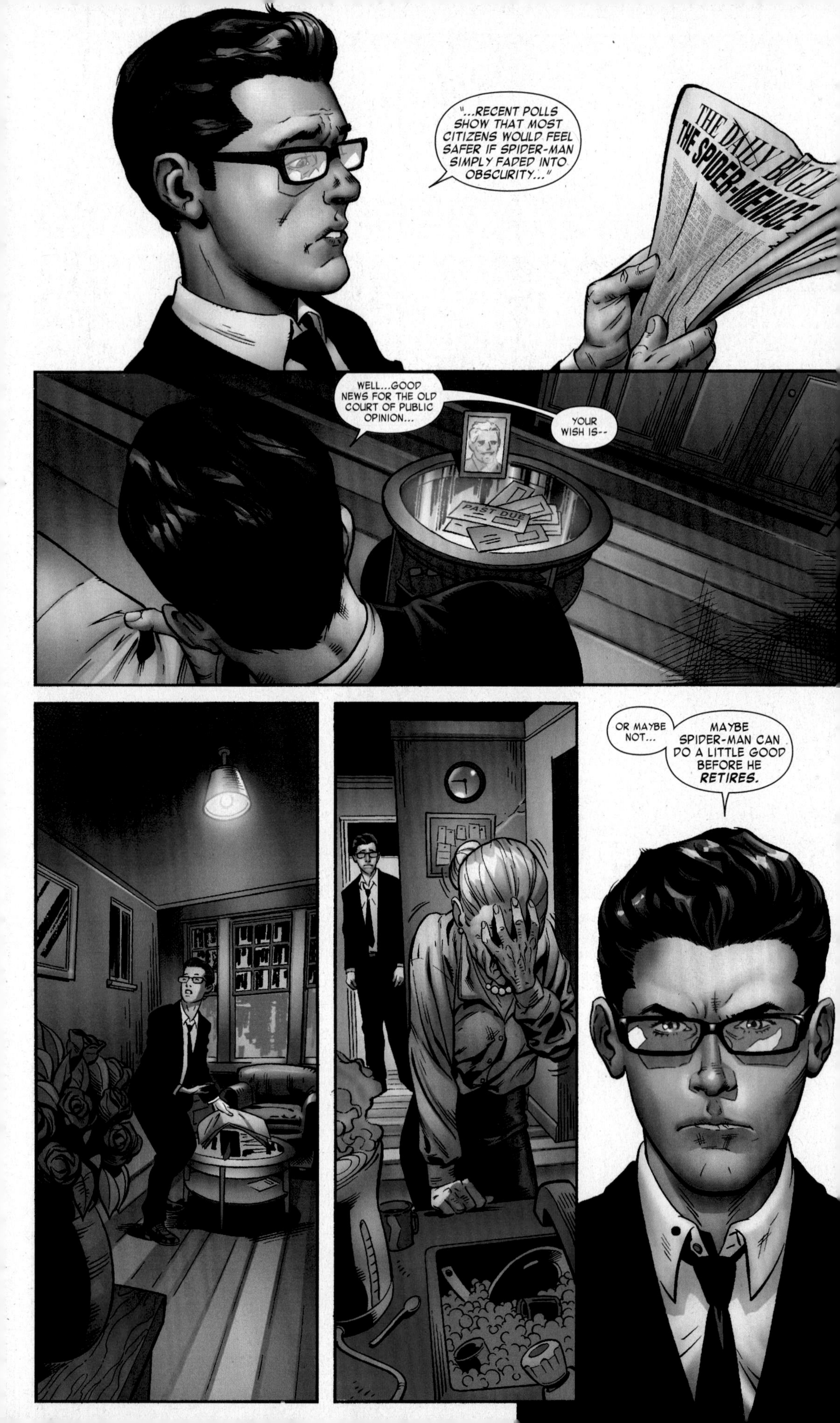
"...RECENT POLLS SHOW THAT MOST CITIZENS WOULD FEEL SAFER IF SPIDER-MAN SIMPLY FADED INTO OBSCURITY..."
THE DAILY BUGLE
THE SPIDER-MENACE
WELL...GOOD NEWS FOR THE OLD COURT OF PUBLIC OPINION...
YOUR WISH IS--
PAST DUE
OR MAYBE NOT...
MAYBE SPIDER-MAN CAN DO A LITTLE GOOD BEFORE HE RETIRES.

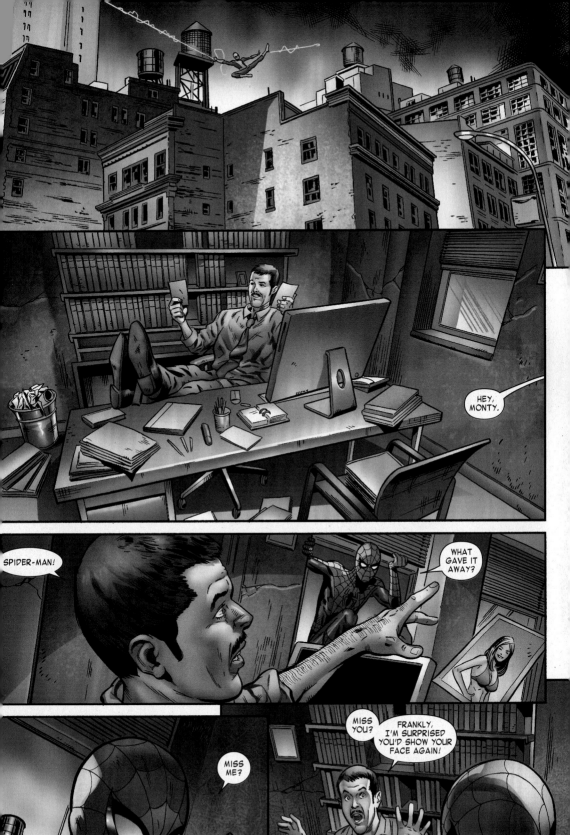

HEY, MONTY.

SPIDER-MAN!

WHAT GAVE IT AWAY?

MISS YOU?

MISS ME?

FRANKLY, I'M SURPRISED YOU'D SHOW YOUR FACE AGAIN!

I KNOW... I KNOW...

I'M SORRY I'VE BEEN FLAKING OUT ON YOU, BUT--

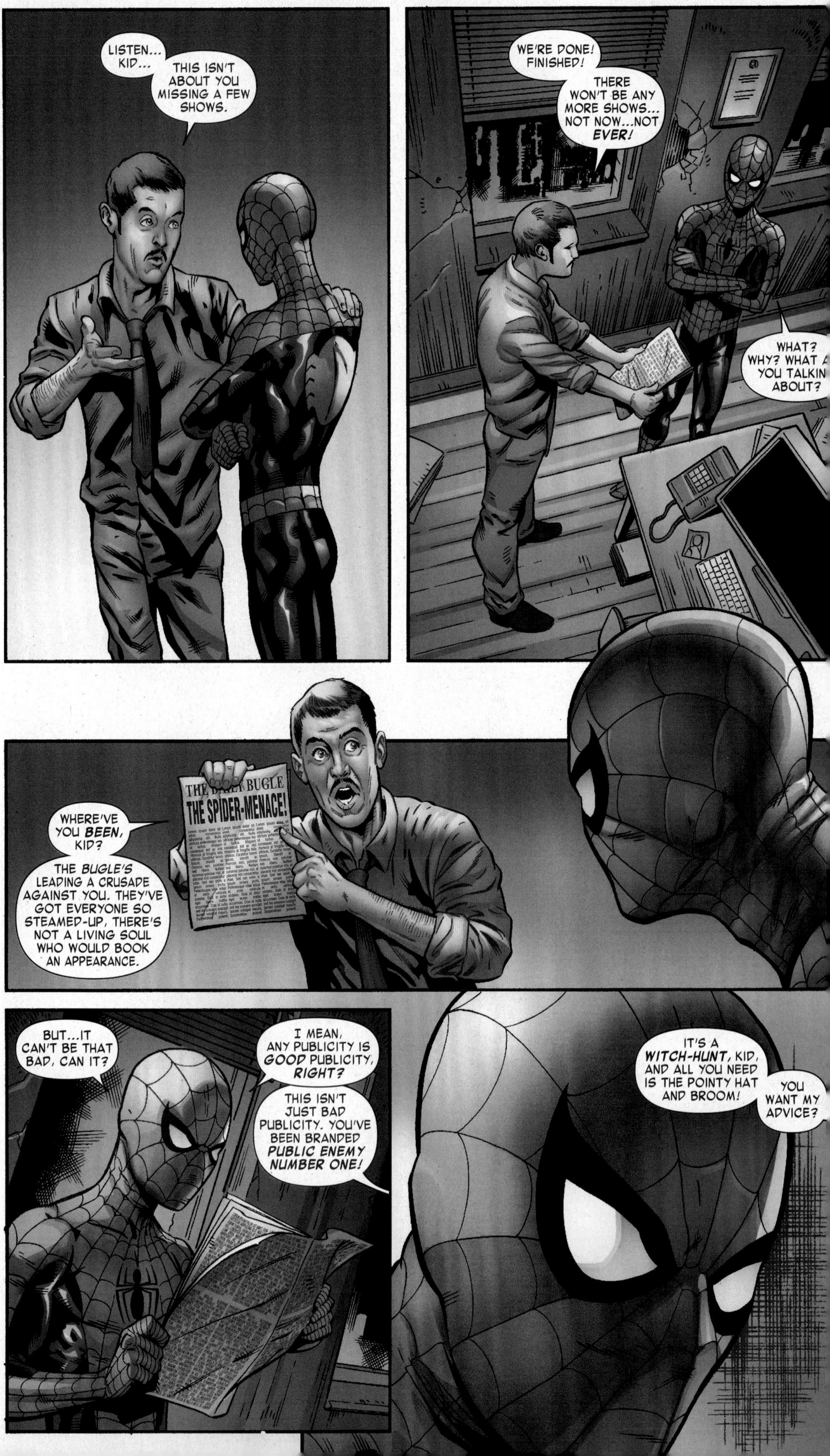
LISTEN... KID...
THIS ISN'T ABOUT YOU MISSING A FEW SHOWS.
WE'RE DONE! FINISHED!
THERE WON'T BE ANY MORE SHOWS... NOT NOW...NOT EVER!
WHAT? WHY? WHAT A YOU TALKIN ABOUT?
THE DAILY BUGLE
THE SPIDER-MENACE!
WHERE'VE YOU BEEN, KID?
THE BUGLE'S LEADING A CRUSADE AGAINST YOU. THEY'VE GOT EVERYONE SO STEAMED-UP, THERE'S NOT A LIVING SOUL WHO WOULD BOOK AN APPEARANCE.
BUT...IT CAN'T BE THAT BAD, CAN IT?
I MEAN, ANY PUBLICITY IS GOOD PUBLICITY, RIGHT?
THIS ISN'T JUST BAD PUBLICITY. YOU'VE BEEN BRANDED PUBLIC ENEMY NUMBER ONE!
IT'S A WITCH-HUNT, KID, AND ALL YOU NEED IS THE POINTY HAT AND BROOM!
YOU WANT MY ADVICE?

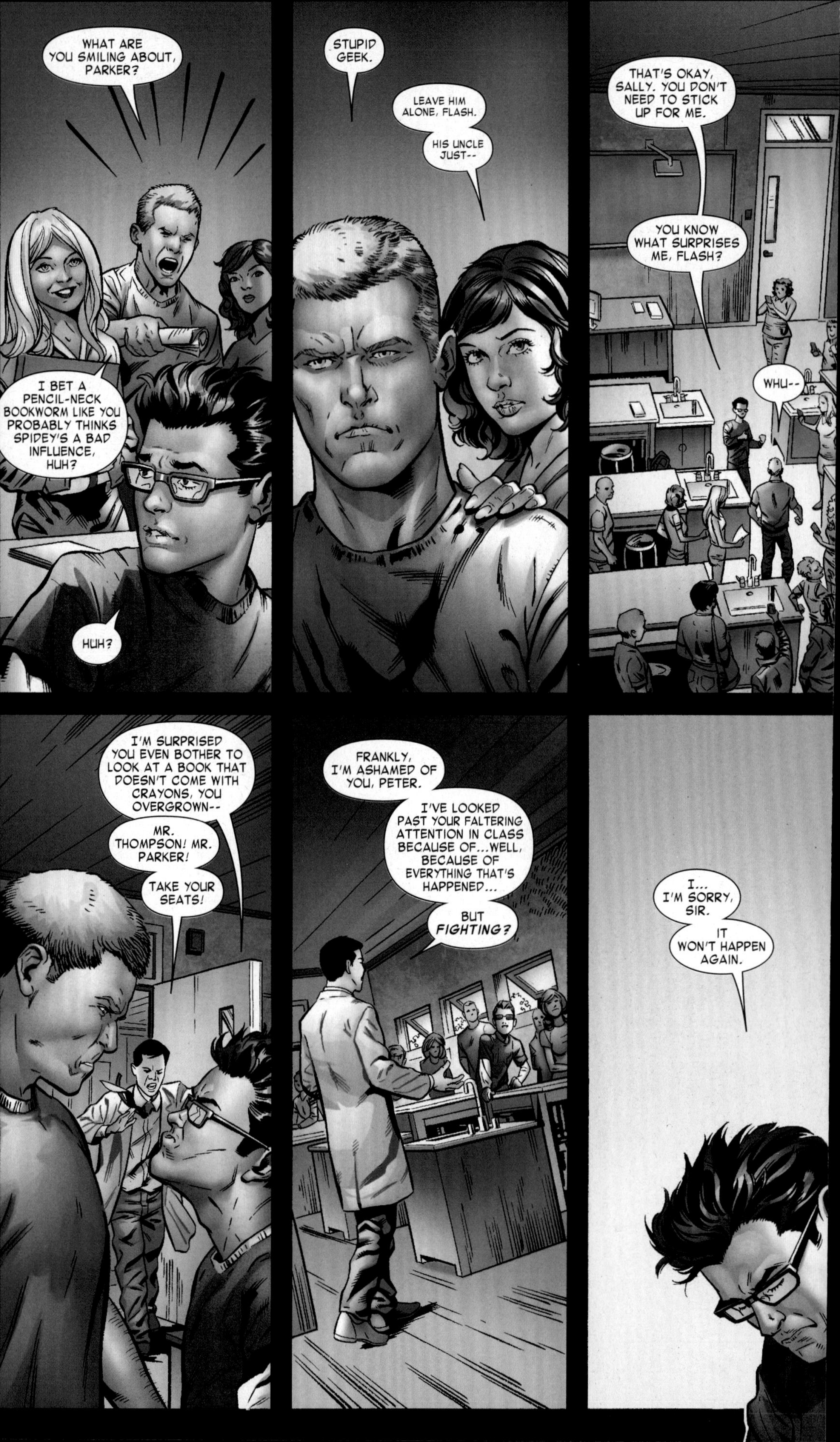
WHAT ARE YOU SMILING ABOUT, PARKER?
I BET A PENCIL-NECK BOOKWORM LIKE YOU PROBABLY THINKS SPIDEY'S A BAD INFLUENCE, HUH?
HUH?
STUPID GEEK.
LEAVE HIM ALONE, FLASH.
HIS UNCLE JUST--
THAT'S OKAY, SALLY. YOU DON'T NEED TO STICK UP FOR ME.
YOU KNOW WHAT SURPRISES ME, FLASH?
WHU--
I'M SURPRISED YOU EVEN BOTHER TO LOOK AT A BOOK THAT DOESN'T COME WITH CRAYONS, YOU OVERGROWN--
MR. THOMPSON! MR. PARKER!
TAKE YOUR SEATS!
FRANKLY, I'M ASHAMED OF YOU, PETER.
I'VE LOOKED PAST YOUR FALTERING ATTENTION IN CLASS BECAUSE OF...WELL, BECAUSE OF EVERYTHING THAT'S HAPPENED...
BUT FIGHTING?
I... I'M SORRY, SIR.
IT WON'T HAPPEN AGAIN.

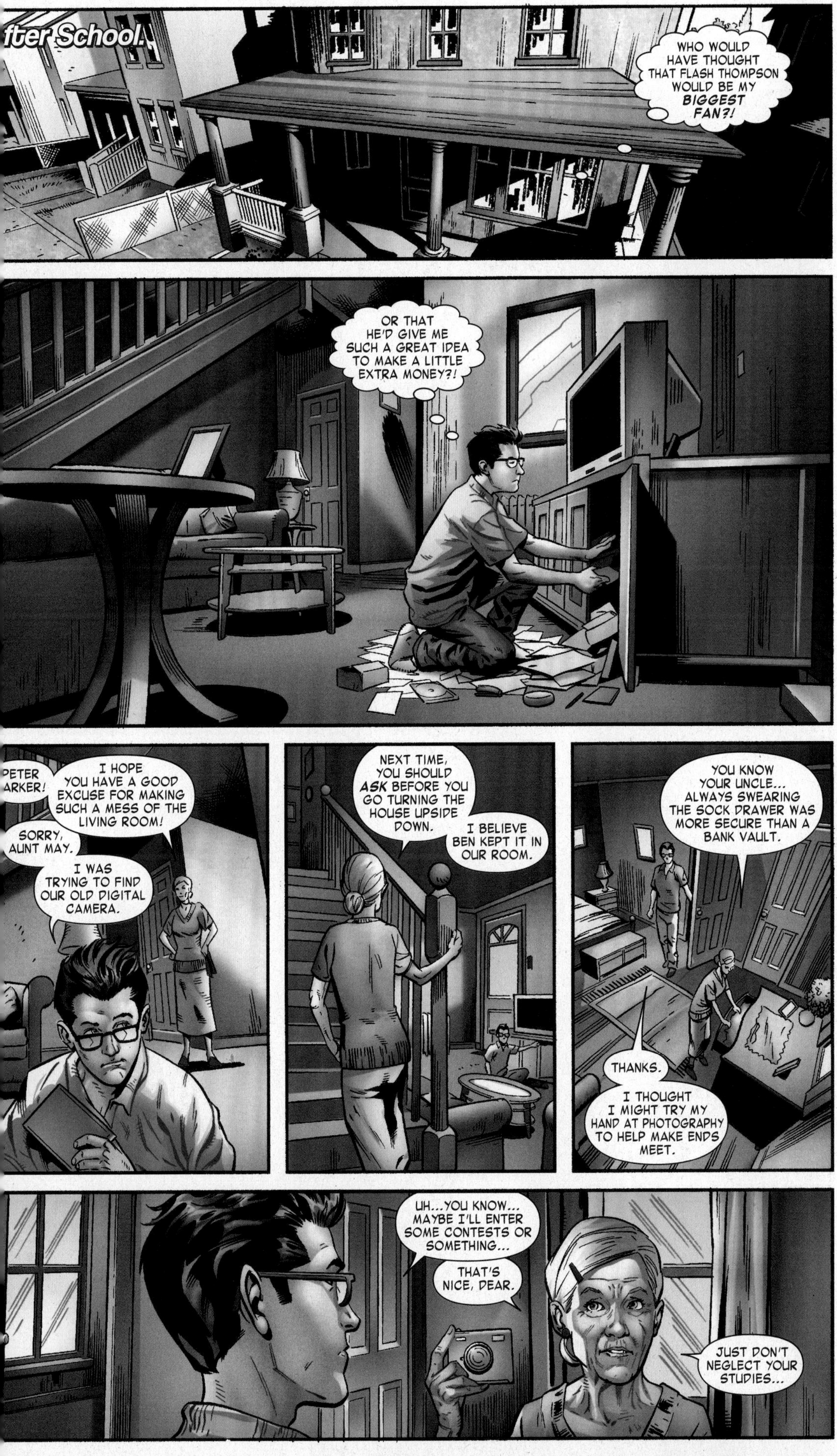
fter School.
WHO WOULD HAVE THOUGHT THAT FLASH THOMPSON WOULD BE MY BIGGEST FAN?!
OR THAT HE'D GIVE ME SUCH A GREAT IDEA TO MAKE A LITTLE EXTRA MONEY?!
PETER ARKER!
I HOPE YOU HAVE A GOOD EXCUSE FOR MAKING SUCH A MESS OF THE LIVING ROOM!
SORRY, AUNT MAY.
I WAS TRYING TO FIND OUR OLD DIGITAL CAMERA.
NEXT TIME, YOU SHOULD ASK BEFORE YOU GO TURNING THE HOUSE UPSIDE DOWN.
I BELIEVE BEN KEPT IT IN OUR ROOM.
YOU KNOW YOUR UNCLE... ALWAYS SWEARING THE SOCK DRAWER WAS MORE SECURE THAN A BANK VAULT.
THANKS.
I THOUGHT I MIGHT TRY MY HAND AT PHOTOGRAPHY TO HELP MAKE ENDS MEET.
UH...YOU KNOW... MAYBE I'LL ENTER SOME CONTESTS OR SOMETHING...
THAT'S NICE, DEAR.
JUST DON'T NEGLECT YOUR STUDIES...

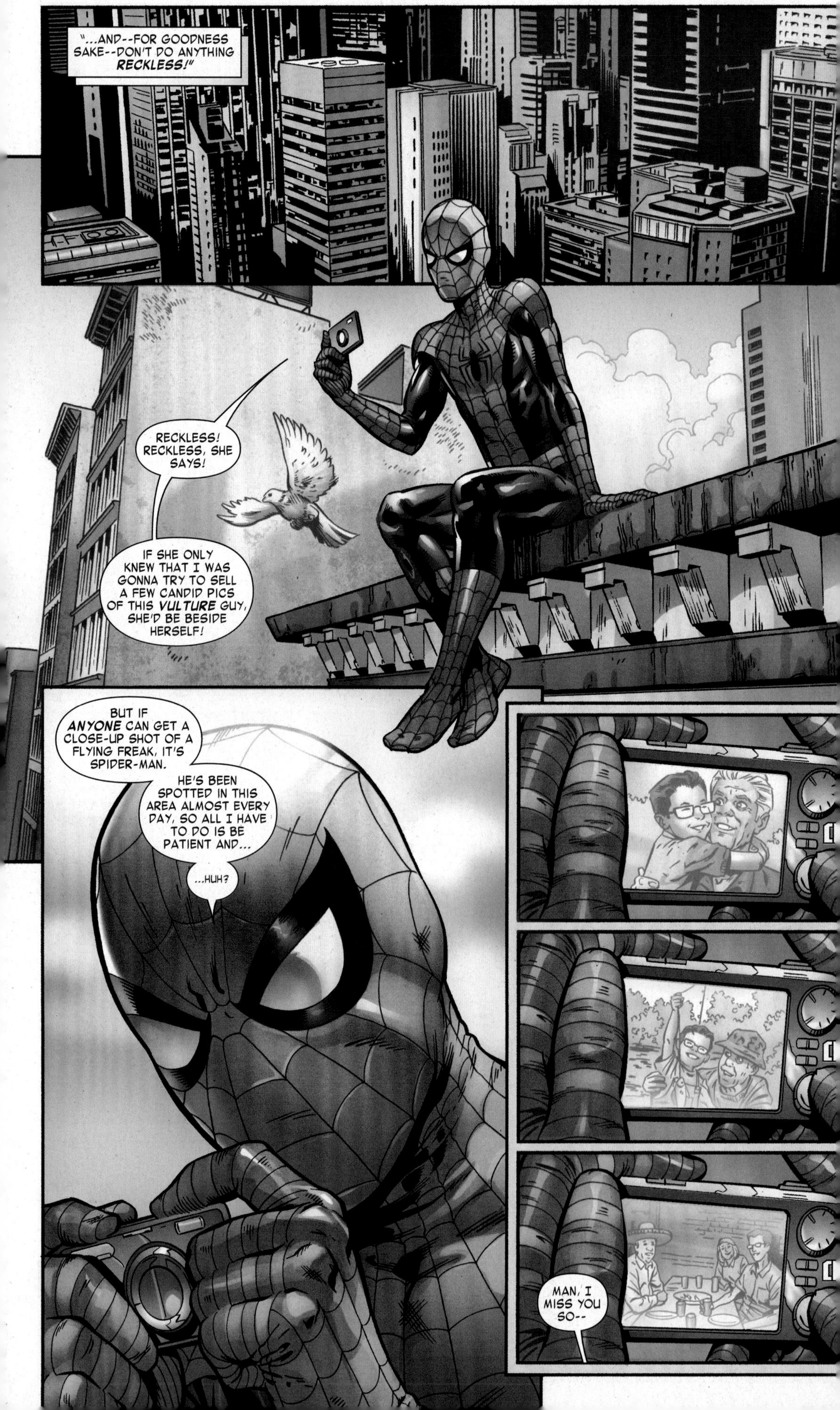
"...AND--FOR GOODNESS SAKE--DON'T DO ANYTHING RECKLESS!"
RECKLESS! RECKLESS, SHE SAYS!
IF SHE ONLY KNEW THAT I WAS GONNA TRY TO SELL A FEW CANDID PICS OF THIS VULTURE GUY, SHE'D BE BESIDE HERSELF!
BUT IF ANYONE CAN GET A CLOSE-UP SHOT OF A FLYING FREAK, IT'S SPIDER-MAN.
HE'S BEEN SPOTTED IN THIS AREA ALMOST EVERY DAY, SO ALL I HAVE TO DO IS BE PATIENT AND...
...HUH?
MAN, I MISS YOU SO--

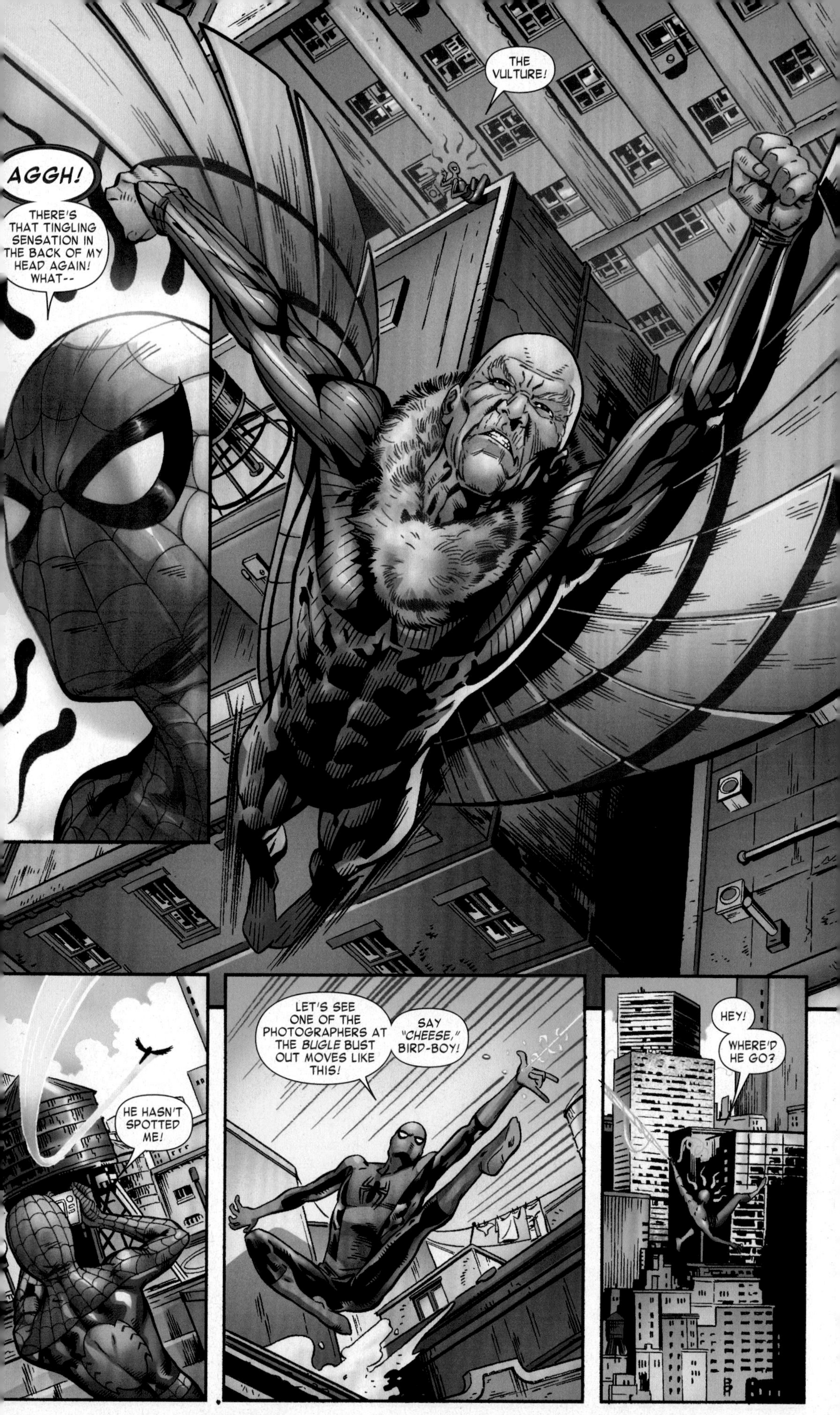
THE VULTURE!
AGGH!
THERE'S THAT TINGLING SENSATION IN THE BACK OF MY HEAD AGAIN! WHAT--
HE HASN'T SPOTTED ME!
LET'S SEE ONE OF THE PHOTOGRAPHERS AT THE *BUGLE* BUST OUT MOVES LIKE THIS!
SAY "CHEESE," BIRD-BOY!
HEY!
WHERE'D HE GO?

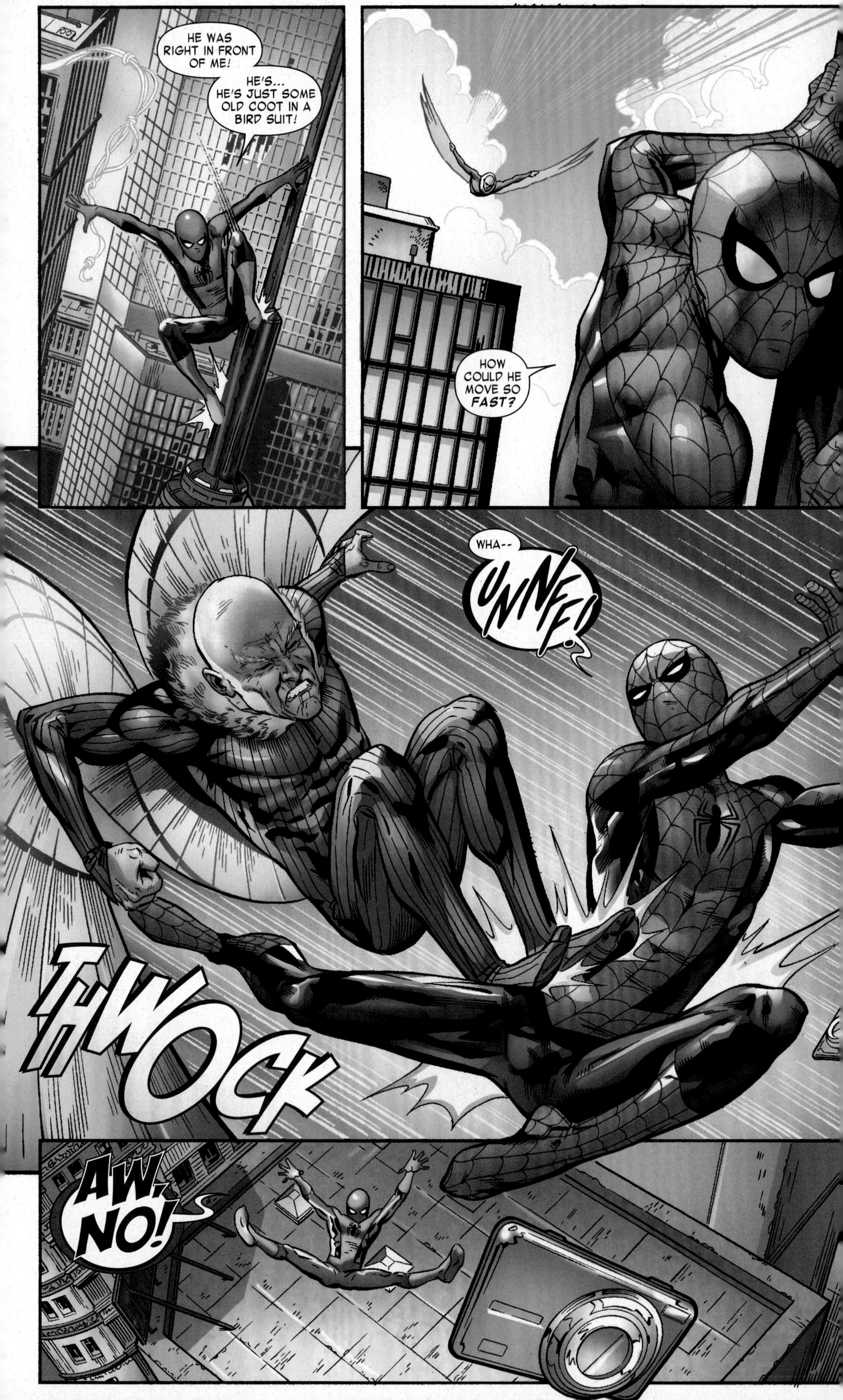
HE WAS RIGHT IN FRONT OF ME!
HE'S... HE'S JUST SOME OLD COOT IN A BIRD SUIT!
HOW COULD HE MOVE SO FAST?
WHA--
UNNF!
THWOCK
AW, NO!

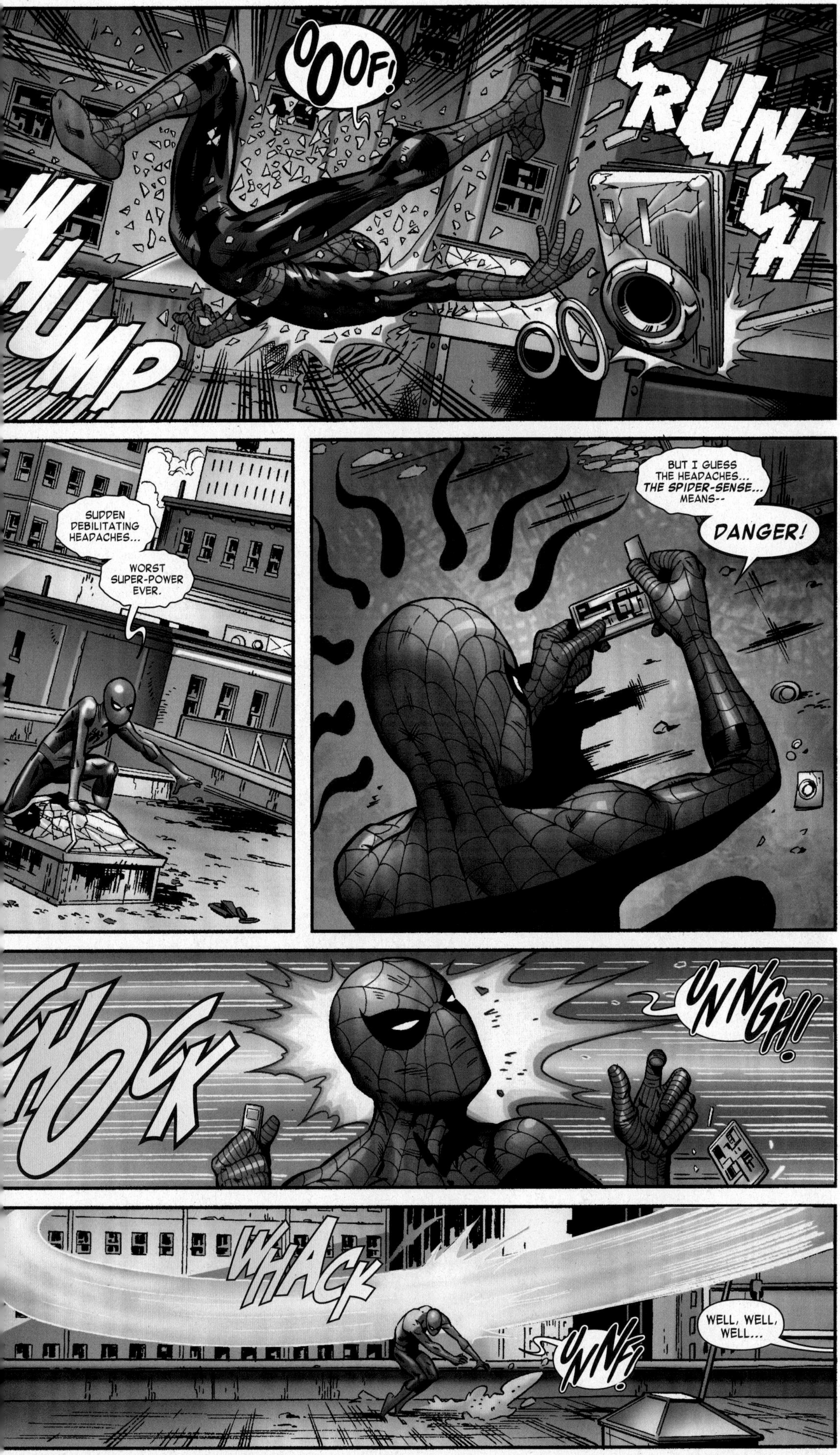

OOOF!
CRUNCH
WHUMP
SUDDEN DEBILITATING HEADACHES...
WORST SUPER-POWER EVER.
BUT I GUESS THE HEADACHES... THE SPIDER-SENSE... MEANS--
DANGER!
CHOCK
UNNGH!
WHACK
UNNF!
WELL, WELL, WELL...

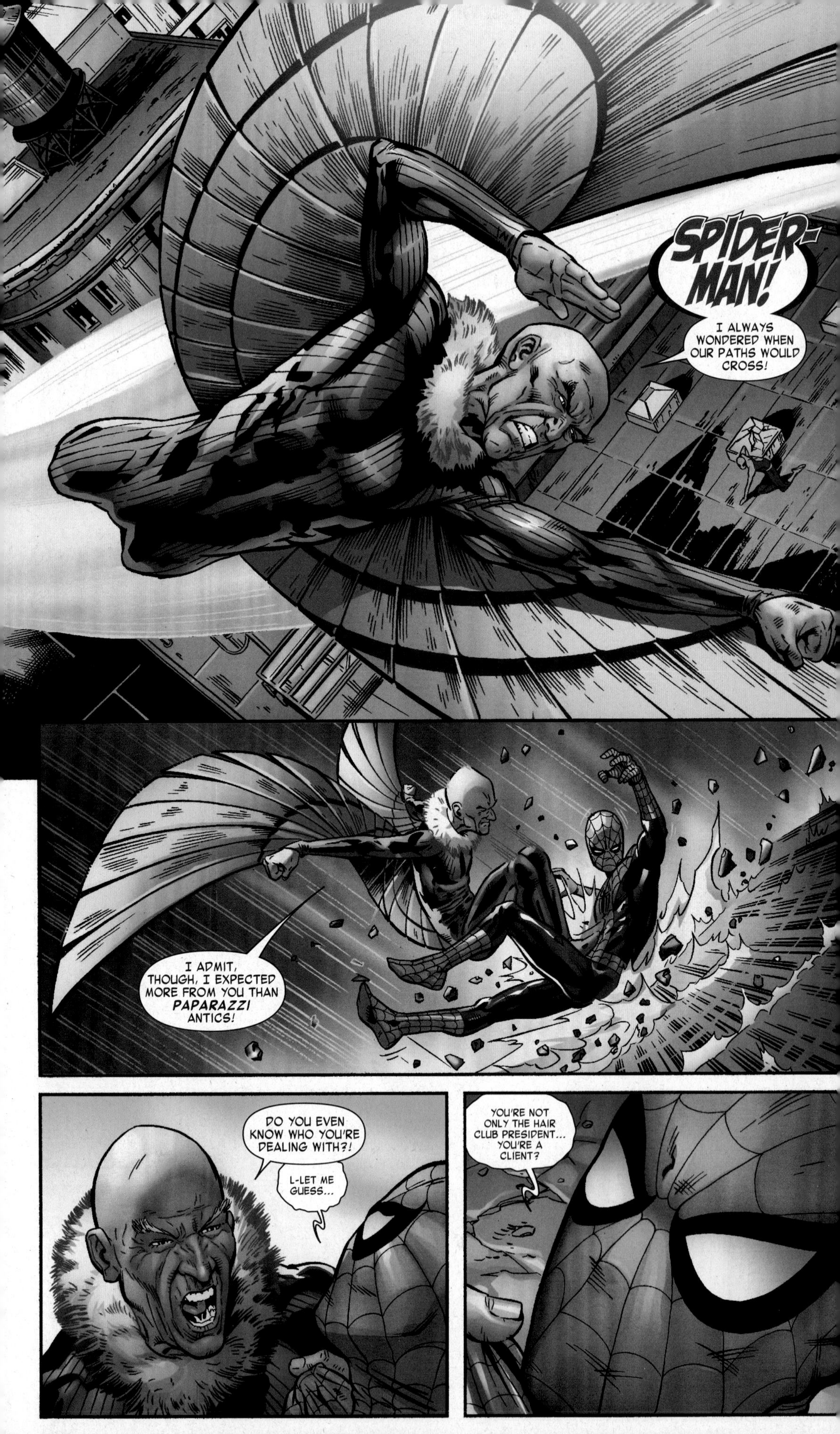
SPIDER-MAN!
I ALWAYS WONDERED WHEN OUR PATHS WOULD CROSS!
I ADMIT, THOUGH, I EXPECTED MORE FROM YOU THAN *PAPARAZZI* ANTICS!
DO YOU EVEN KNOW WHO YOU'RE DEALING WITH?!
L-LET ME GUESS...
YOU'RE NOT ONLY THE HAIR CLUB PRESIDENT... YOU'RE A CLIENT?

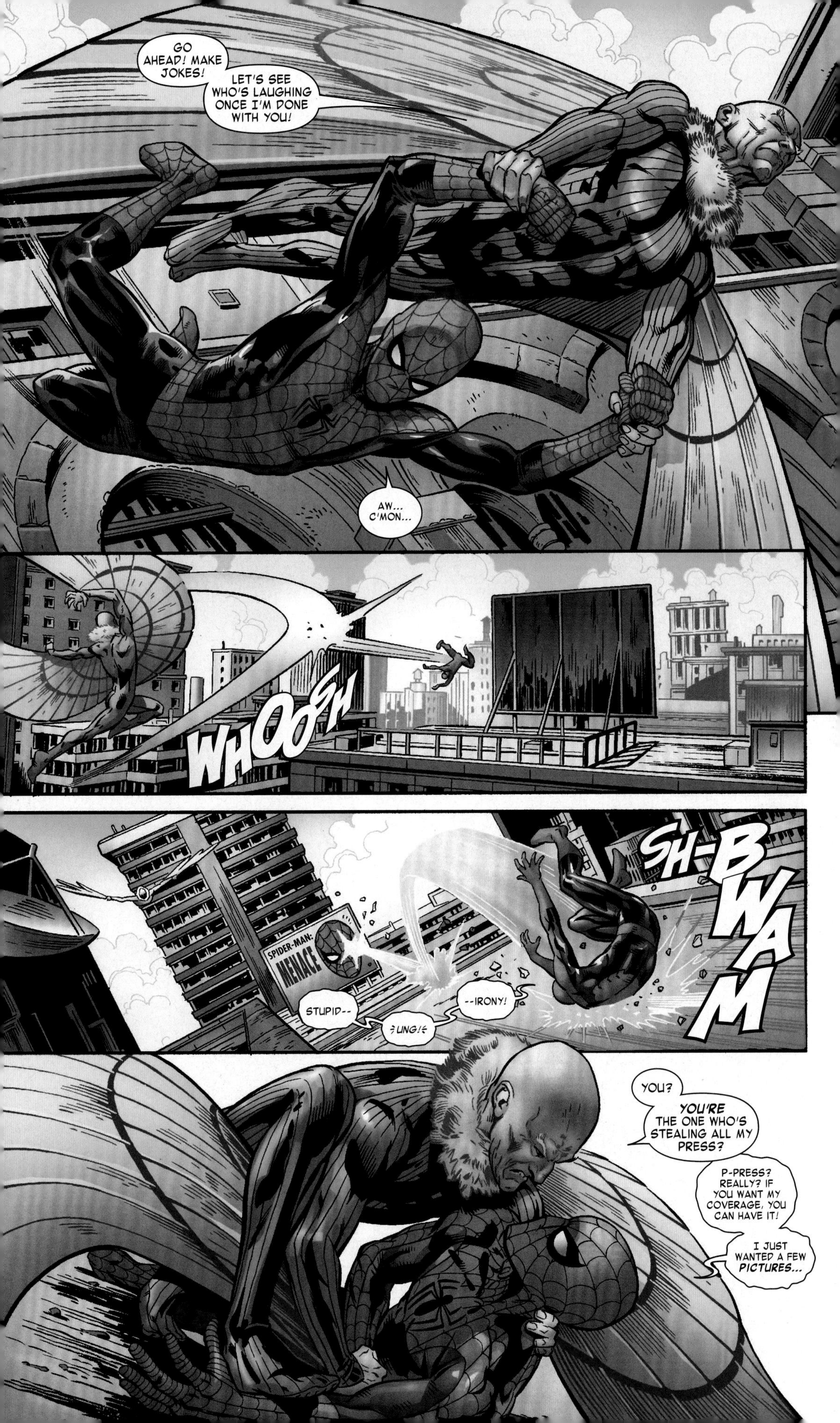

GO AHEAD! MAKE JOKES!
LET'S SEE WHO'S LAUGHING ONCE I'M DONE WITH YOU!
AW... C'MON...
WHOOSH
SH-BWAM
STUPID--
UNG!
--IRONY!
SPIDER-MAN: MENACE
YOU?
YOU'RE THE ONE WHO'S STEALING ALL MY PRESS?
P-PRESS? REALLY? IF YOU WANT MY COVERAGE, YOU CAN HAVE IT!
I JUST WANTED A FEW PICTURES...

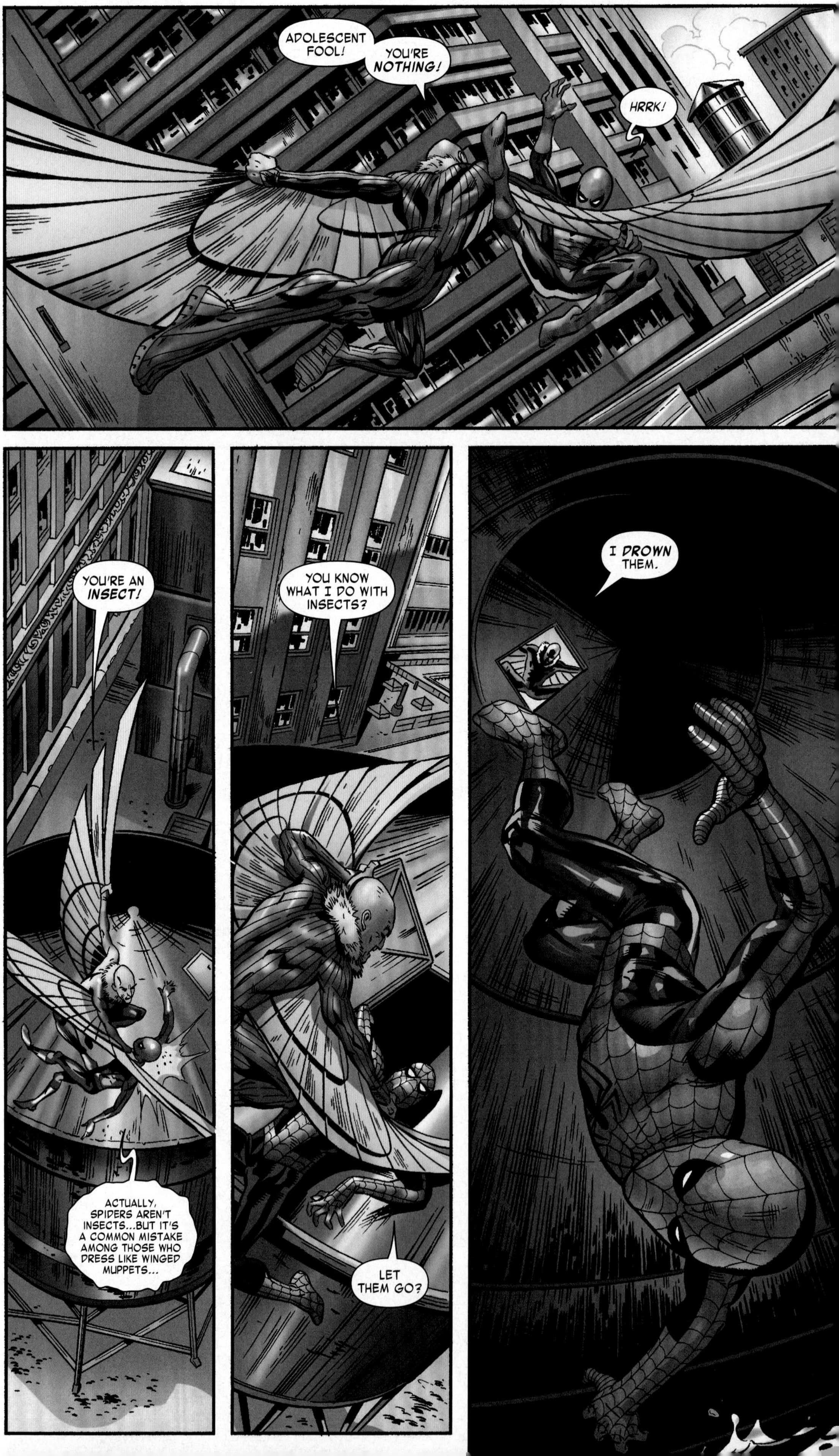
ADOLESCENT FOOL!
YOU'RE NOTHING!
HRRK!
YOU'RE AN INSECT!
ACTUALLY, SPIDERS AREN'T INSECTS...BUT IT'S A COMMON MISTAKE AMONG THOSE WHO DRESS LIKE WINGED MUPPETS...
YOU KNOW WHAT I DO WITH INSECTS?
LET THEM GO?
I DROWN THEM.

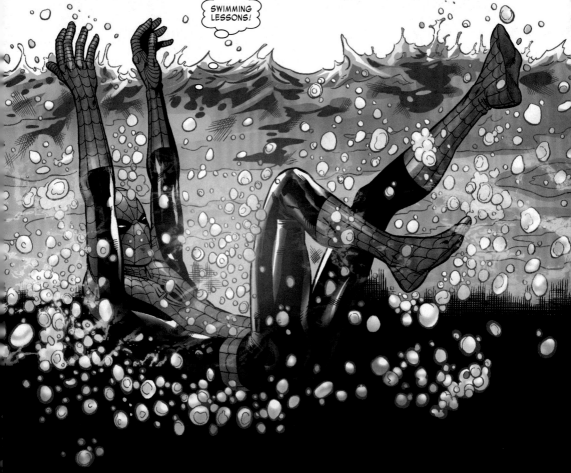

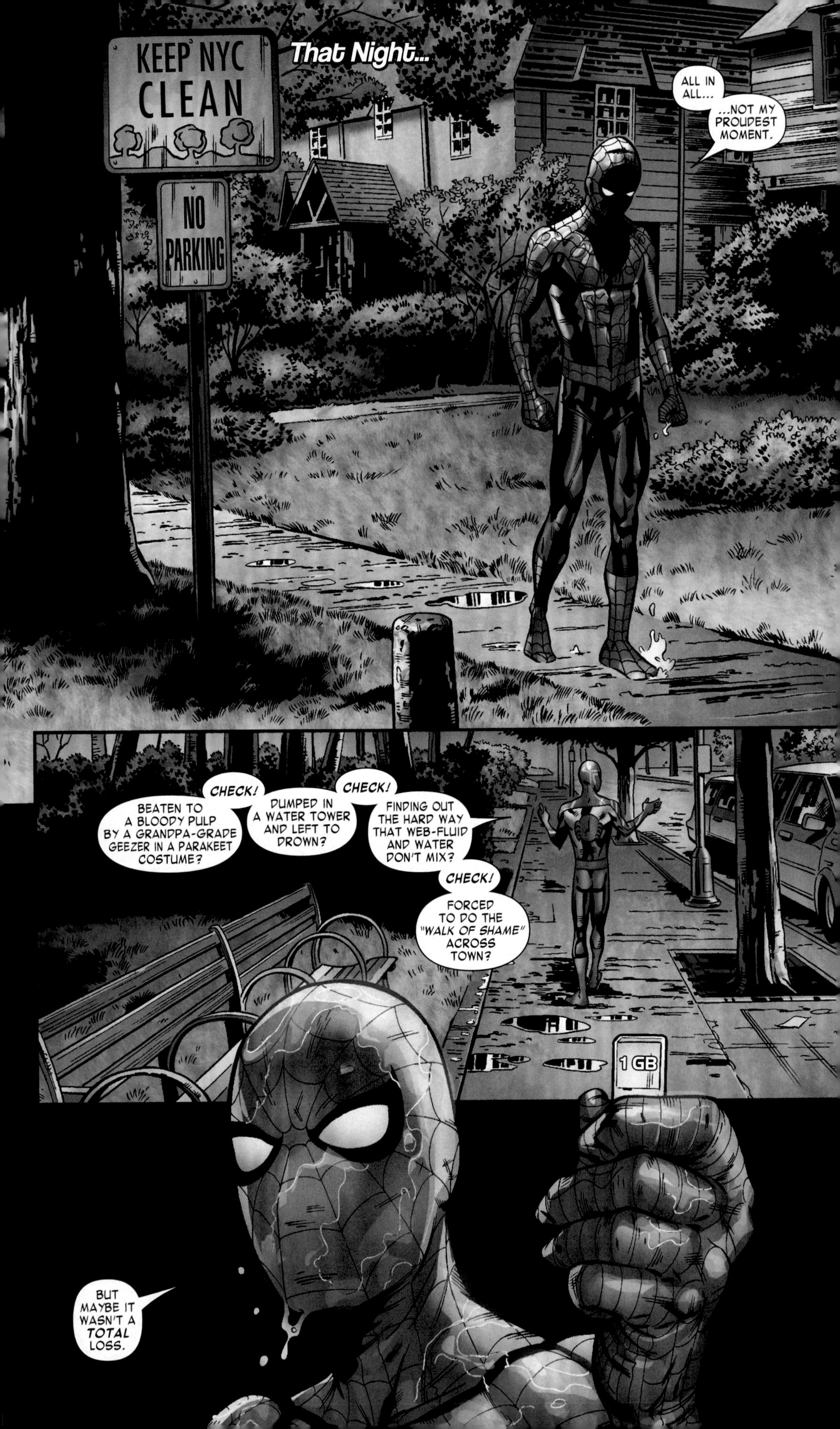
KEEP NYC CLEAN
NO PARKING
That Night...
ALL IN ALL...
...NOT MY PROUDEST MOMENT.
BEATEN TO A BLOODY PULP BY A GRANDPA-GRADE GEEZER IN A PARAKEET COSTUME?
CHECK!
DUMPED IN A WATER TOWER AND LEFT TO DROWN?
CHECK!
FINDING OUT THE HARD WAY THAT WEB-FLUID AND WATER DON'T MIX?
CHECK!
FORCED TO DO THE "WALK OF SHAME" ACROSS TOWN?
1 GB
BUT MAYBE IT WASN'T A TOTAL LOSS.

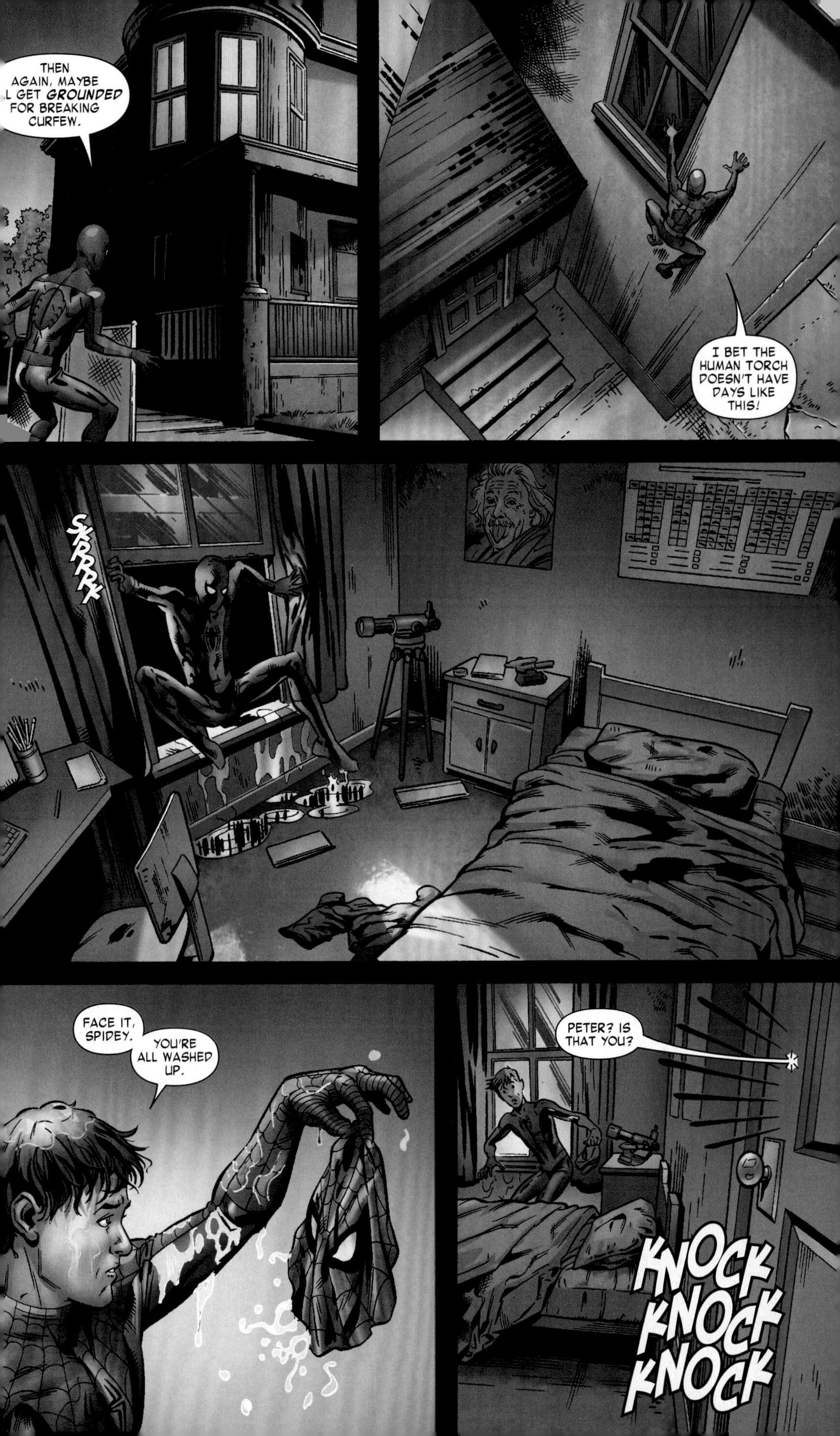
THEN AGAIN, MAYBE
L GET GROUNDED FOR BREAKING CURFEW.
I BET THE HUMAN TORCH DOESN'T HAVE DAYS LIKE THIS!
SKRRRK
FACE IT, SPIDEY.
YOU'RE ALL WASHED UP.
PETER? IS THAT YOU?
KNOCK KNOCK KNOCK

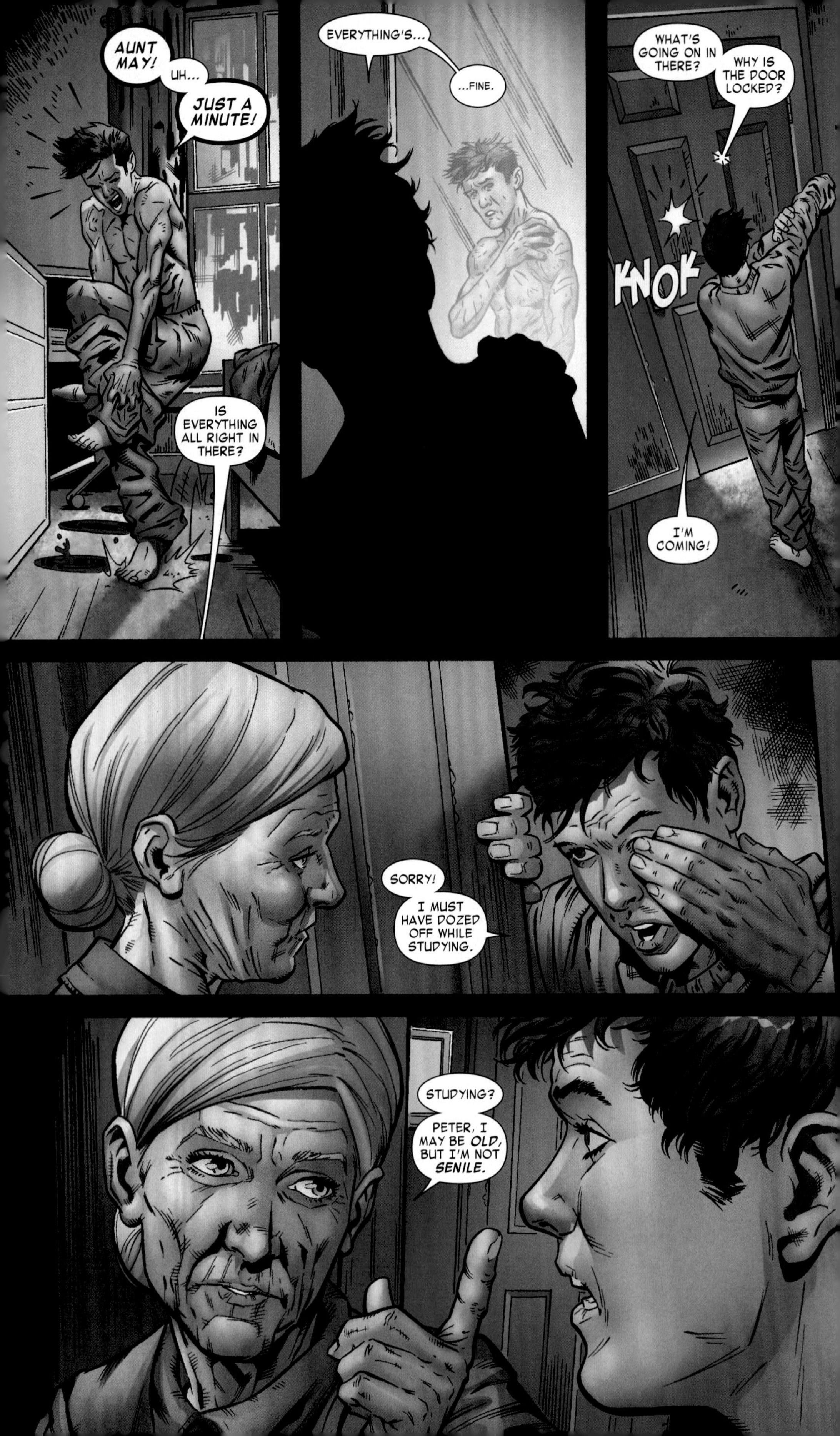
AUNT MAY!
UH...
JUST A MINUTE!
IS EVERYTHING ALL RIGHT IN THERE?
EVERYTHING'S...
...FINE.
WHAT'S GOING ON IN THERE?
WHY IS THE DOOR LOCKED?
KNOK
I'M COMING!
SORRY!
I MUST HAVE DOZED OFF WHILE STUDYING.
STUDYING?
PETER, I MAY BE OLD, BUT I'M NOT SENILE.

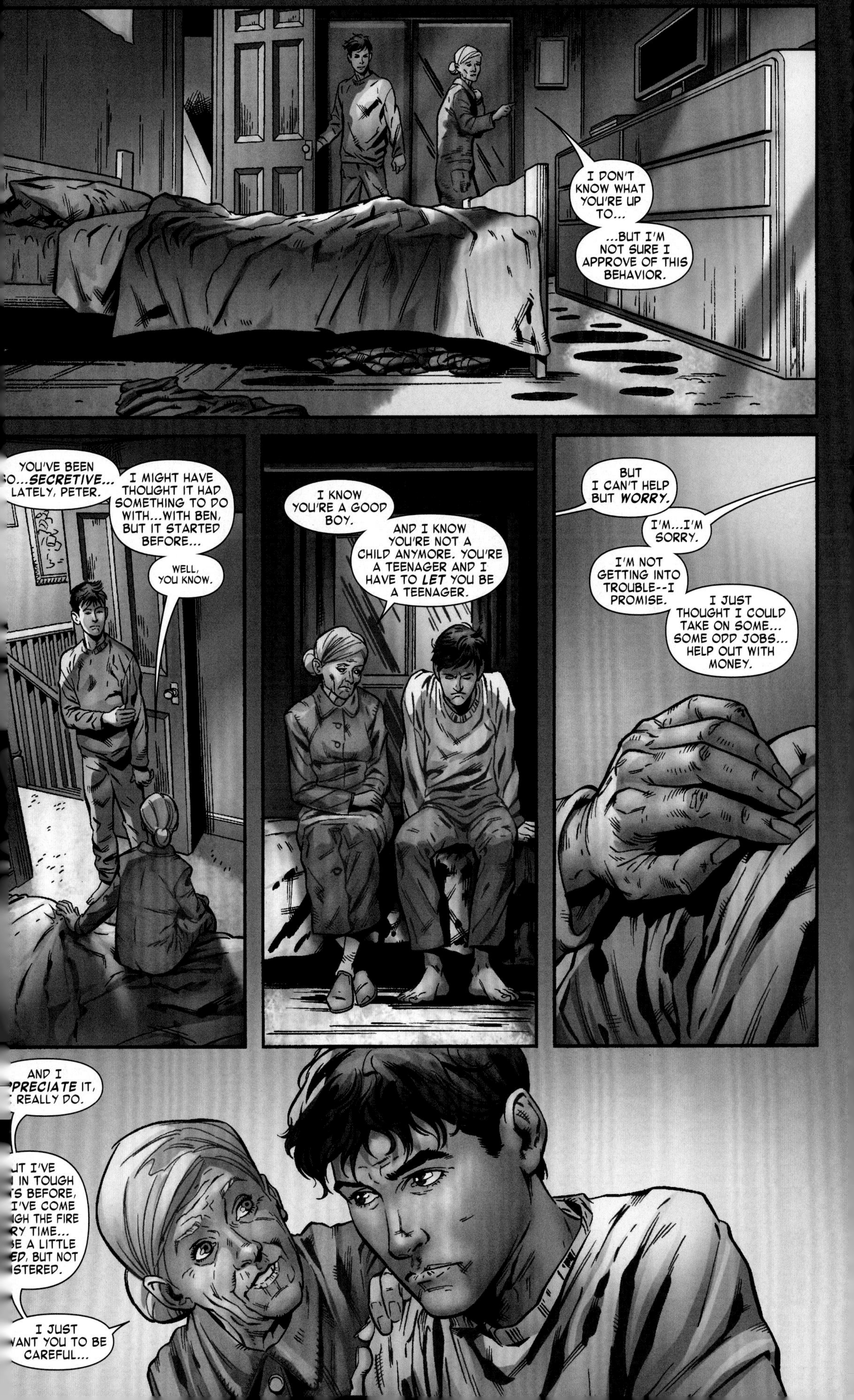

I DON'T KNOW WHAT YOU'RE UP TO...
...BUT I'M NOT SURE I APPROVE OF THIS BEHAVIOR.
YOU'VE BEEN O...SECRETIVE... LATELY, PETER.
I MIGHT HAVE THOUGHT IT HAD SOMETHING TO DO WITH...WITH BEN, BUT IT STARTED BEFORE...
WELL, YOU KNOW.
I KNOW YOU'RE A GOOD BOY.
AND I KNOW YOU'RE NOT A CHILD ANYMORE. YOU'RE A TEENAGER AND I HAVE TO LET YOU BE A TEENAGER.
BUT I CAN'T HELP BUT WORRY.
I'M...I'M SORRY.
I'M NOT GETTING INTO TROUBLE--I PROMISE.
I JUST THOUGHT I COULD TAKE ON SOME... SOME ODD JOBS... HELP OUT WITH MONEY.
AND I PRECIATE IT, REALLY DO.
UT I'VE IN TOUGH S BEFORE, I'VE COME IGH THE FIRE RY TIME... E A LITTLE ED, BUT NOT STERED.
I JUST WANT YOU TO BE CAREFUL...

"...THERE ARE PLENTY OF PEOPLE IN THE WORLD WHO LIVE FOR NOTHING MORE THAN TO DO OTHERS HARM."

I HATE TO SAY IT...

...BUT THESE PHOTOS AREN'T BAD.

NOT BAD AT ALL.

IF THEY'RE *FREE*, THEY'RE EVEN BETTER!

THEY'RE NOT *FREE*, BUT I'M SURE YOU COULD *LOW-BALL* THE PHOTOGRAPHER.

A FEW SHOTS LIKE THIS OF SPIDER-MAN IN ACTION COULDN'T HURT.

THANKS FOR THE ADVICE, KIERNAN. WHO IS THIS MODERN DAY ANSEL ADAMS, ANYWAY?

HE'S IN THE LOBBY. YOU CAN MEET HIM YOURSELF.

BEFORE YOU DO THAT, SIR, YOU SHOULD PROBABLY--

WELL, DON'T JUST STAND THERE. SEND HIM IN.

J. JONAH JAMESON...MEET PETER PARKER...

WHAT IS THIS, A *JOKE*?

HI.

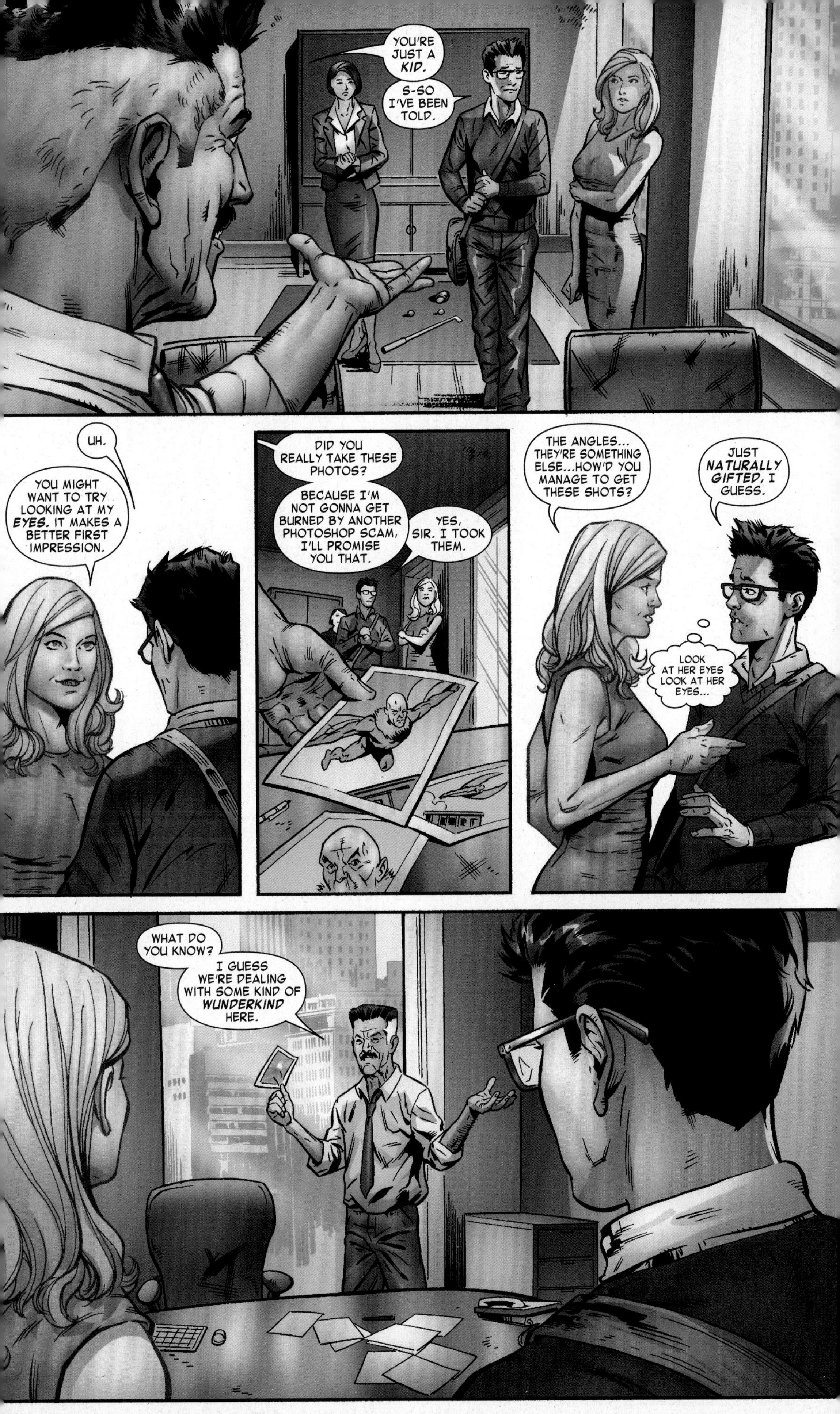
YOU'RE JUST A *KID.*
S-SO I'VE BEEN TOLD.
UH.
YOU MIGHT WANT TO TRY LOOKING AT MY *EYES.* IT MAKES A BETTER FIRST IMPRESSION.
DID YOU REALLY TAKE THESE PHOTOS?
BECAUSE I'M NOT GONNA GET BURNED BY ANOTHER PHOTOSHOP SCAM, I'LL PROMISE YOU THAT.
YES, SIR. I TOOK THEM.
THE ANGLES... THEY'RE SOMETHING ELSE...HOW'D YOU MANAGE TO GET THESE SHOTS?
JUST *NATURALLY GIFTED,* I GUESS.
LOOK AT HER EYES LOOK AT HER EYES...
WHAT DO YOU KNOW?
I GUESS WE'RE DEALING WITH SOME KIND OF *WUNDERKIND* HERE.

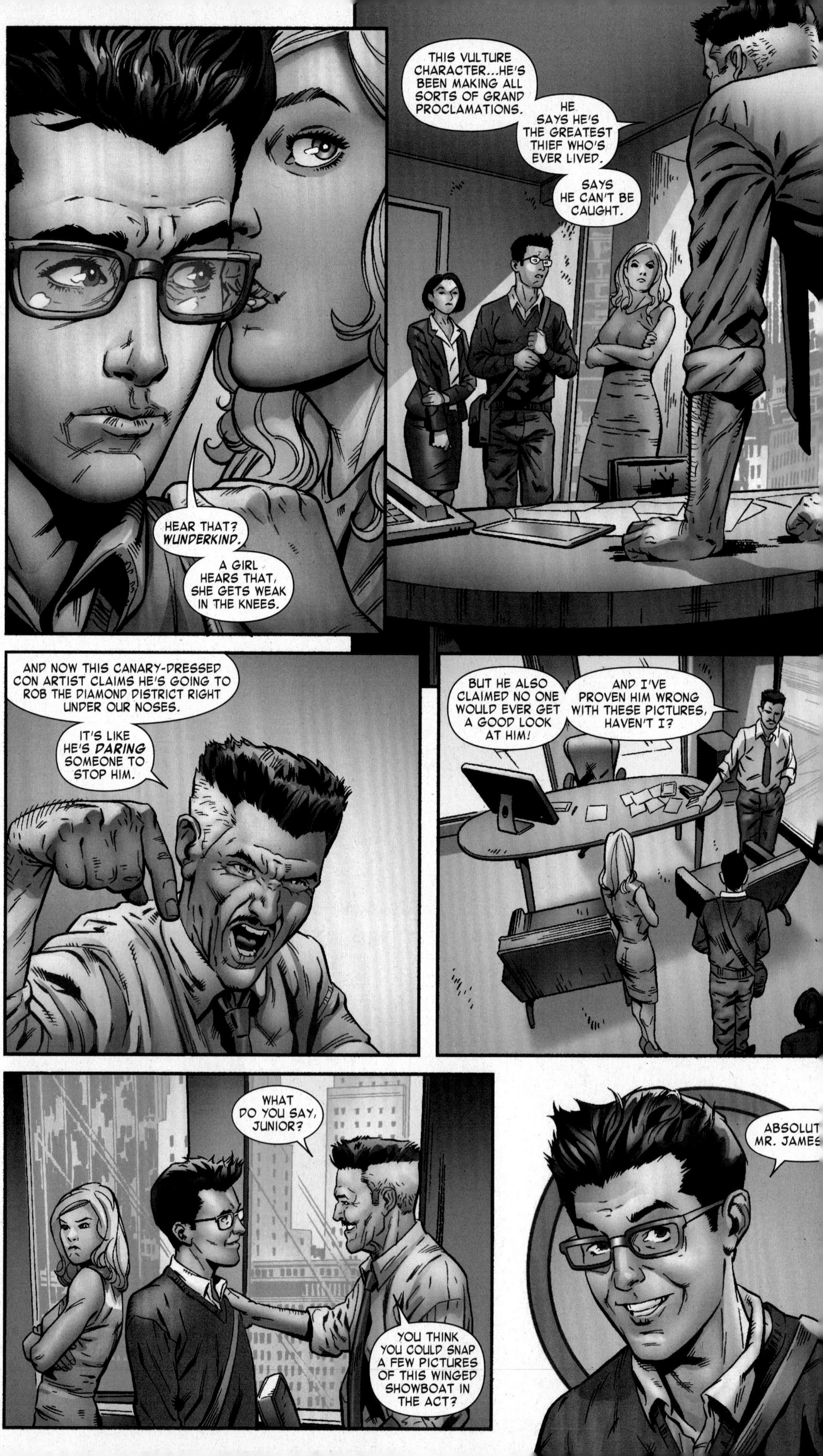
HEAR THAT? WUNDERKIND.
A GIRL HEARS THAT, SHE GETS WEAK IN THE KNEES.
THIS VULTURE CHARACTER...HE'S BEEN MAKING ALL SORTS OF GRAND PROCLAMATIONS.
HE SAYS HE'S THE GREATEST THIEF WHO'S EVER LIVED.
SAYS HE CAN'T BE CAUGHT.
AND NOW THIS CANARY-DRESSED CON ARTIST CLAIMS HE'S GOING TO ROB THE DIAMOND DISTRICT RIGHT UNDER OUR NOSES.
IT'S LIKE HE'S DARING SOMEONE TO STOP HIM.
BUT HE ALSO CLAIMED NO ONE WOULD EVER GET A GOOD LOOK AT HIM!
AND I'VE PROVEN HIM WRONG WITH THESE PICTURES, HAVEN'T I?
WHAT DO YOU SAY, JUNIOR?
YOU THINK YOU COULD SNAP A FEW PICTURES OF THIS WINGED SHOWBOAT IN THE ACT?
ABSOLUT
MR. JAMES

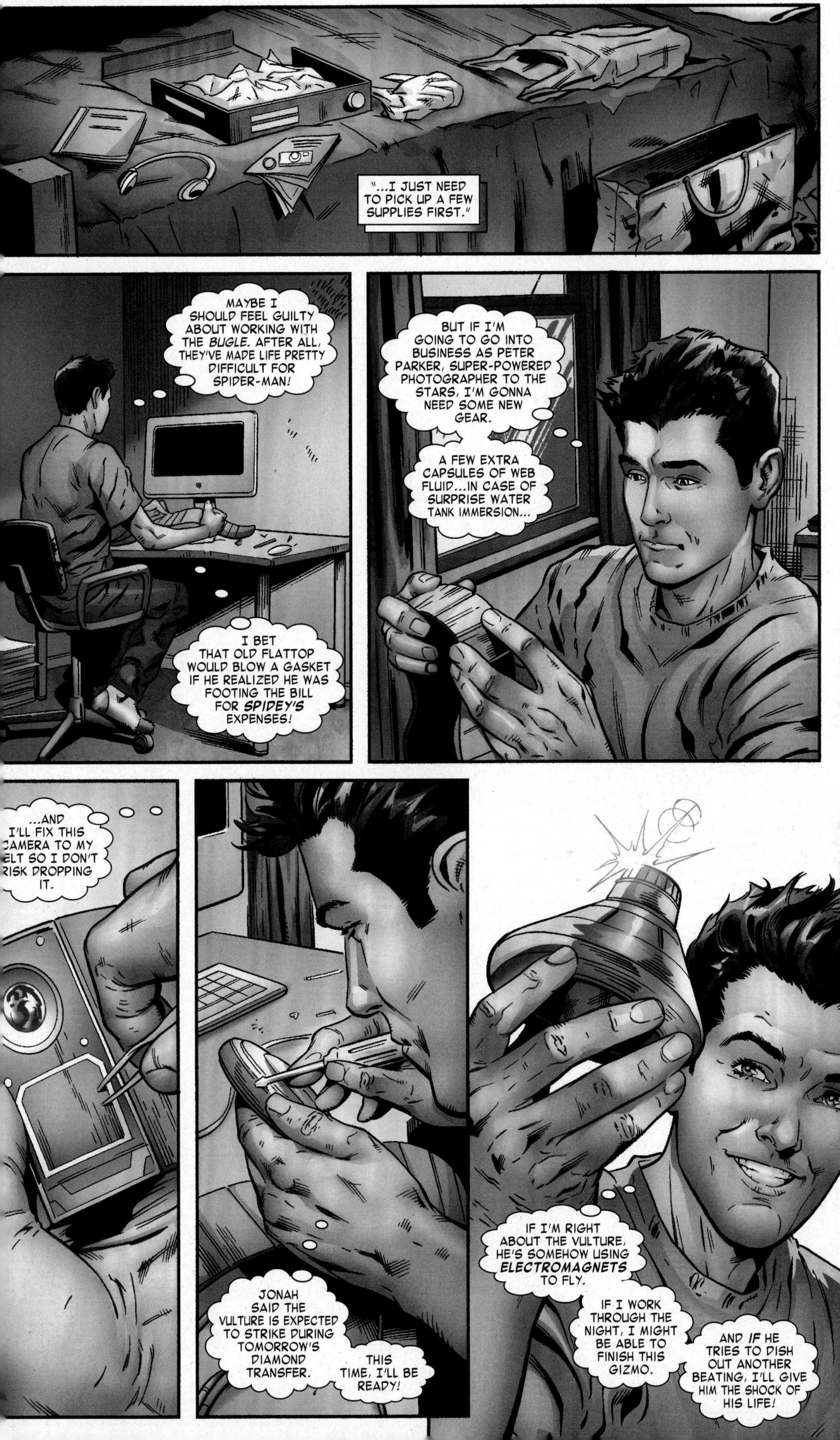
"...I JUST NEED TO PICK UP A FEW SUPPLIES FIRST."
MAYBE I SHOULD FEEL GUILTY ABOUT WORKING WITH THE *BUGLE.* AFTER ALL, THEY'VE MADE LIFE PRETTY DIFFICULT FOR SPIDER-MAN!
I BET THAT OLD FLATTOP WOULD BLOW A GASKET IF HE REALIZED HE WAS FOOTING THE BILL FOR *SPIDEY'S* EXPENSES!
BUT IF I'M GOING TO GO INTO BUSINESS AS PETER PARKER, SUPER-POWERED PHOTOGRAPHER TO THE STARS, I'M GONNA NEED SOME NEW GEAR.
A FEW EXTRA CAPSULES OF WEB FLUID...IN CASE OF SURPRISE WATER TANK IMMERSION...
...AND I'LL FIX THIS CAMERA TO MY ELT SO I DON'T RISK DROPPING IT.
JONAH SAID THE VULTURE IS EXPECTED TO STRIKE DURING TOMORROW'S DIAMOND TRANSFER.
THIS TIME, I'LL BE READY!
IF I'M RIGHT ABOUT THE VULTURE, HE'S SOMEHOW USING ***ELECTROMAGNETS*** TO FLY.
IF I WORK THROUGH THE NIGHT, I MIGHT BE ABLE TO FINISH THIS GIZMO.
AND *IF* HE TRIES TO DISH OUT ANOTHER BEATING, I'LL GIVE HIM THE SHOCK OF HIS LIFE!

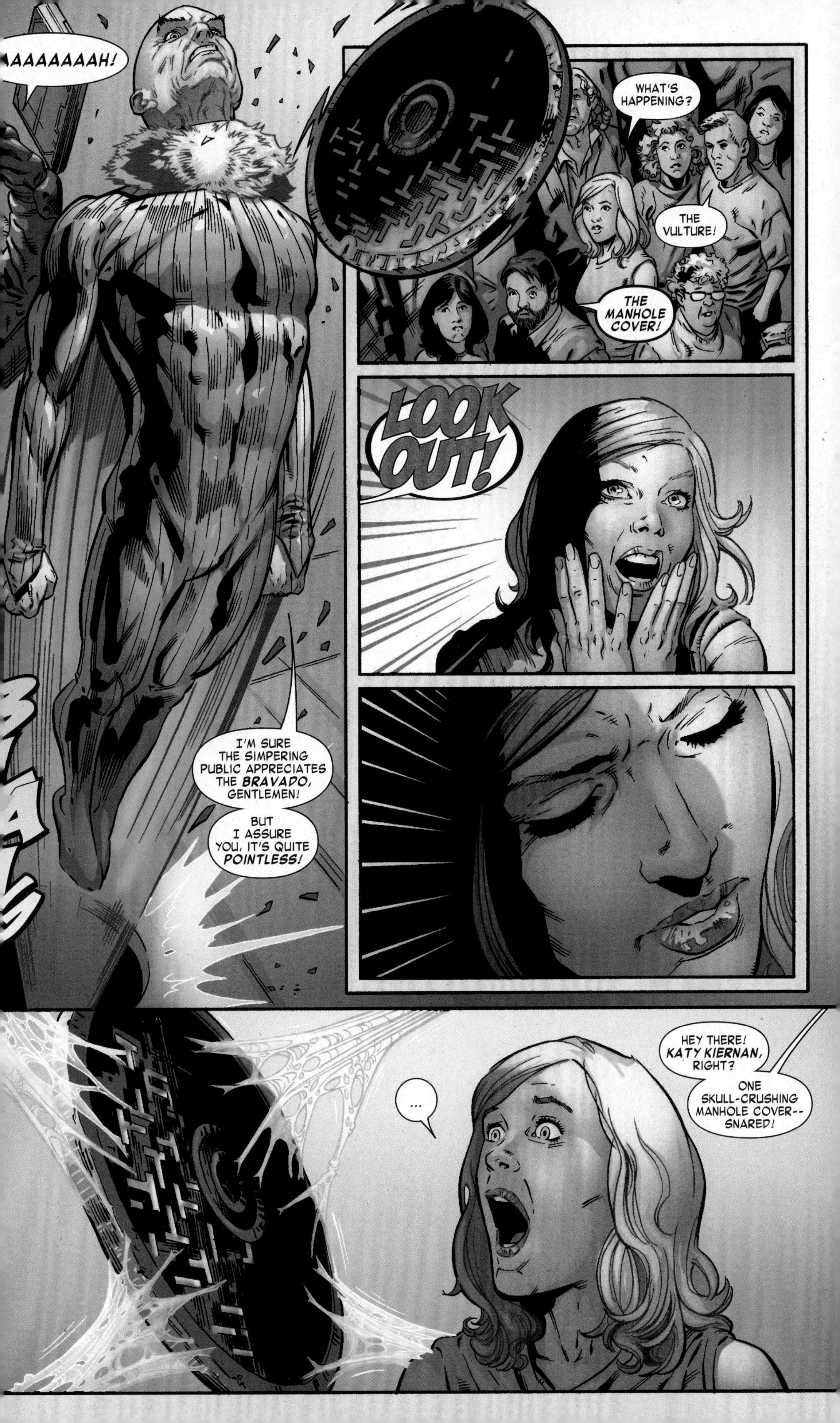
AAAAAAAAH!
WHAT'S HAPPENING?
THE VULTURE!
THE MANHOLE COVER!
LOOK OUT!
I'M SURE THE SIMPERING PUBLIC APPRECIATES THE BRAVADO, GENTLEMEN!
BUT I ASSURE YOU, IT'S QUITE POINTLESS!
HEY THERE! KATY KIERNAN, RIGHT?
ONE SKULL-CRUSHING MANHOLE COVER--SNARED!
...

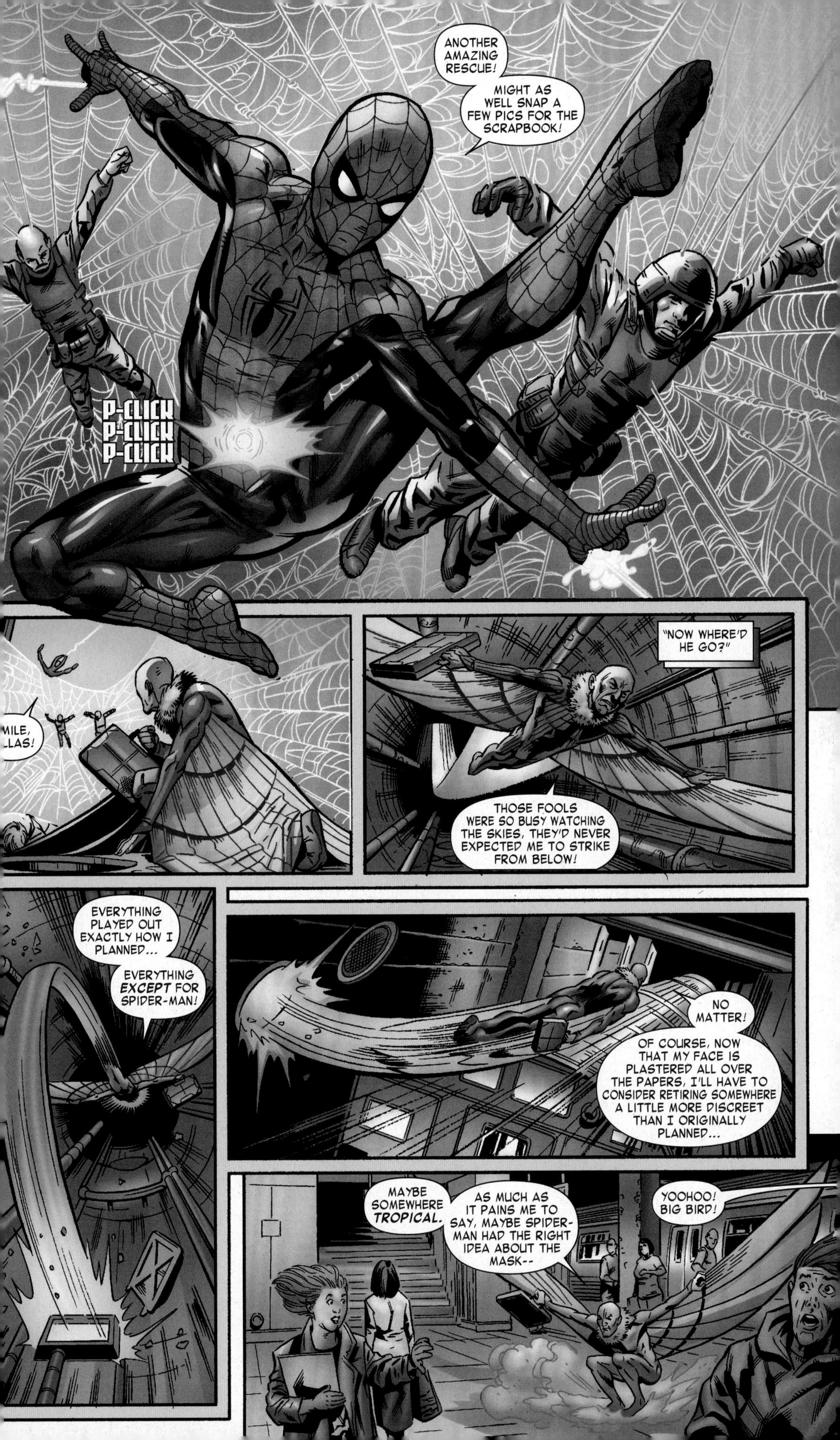
ANOTHER AMAZING RESCUE!
MIGHT AS WELL SNAP A FEW PICS FOR THE SCRAPBOOK!
P-CLICK P-CLICK P-CLICK
MILE, LLAS!
"NOW WHERE'D HE GO?"
THOSE FOOLS WERE SO BUSY WATCHING THE SKIES, THEY'D NEVER EXPECTED ME TO STRIKE FROM BELOW!
EVERYTHING PLAYED OUT EXACTLY HOW I PLANNED...
EVERYTHING *EXCEPT* FOR SPIDER-MAN!
NO MATTER!
OF COURSE, NOW THAT MY FACE IS PLASTERED ALL OVER THE PAPERS, I'LL HAVE TO CONSIDER RETIRING SOMEWHERE A LITTLE MORE DISCREET THAN I ORIGINALLY PLANNED...
MAYBE SOMEWHERE *TROPICAL*.
AS MUCH AS IT PAINS ME TO SAY, MAYBE SPIDER-MAN HAD THE RIGHT IDEA ABOUT THE MASK--
YOOHOO! BIG BIRD!

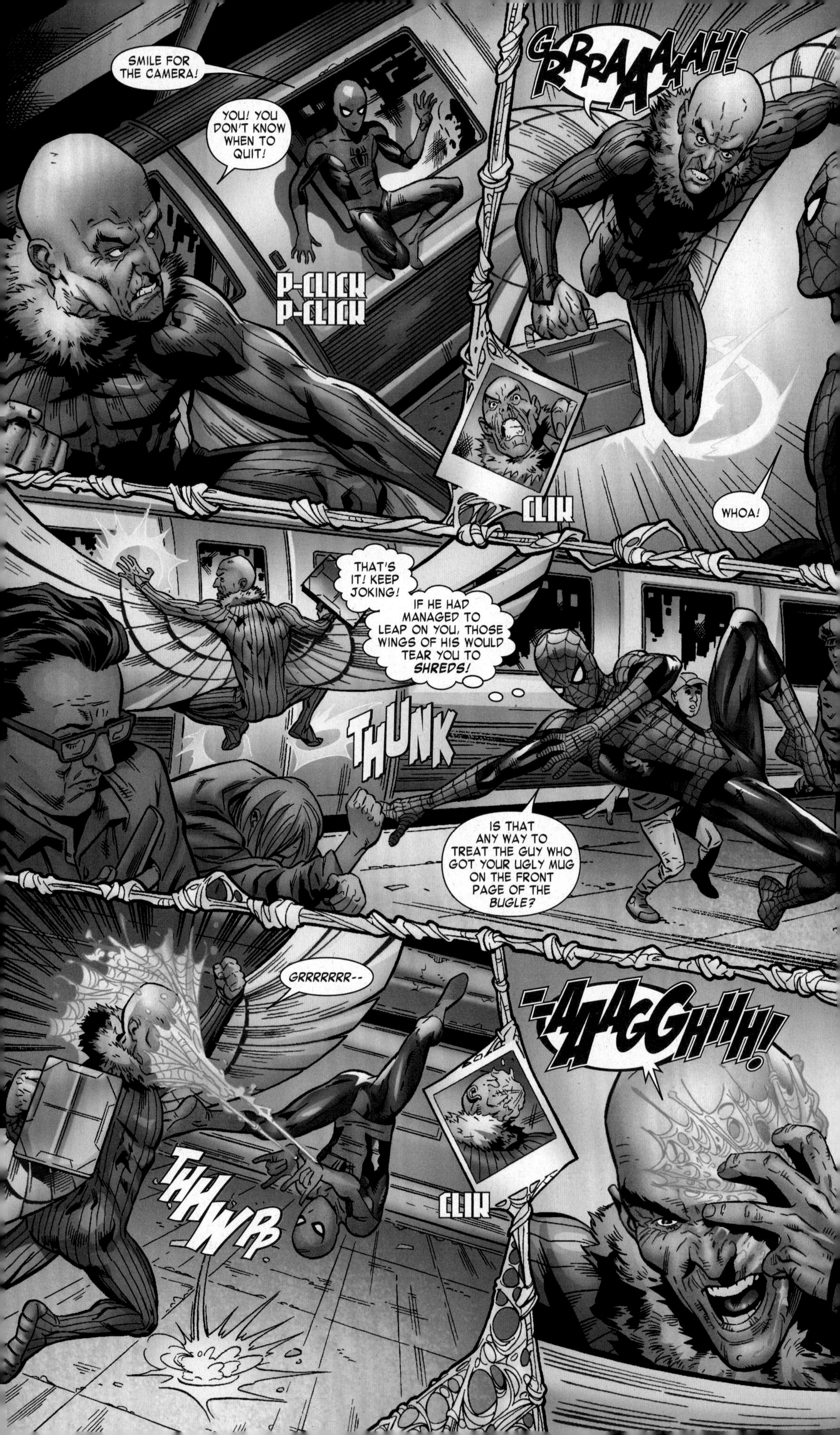
SMILE FOR THE CAMERA!
YOU! YOU DON'T KNOW WHEN TO QUIT!
P-CLICK P-CLICK
GRRRAAAAAAH!
CLIK
WHOA!
THAT'S IT! KEEP JOKING!
IF HE HAD MANAGED TO LEAP ON YOU, THOSE WINGS OF HIS WOULD TEAR YOU TO *SHREDS!*
THUNK
IS THAT ANY WAY TO TREAT THE GUY WHO GOT YOUR UGLY MUG ON THE FRONT PAGE OF THE *BUGLE?*
GRRRRRRR--
--AAAGGHHH!
THHWPP
CLIK

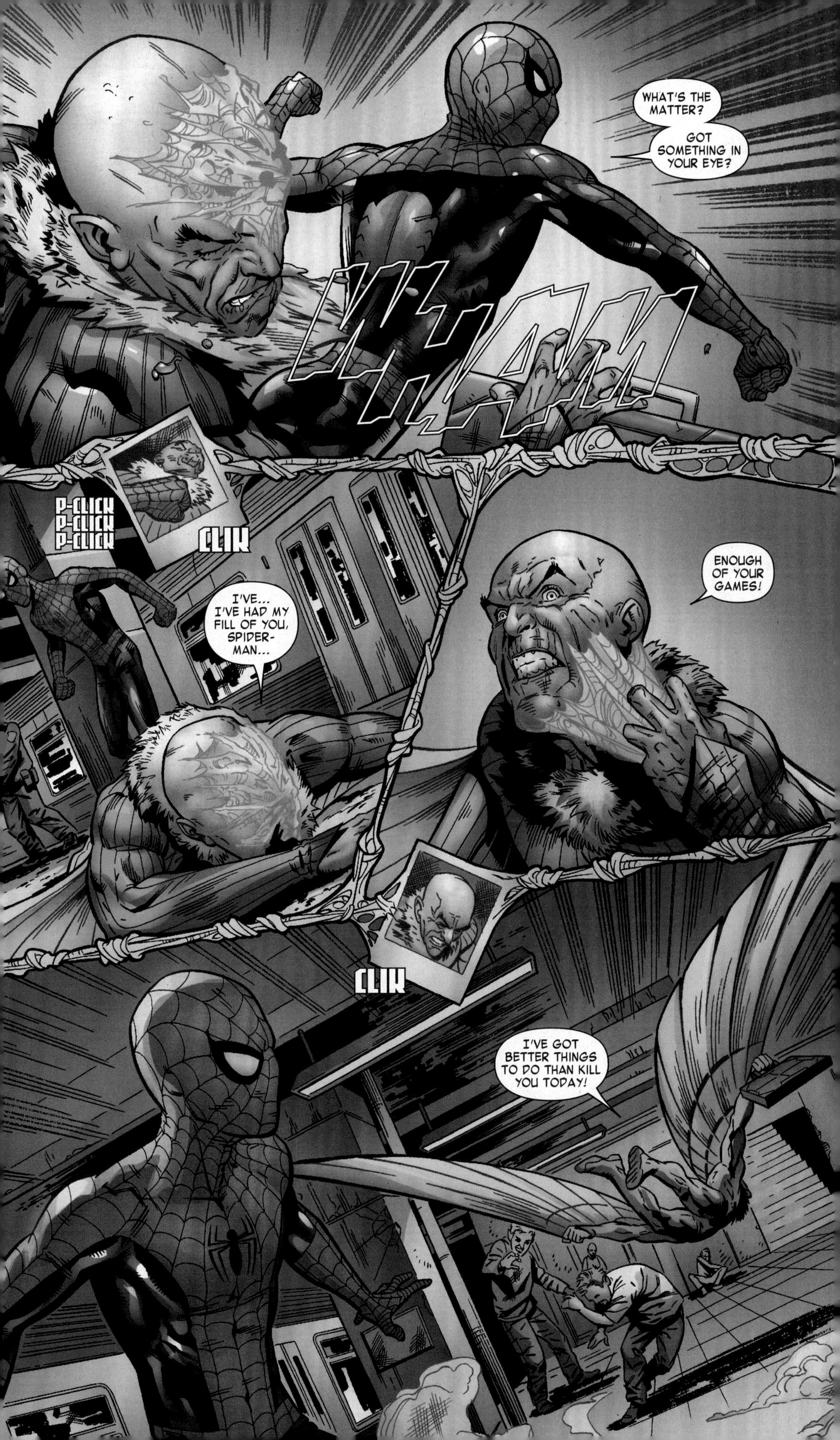
WHAT'S THE MATTER?
GOT SOMETHING IN YOUR EYE?
WHAM
P-CLICK P-CLICK P-CLICK
CLIK
I'VE... I'VE HAD MY FILL OF YOU, SPIDER-MAN...
ENOUGH OF YOUR GAMES!
CLIK
I'VE GOT BETTER THINGS TO DO THAN KILL YOU TODAY!

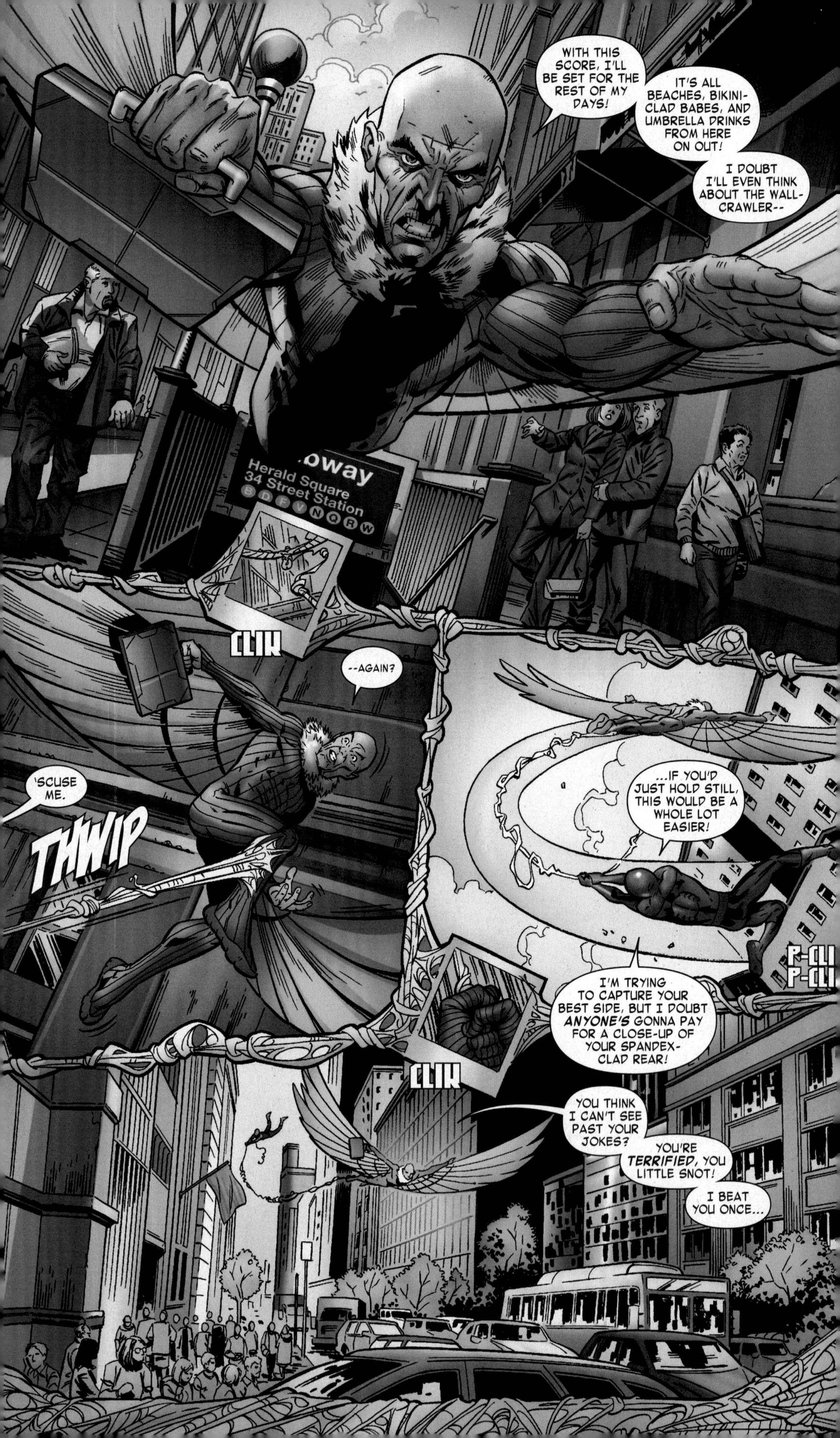
WITH THIS SCORE, I'LL BE SET FOR THE REST OF MY DAYS!
IT'S ALL BEACHES, BIKINI-CLAD BABES, AND UMBRELLA DRINKS FROM HERE ON OUT!
I DOUBT I'LL EVEN THINK ABOUT THE WALL-CRAWLER--
Herald Square
34 Street Station
CLIK
--AGAIN?
'SCUSE ME.
THWIP
...IF YOU'D JUST HOLD STILL, THIS WOULD BE A WHOLE LOT EASIER!
P-CLI
P-CLI
I'M TRYING TO CAPTURE YOUR BEST SIDE, BUT I DOUBT ANYONE'S GONNA PAY FOR A CLOSE-UP OF YOUR SPANDEX-CLAD REAR!
CLIK
YOU THINK I CAN'T SEE PAST YOUR JOKES?
YOU'RE TERRIFIED, YOU LITTLE SNOT!
I BEAT YOU ONCE...

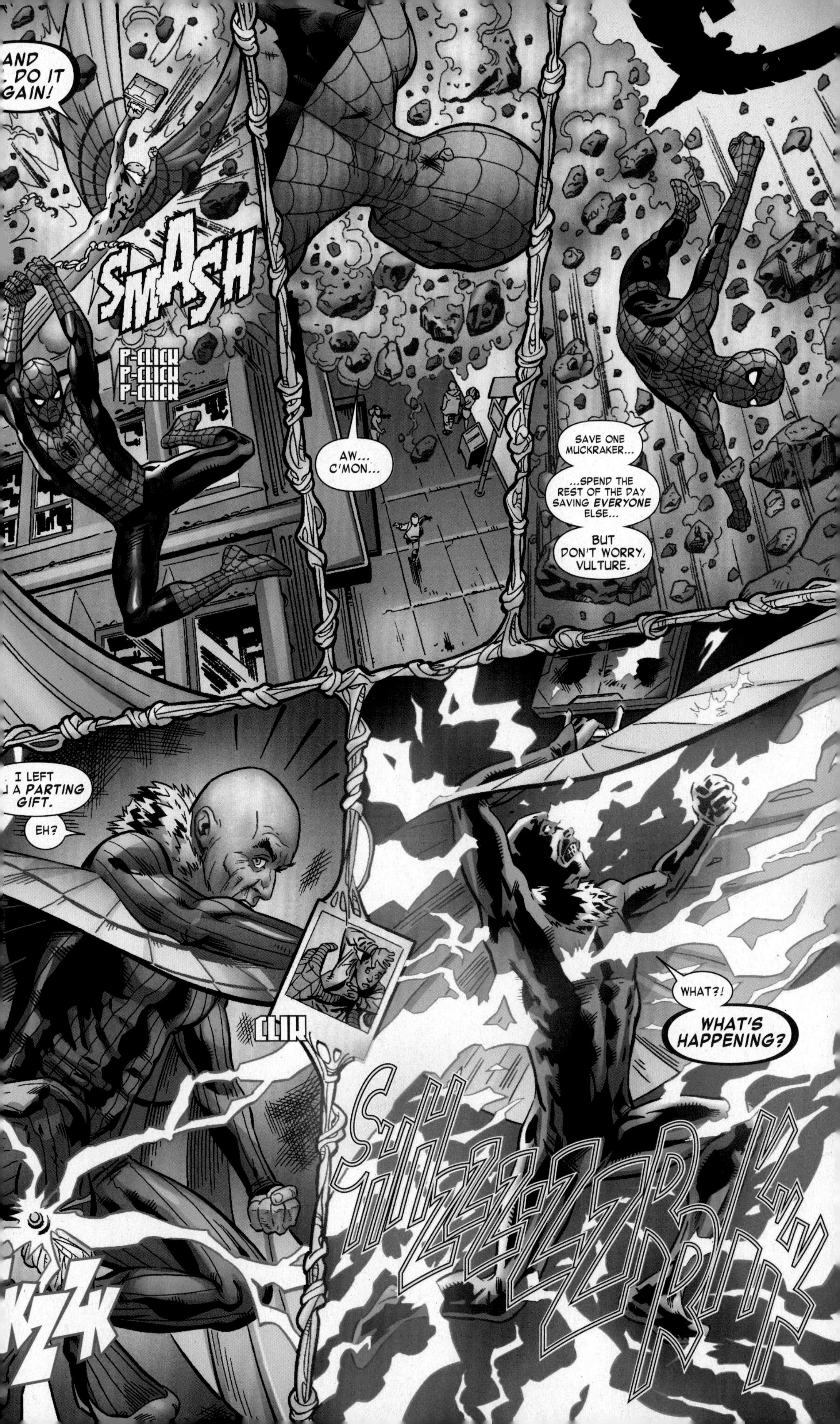
AND
DO IT
GAIN!
SMASH
P-CLICK
P-CLICK
P-CLICK
AW... C'MON...
SAVE ONE MUCKRAKER...
...SPEND THE REST OF THE DAY SAVING EVERYONE ELSE...
BUT DON'T WORRY, VULTURE.
I LEFT A PARTING GIFT.
EH?
CLIK
WHAT?!
WHAT'S HAPPENING?
KZZK

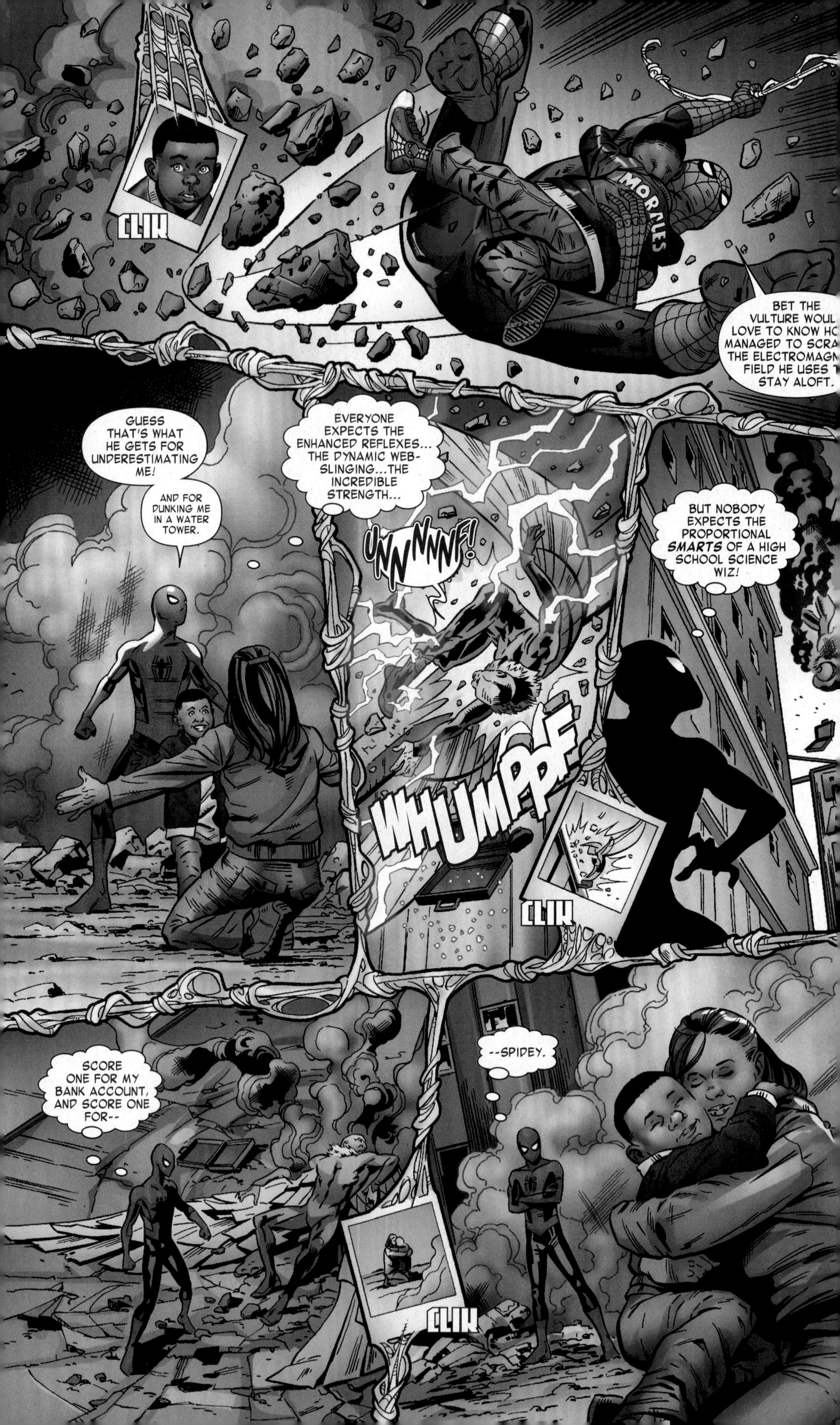
CLIK
BET THE VULTURE WOUL LOVE TO KNOW HO MANAGED TO SCRA THE ELECTROMAGN FIELD HE USES T STAY ALOFT.
GUESS THAT'S WHAT HE GETS FOR UNDERESTIMATING ME!
AND FOR DUNKING ME IN A WATER TOWER.
EVERYONE EXPECTS THE ENHANCED REFLEXES... THE DYNAMIC WEB-SLINGING...THE INCREDIBLE STRENGTH...
UNNNNNF!
BUT NOBODY EXPECTS THE PROPORTIONAL SMARTS OF A HIGH SCHOOL SCIENCE WIZ!
WHUMPPF
CLIK
SCORE ONE FOR MY BANK ACCOUNT, AND SCORE ONE FOR--
--SPIDEY.
CLIK

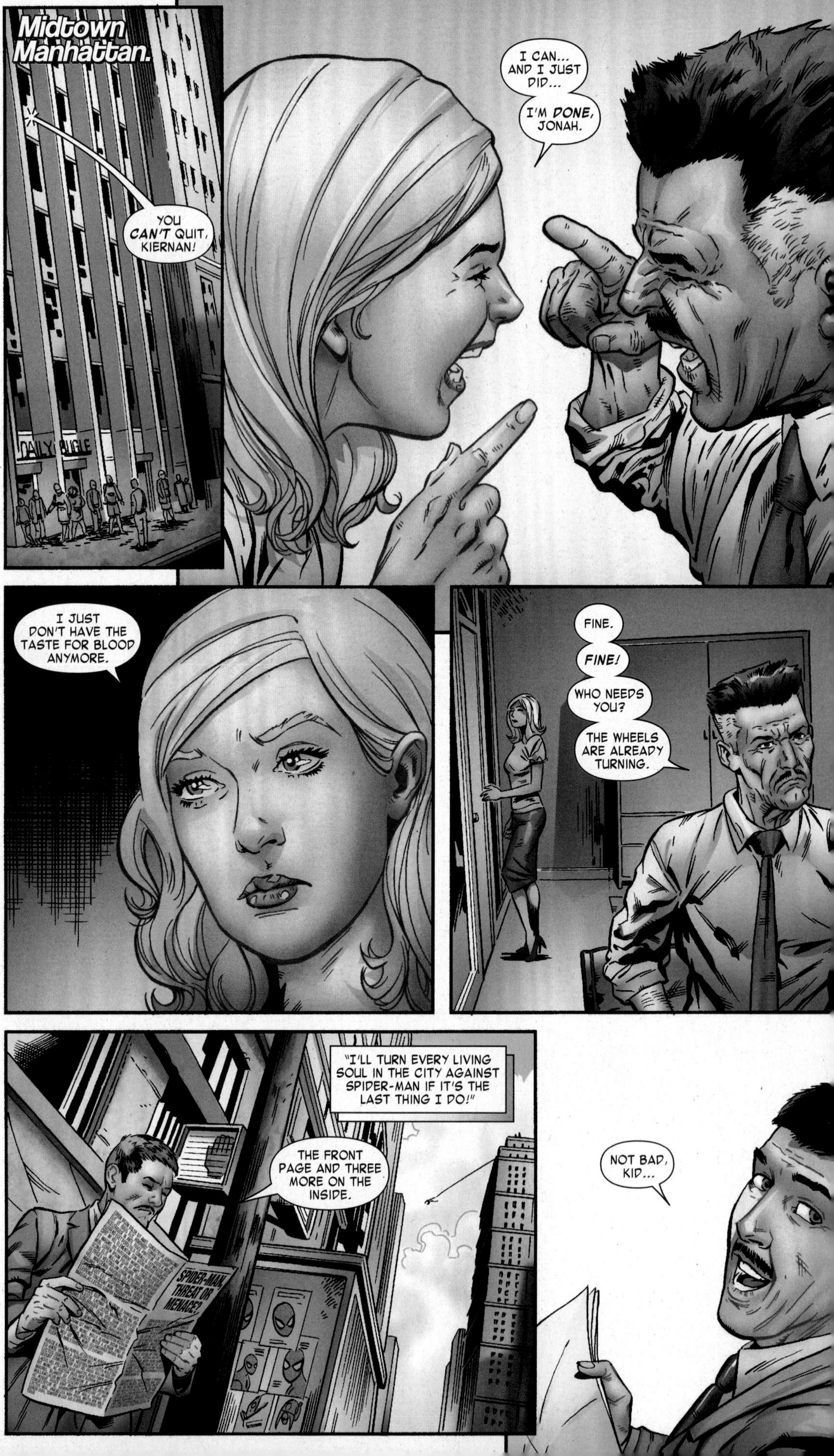

Midtown Manhattan.
YOU CAN'T QUIT, KIERNAN!
I CAN... AND I JUST DID...
I'M DONE, JONAH.
I JUST DON'T HAVE THE TASTE FOR BLOOD ANYMORE.
FINE.
FINE!
WHO NEEDS YOU?
THE WHEELS ARE ALREADY TURNING.
"I'LL TURN EVERY LIVING SOUL IN THE CITY AGAINST SPIDER-MAN IF IT'S THE LAST THING I DO!"
THE FRONT PAGE AND THREE MORE ON THE INSIDE.
SPIDER-MAN: THREAT OR MENACE?
NOT BAD, KID...

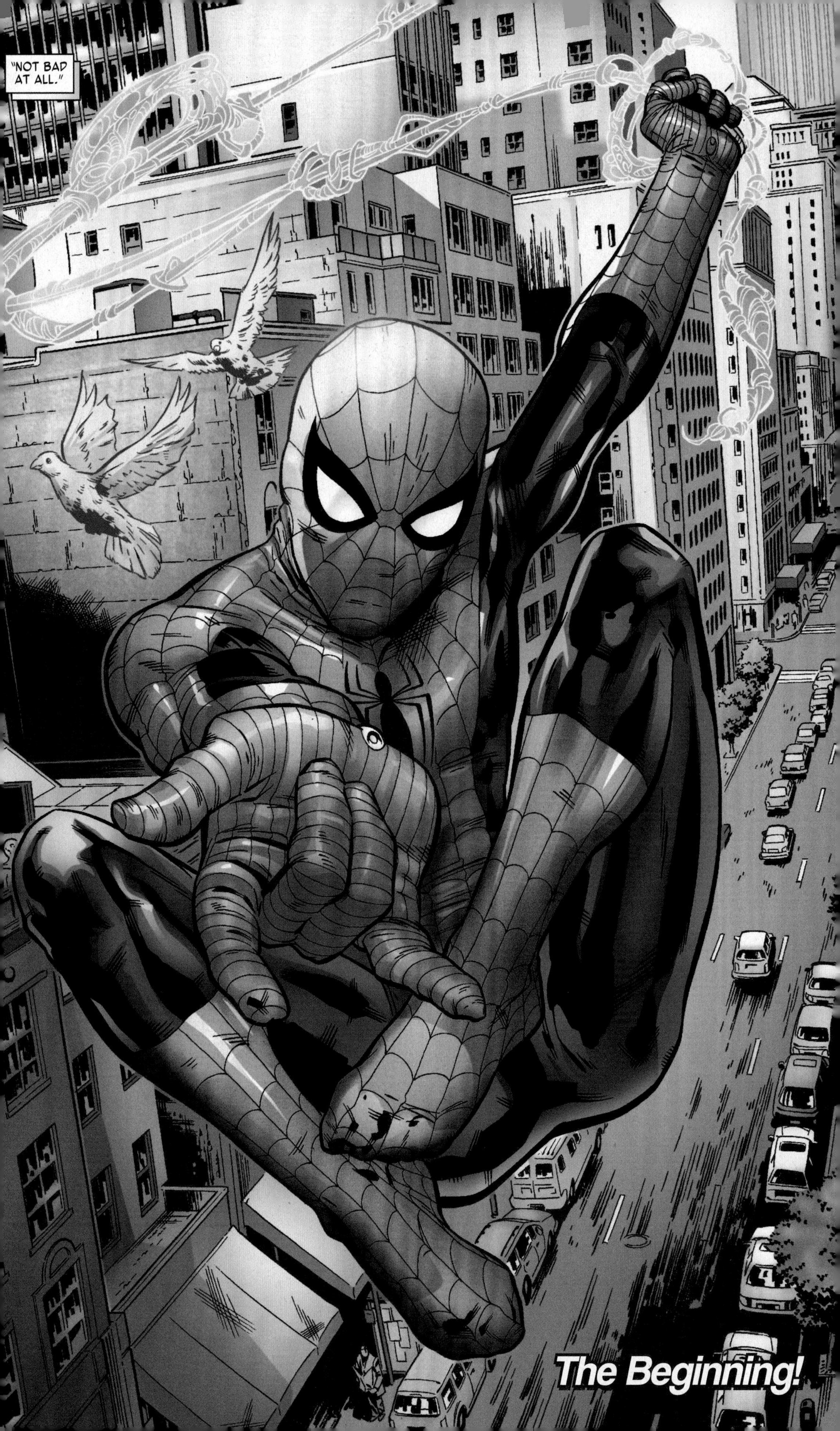
"NOT BAD AT ALL."
The Beginning!

THINK YOU KNOW EVERYTHING ABOUT PETER PARKER'S EARLY DAYS? THINK AGAIN. TAKE A RIP-ROARING ROMP THROUGH THE WEB-SLINGER'S WONDER YEARS IN *SPIDEY #1*, FEATURING ACTION AND ADVENTURE IN THE CLASSIC MARVEL STYLE!

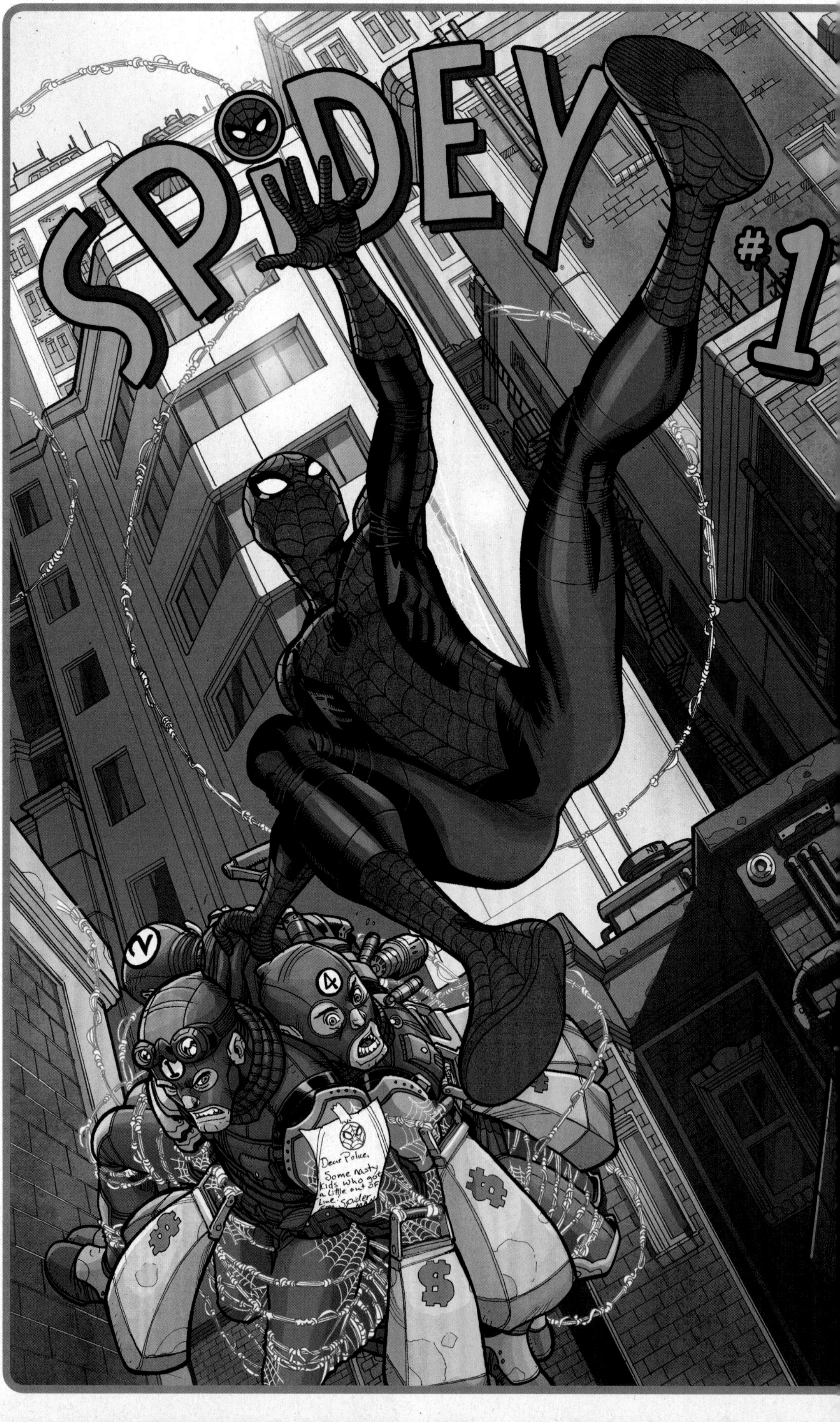

SPIDEY
#1
Dear Police,
Some nasty kids who got a little out of line.

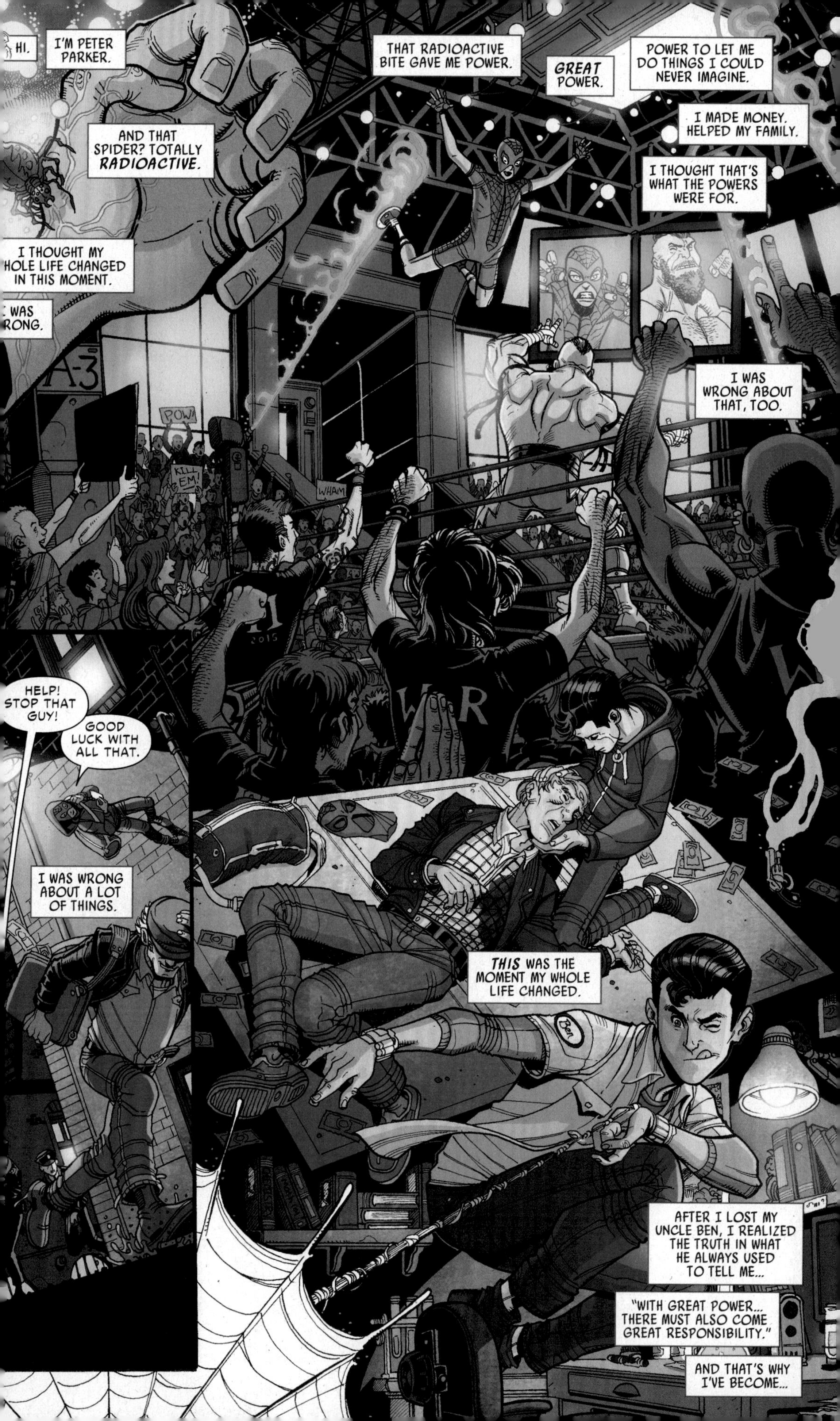
HI.
I'M PETER PARKER.
AND THAT SPIDER? TOTALLY RADIOACTIVE.
I THOUGHT MY WHOLE LIFE CHANGED IN THIS MOMENT.
I WAS WRONG.
THAT RADIOACTIVE BITE GAVE ME POWER.
GREAT POWER.
POWER TO LET ME DO THINGS I COULD NEVER IMAGINE.
I MADE MONEY. HELPED MY FAMILY.
I THOUGHT THAT'S WHAT THE POWERS WERE FOR.
POW!
KILL 'EM!
WHAM
I WAS WRONG ABOUT THAT, TOO.
HELP! STOP THAT GUY!
GOOD LUCK WITH ALL THAT.
I WAS WRONG ABOUT A LOT OF THINGS.
THIS WAS THE MOMENT MY WHOLE LIFE CHANGED.
AFTER I LOST MY UNCLE BEN, I REALIZED THE TRUTH IN WHAT HE ALWAYS USED TO TELL ME...
"WITH GREAT POWER... THERE MUST ALSO COME GREAT RESPONSIBILITY."
AND THAT'S WHY I'VE BECOME...

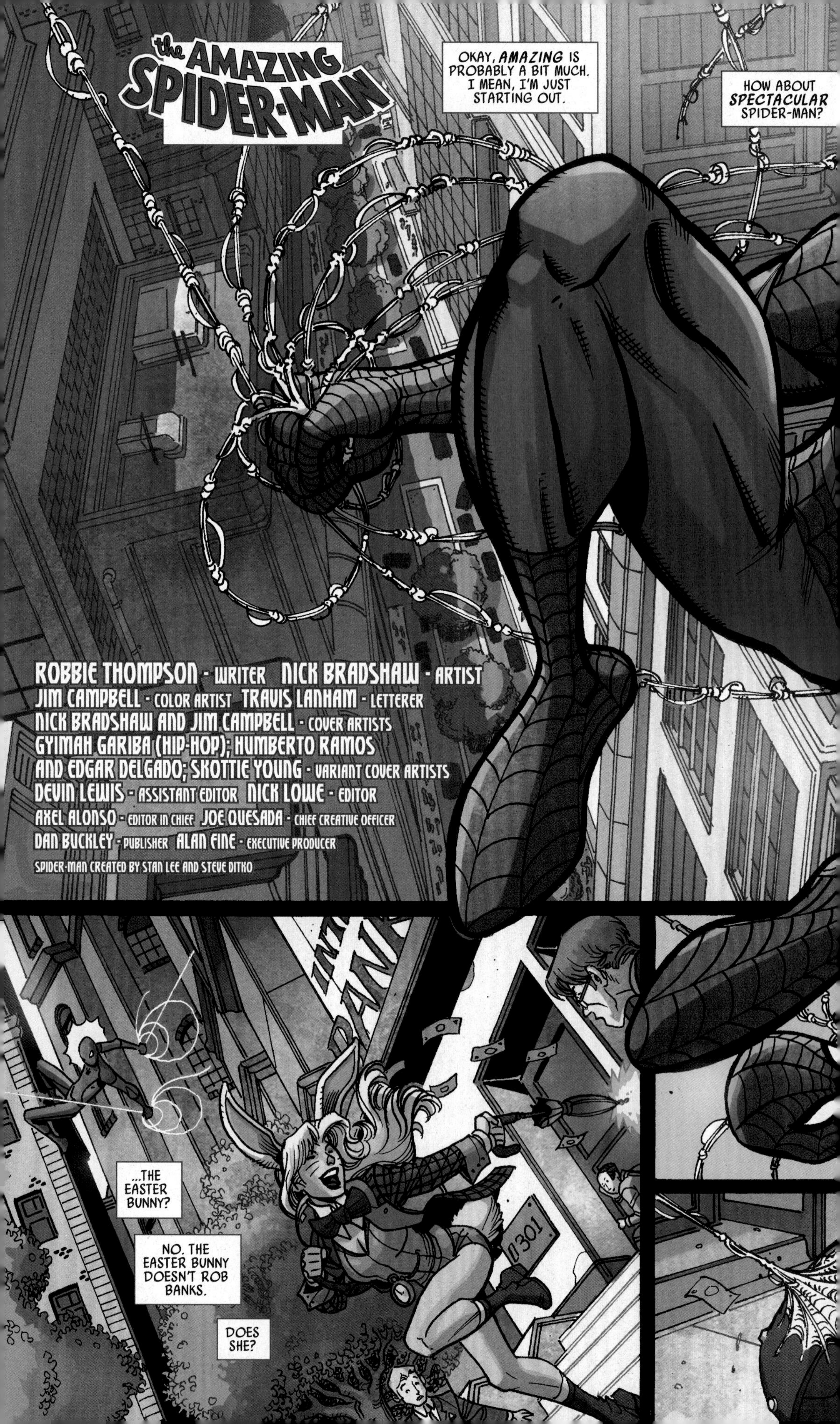
the AMAZING SPIDER-MAN
OKAY, AMAZING IS PROBABLY A BIT MUCH. I MEAN, I'M JUST STARTING OUT.
HOW ABOUT SPECTACULAR SPIDER-MAN?
ROBBIE THOMPSON - WRITER NICK BRADSHAW - ARTIST
JIM CAMPBELL - COLOR ARTIST TRAVIS LANHAM - LETTERER
NICK BRADSHAW AND JIM CAMPBELL - COVER ARTISTS
GYIMAH GARIBA (HIP-HOP); HUMBERTO RAMOS AND EDGAR DELGADO; SKOTTIE YOUNG - VARIANT COVER ARTISTS
DEVIN LEWIS - ASSISTANT EDITOR NICK LOWE - EDITOR
AXEL ALONSO - EDITOR IN CHIEF JOE QUESADA - CHIEF CREATIVE OFFICER
DAN BUCKLEY - PUBLISHER ALAN FINE - EXECUTIVE PRODUCER
SPIDER-MAN CREATED BY STAN LEE AND STEVE DITKO
...THE EASTER BUNNY?
NO. THE EASTER BUNNY DOESN'T ROB BANKS.
DOES SHE?
301

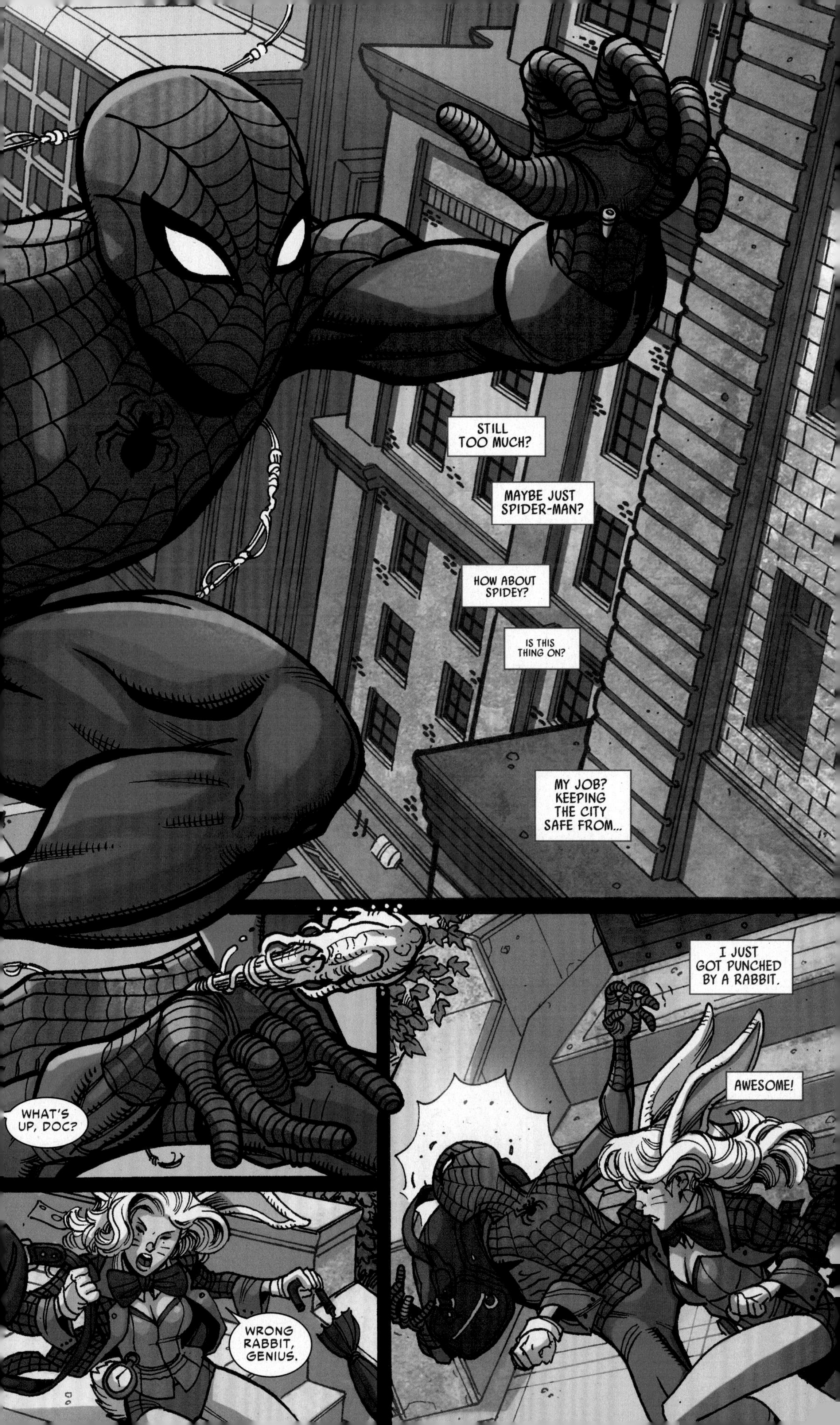
STILL TOO MUCH?
MAYBE JUST SPIDER-MAN?
HOW ABOUT SPIDEY?
IS THIS THING ON?
MY JOB? KEEPING THE CITY SAFE FROM...
WHAT'S UP, DOC?
I JUST GOT PUNCHED BY A RABBIT.
AWESOME!
WRONG RABBIT, GENIUS.

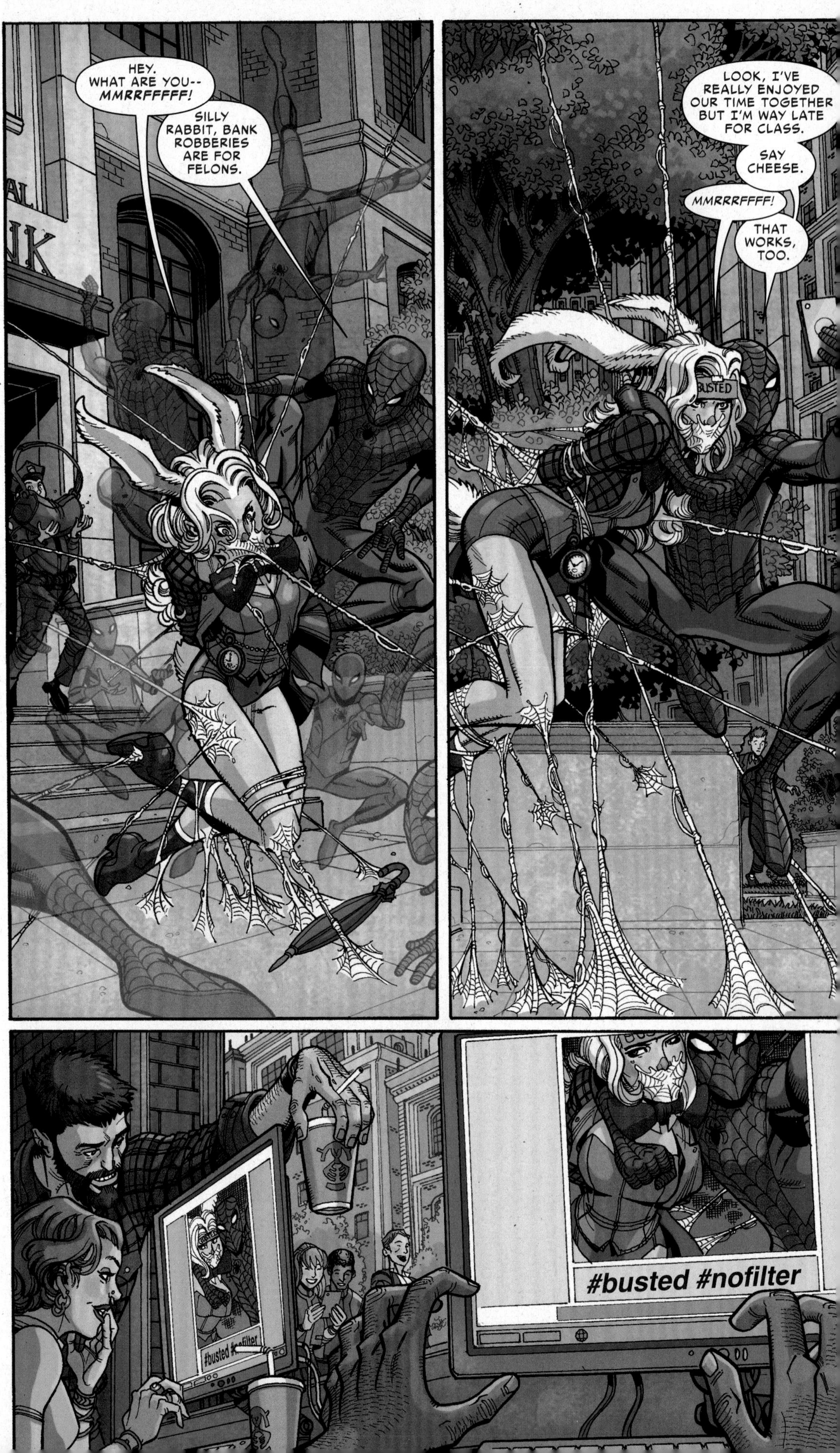
HEY. WHAT ARE YOU-- MMRRFFFFF!
SILLY RABBIT, BANK ROBBERIES ARE FOR FELONS.
LOOK, I'VE REALLY ENJOYED OUR TIME TOGETHER BUT I'M WAY LATE FOR CLASS.
SAY CHEESE.
MMRRRFFFF!
THAT WORKS, TOO.
BUSTED
#busted #nofilter
#busted #nofilter

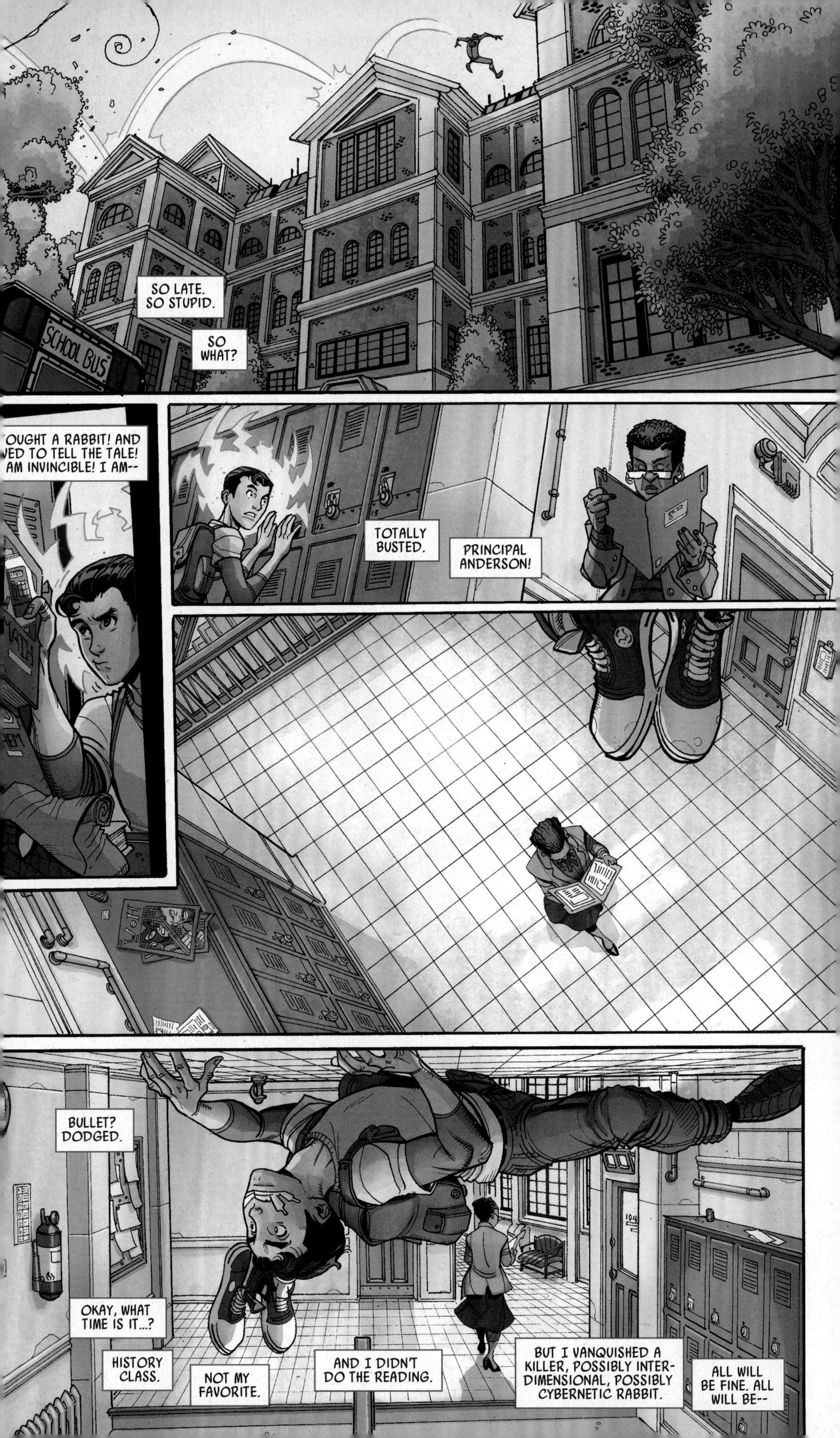
SO LATE. SO STUPID.
SO WHAT?
SCHOOL BUS
FOUGHT A RABBIT! AND LIVED TO TELL THE TALE! I AM INVINCIBLE! I AM--
TOTALLY BUSTED.
PRINCIPAL ANDERSON!
BULLET? DODGED.
OKAY, WHAT TIME IS IT...?
HISTORY CLASS.
NOT MY FAVORITE.
AND I DIDN'T DO THE READING.
BUT I VANQUISHED A KILLER, POSSIBLY INTER-DIMENSIONAL, POSSIBLY CYBERNETIC RABBIT.
ALL WILL BE FINE. ALL WILL BE--

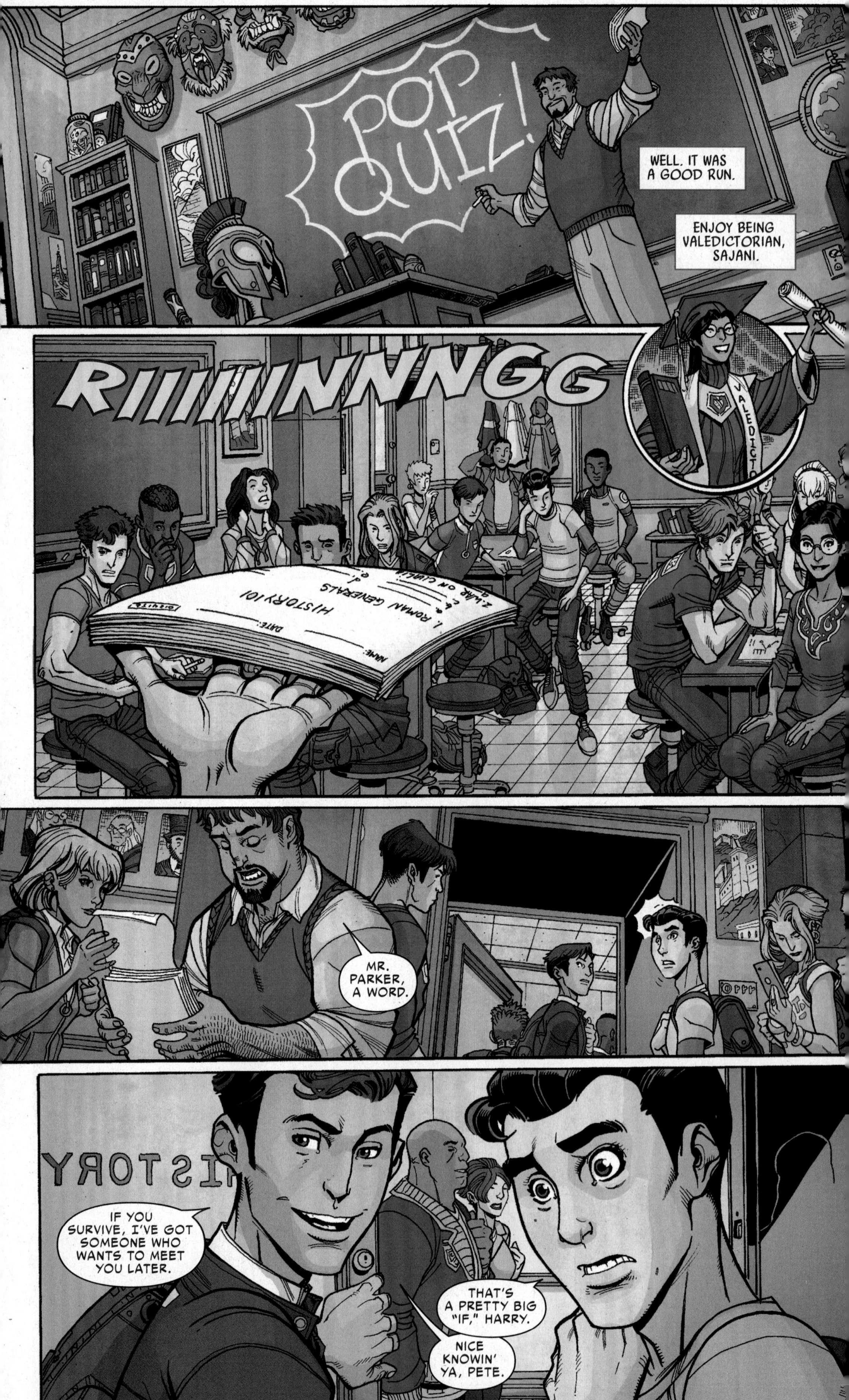
POP QUIZ!
WELL. IT WAS A GOOD RUN.
ENJOY BEING VALEDICTORIAN, SAJANI.
VALEDICTO
RIIIIIINNNNGG
HISTORY 101
NAME:
DATE:
1. ROMAN GENERALS
2. WAR ON CURLIA
MR. PARKER, A WORD.
HISTORY
IF YOU SURVIVE, I'VE GOT SOMEONE WHO WANTS TO MEET YOU LATER.
THAT'S A PRETTY BIG "IF," HARRY.
NICE KNOWIN' YA, PETE.

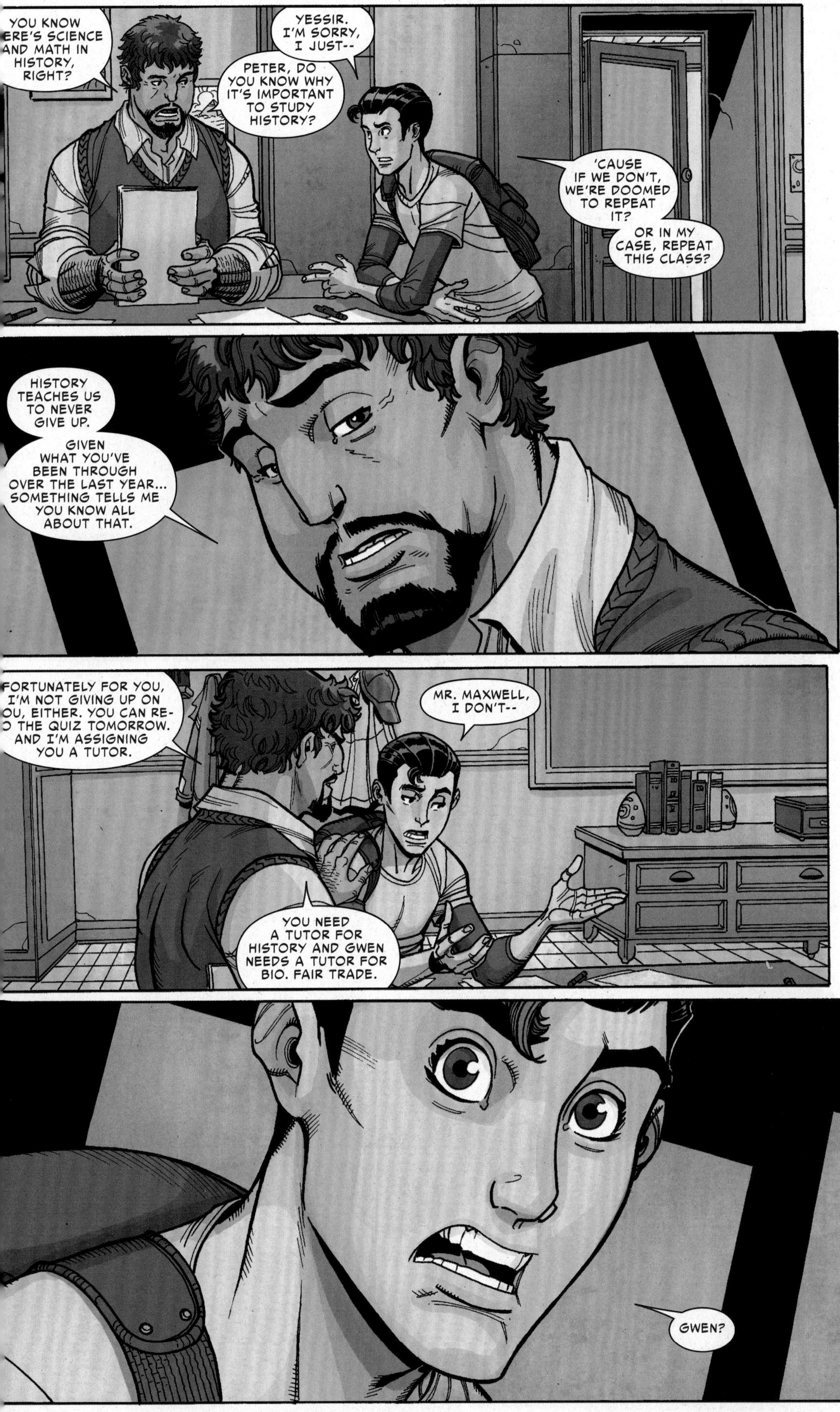

YOU KNOW ERE'S SCIENCE AND MATH IN HISTORY, RIGHT?
YESSIR. I'M SORRY, I JUST--
PETER, DO YOU KNOW WHY IT'S IMPORTANT TO STUDY HISTORY?
'CAUSE IF WE DON'T, WE'RE DOOMED TO REPEAT IT?
OR IN MY CASE, REPEAT THIS CLASS?
HISTORY TEACHES US TO NEVER GIVE UP.
GIVEN WHAT YOU'VE BEEN THROUGH OVER THE LAST YEAR... SOMETHING TELLS ME YOU KNOW ALL ABOUT THAT.
FORTUNATELY FOR YOU, I'M NOT GIVING UP ON OU, EITHER. YOU CAN RE- O THE QUIZ TOMORROW. AND I'M ASSIGNING YOU A TUTOR.
MR. MAXWELL, I DON'T--
YOU NEED A TUTOR FOR HISTORY AND GWEN NEEDS A TUTOR FOR BIO. FAIR TRADE.
GWEN?

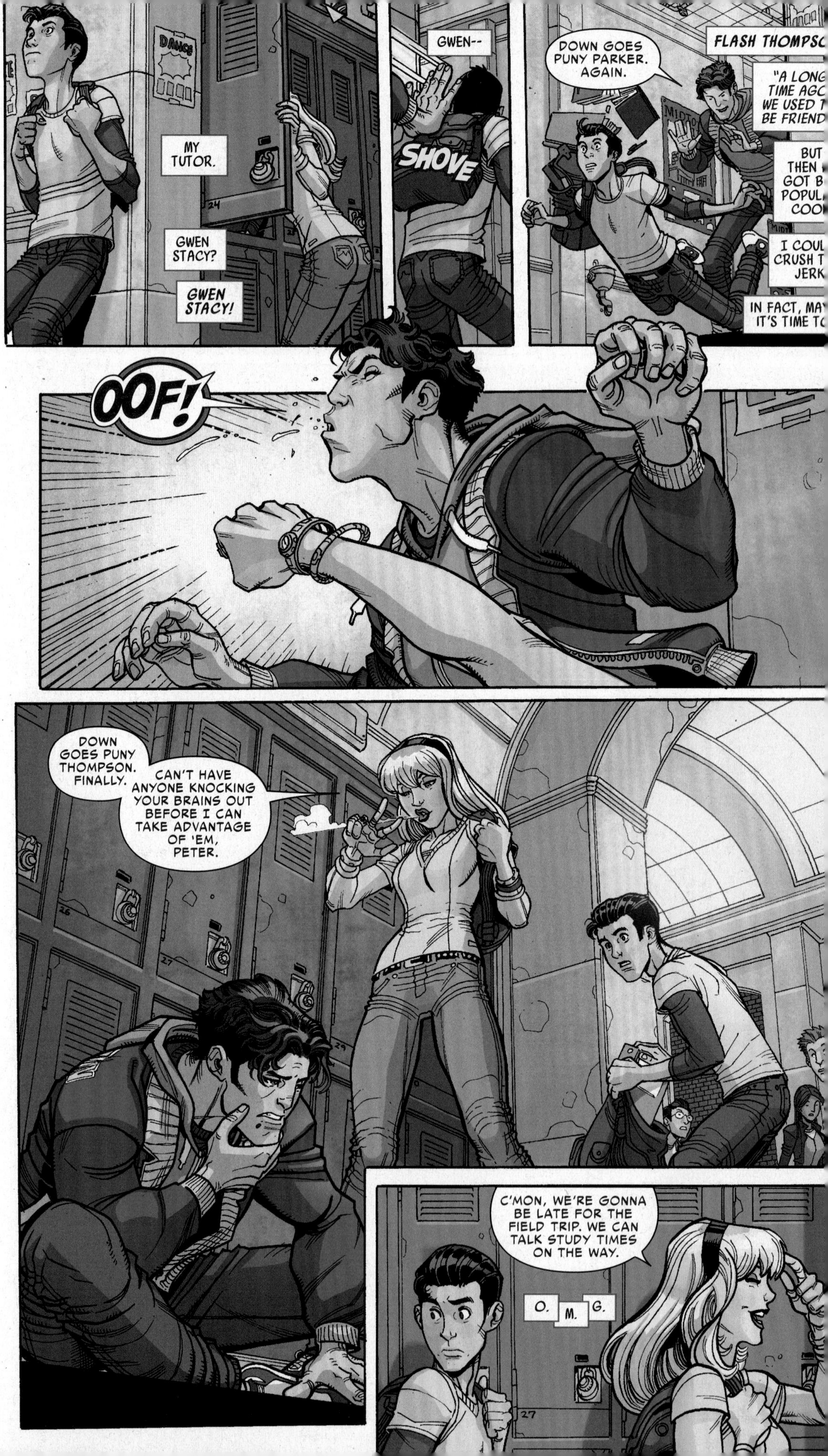
MY TUTOR.
GWEN STACY?
GWEN STACY!
GWEN--
SHOVE
DOWN GOES PUNY PARKER. AGAIN.
OOF!
DOWN GOES PUNY THOMPSON. FINALLY.
CAN'T HAVE ANYONE KNOCKING YOUR BRAINS OUT BEFORE I CAN TAKE ADVANTAGE OF 'EM, PETER.
C'MON, WE'RE GONNA BE LATE FOR THE FIELD TRIP. WE CAN TALK STUDY TIMES ON THE WAY.
O.
M.
G.

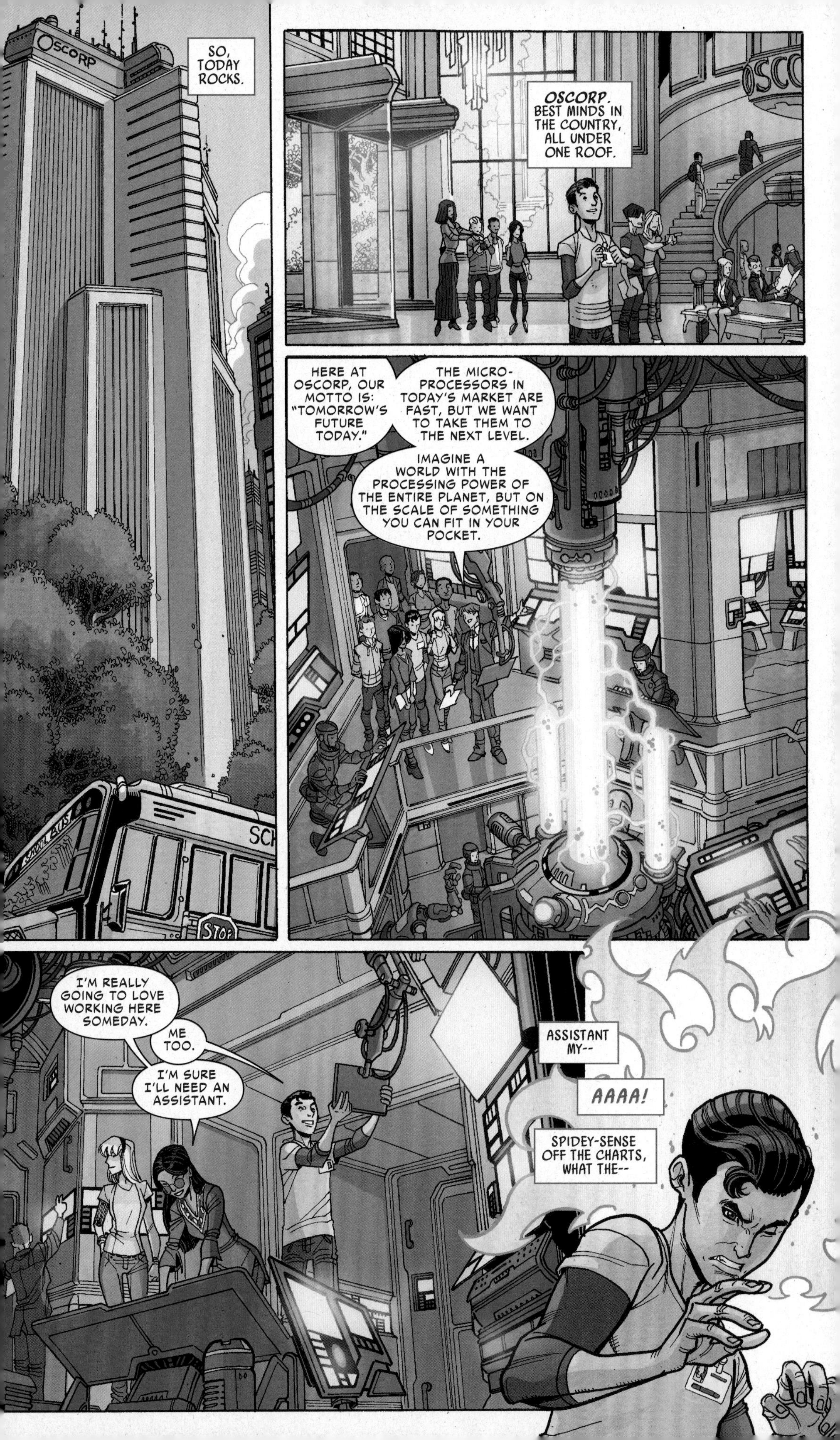
OSCORP
SO, TODAY ROCKS.
SCHOOL BUS
STOP
OSCORP. BEST MINDS IN THE COUNTRY, ALL UNDER ONE ROOF.
HERE AT OSCORP, OUR MOTTO IS: "TOMORROW'S FUTURE TODAY."
THE MICRO-PROCESSORS IN TODAY'S MARKET ARE FAST, BUT WE WANT TO TAKE THEM TO THE NEXT LEVEL.
IMAGINE A WORLD WITH THE PROCESSING POWER OF THE ENTIRE PLANET, BUT ON THE SCALE OF SOMETHING YOU CAN FIT IN YOUR POCKET.
I'M REALLY GOING TO LOVE WORKING HERE SOMEDAY.
ME TOO.
I'M SURE I'LL NEED AN ASSISTANT.
ASSISTANT MY--
AAAA!
SPIDEY-SENSE OFF THE CHARTS, WHAT THE--

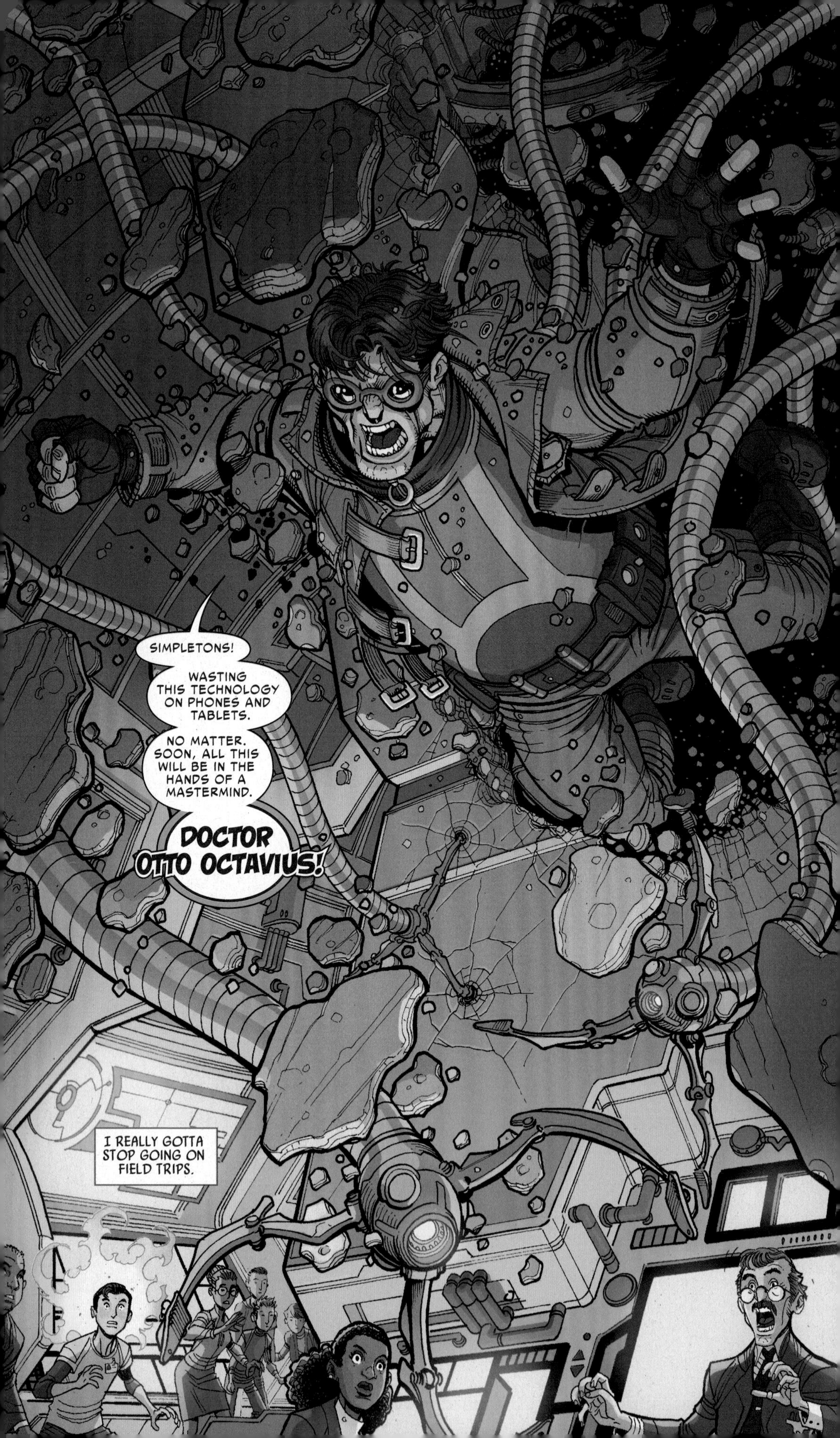
SIMPLETONS!
WASTING THIS TECHNOLOGY ON PHONES AND TABLETS.
NO MATTER. SOON, ALL THIS WILL BE IN THE HANDS OF A MASTERMIND.
DOCTOR OTTO OCTAVIUS!
I REALLY GOTTA STOP GOING ON FIELD TRIPS.

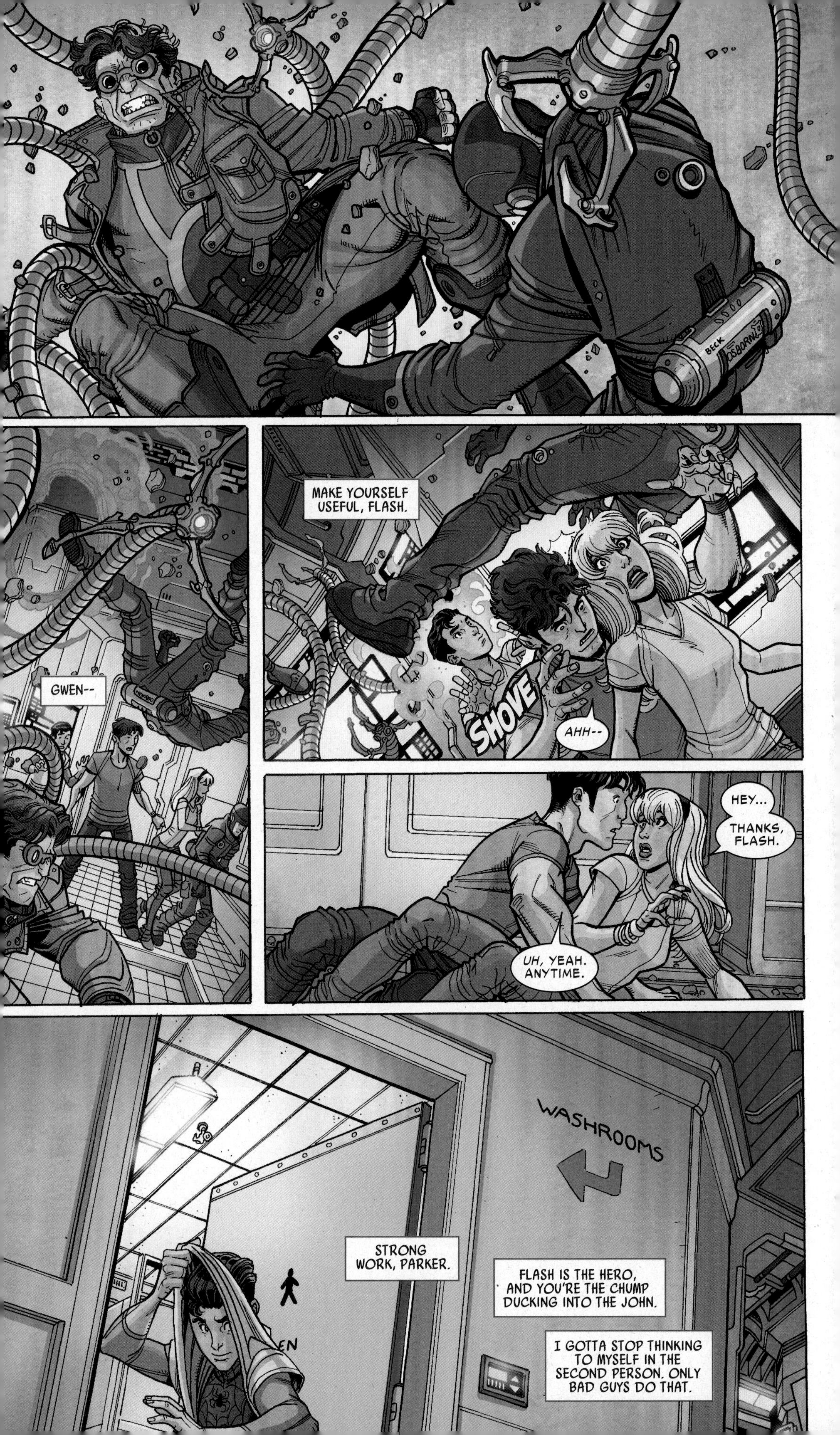
BECK
OSBORN
MAKE YOURSELF USEFUL, FLASH.
GWEN--
SHOVE
AHH--
HEY...
THANKS, FLASH.
UH, YEAH. ANYTIME.
WASHROOMS
STRONG WORK, PARKER.
FLASH IS THE HERO, AND YOU'RE THE CHUMP DUCKING INTO THE JOHN.
I GOTTA STOP THINKING TO MYSELF IN THE SECOND PERSON. ONLY BAD GUYS DO THAT.

I HAVE TO GET BACK OUT THERE. DOC OCK IS NOTHING BUT TROUBLE.

DOORS ARE LOCKED. BUT THE VENTS LEAD BACK INTO THE LAB.

SORRY FOR THE DAMAGE, FUTURE EMPLOYER!

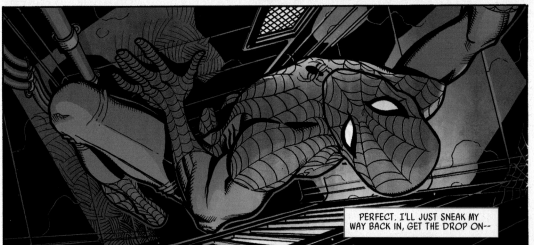

PERFECT. I'LL JUST SNEAK MY WAY BACK IN, GET THE DROP ON--

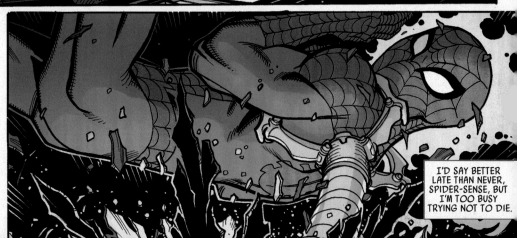

I'D SAY BETTER LATE THAN NEVER, SPIDER-SENSE, BUT I'M TOO BUSY TRYING NOT TO DIE.

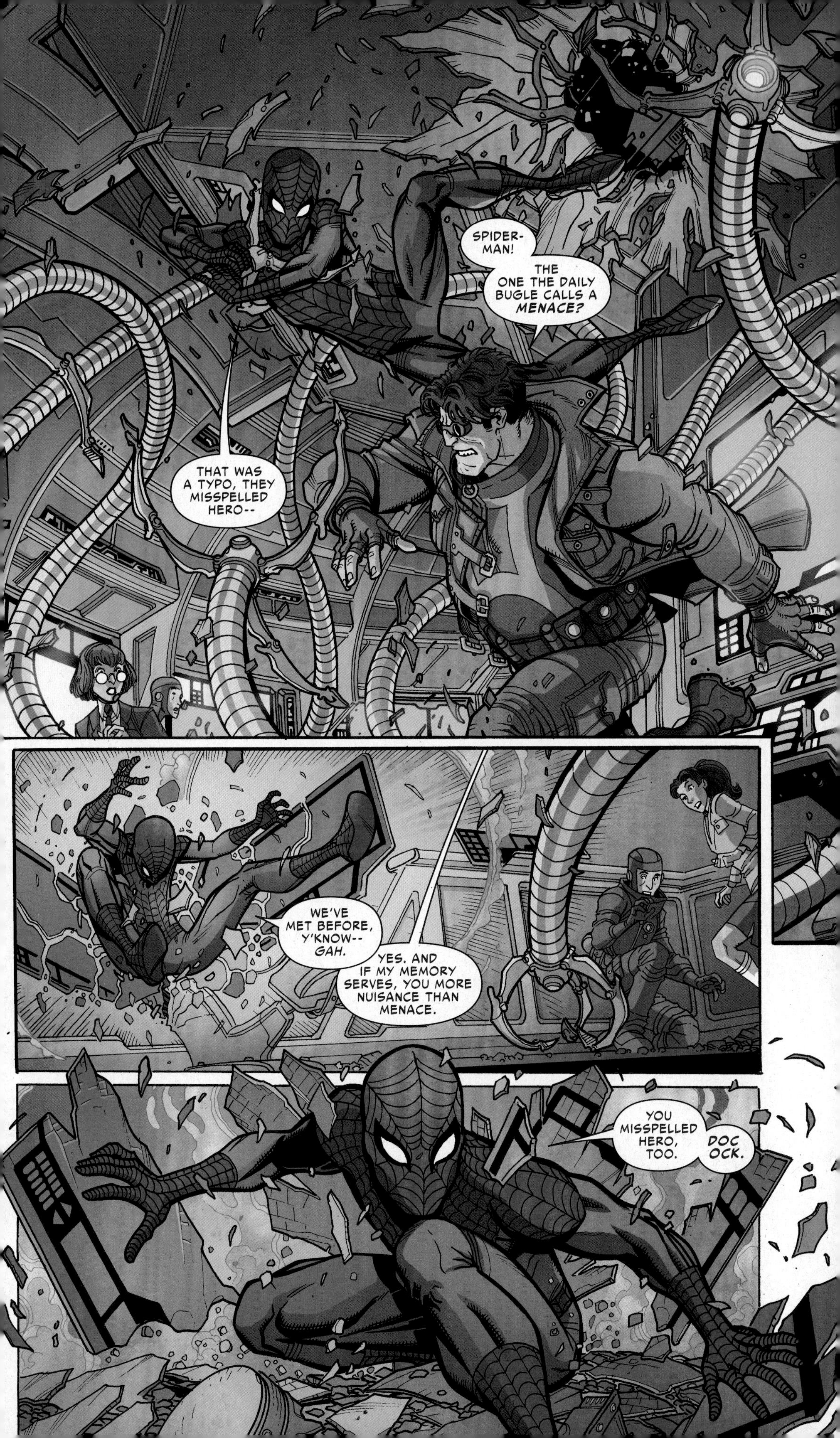
SPIDER-MAN!
THE ONE THE DAILY BUGLE CALLS A *MENACE?*
THAT WAS A TYPO, THEY MISSPELLED HERO--
WE'VE MET BEFORE, Y'KNOW-- GAH.
YES. AND IF MY MEMORY SERVES, YOU MORE NUISANCE THAN MENACE.
YOU MISSPELLED HERO, TOO.
DOC OCK.

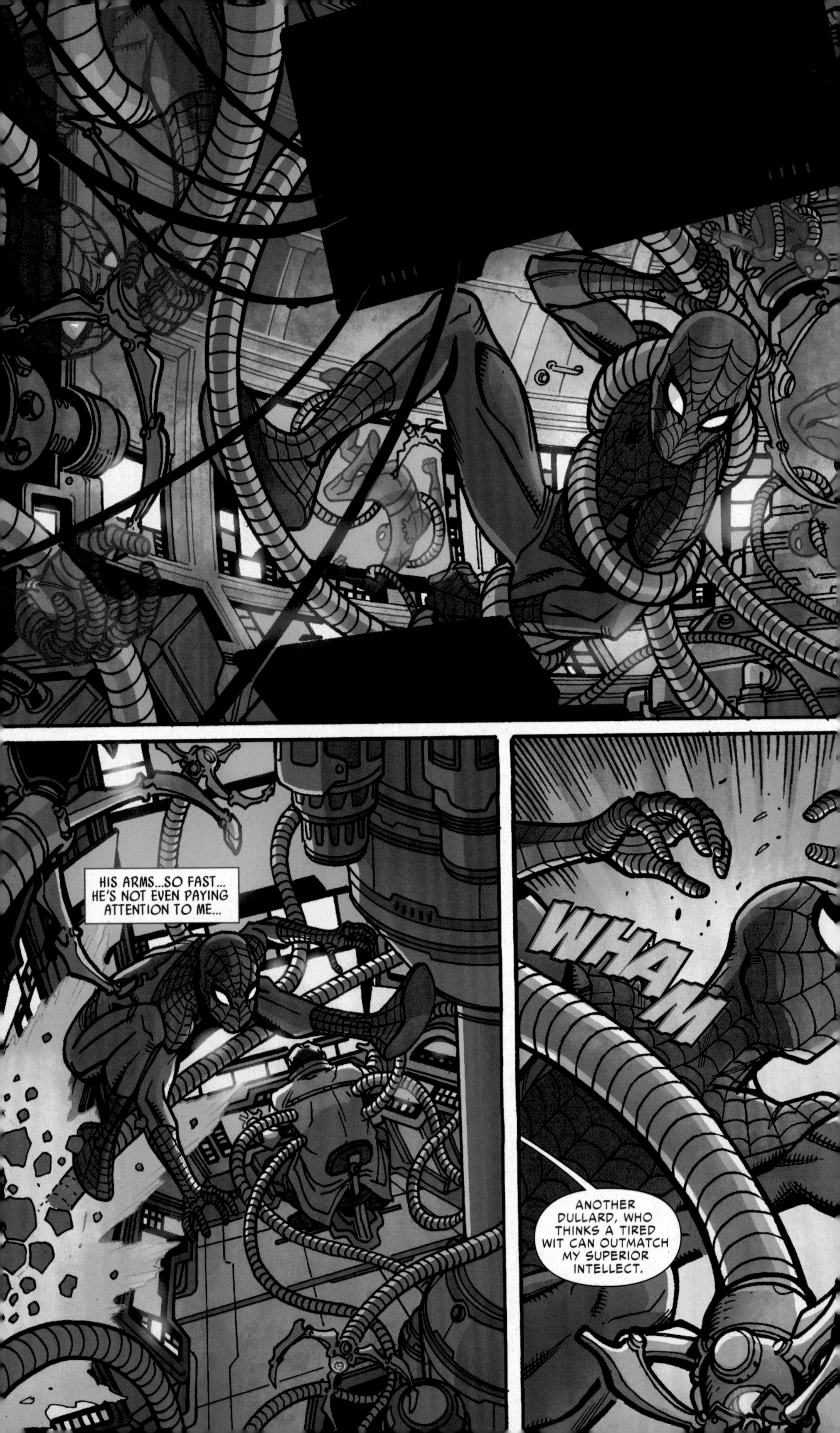
HIS ARMS...SO FAST...
HE'S NOT EVEN PAYING
ATTENTION TO ME...
WHAM
ANOTHER
DULLARD, WHO
THINKS A TIRED
WIT CAN OUTMATCH
MY SUPERIOR
INTELLECT.

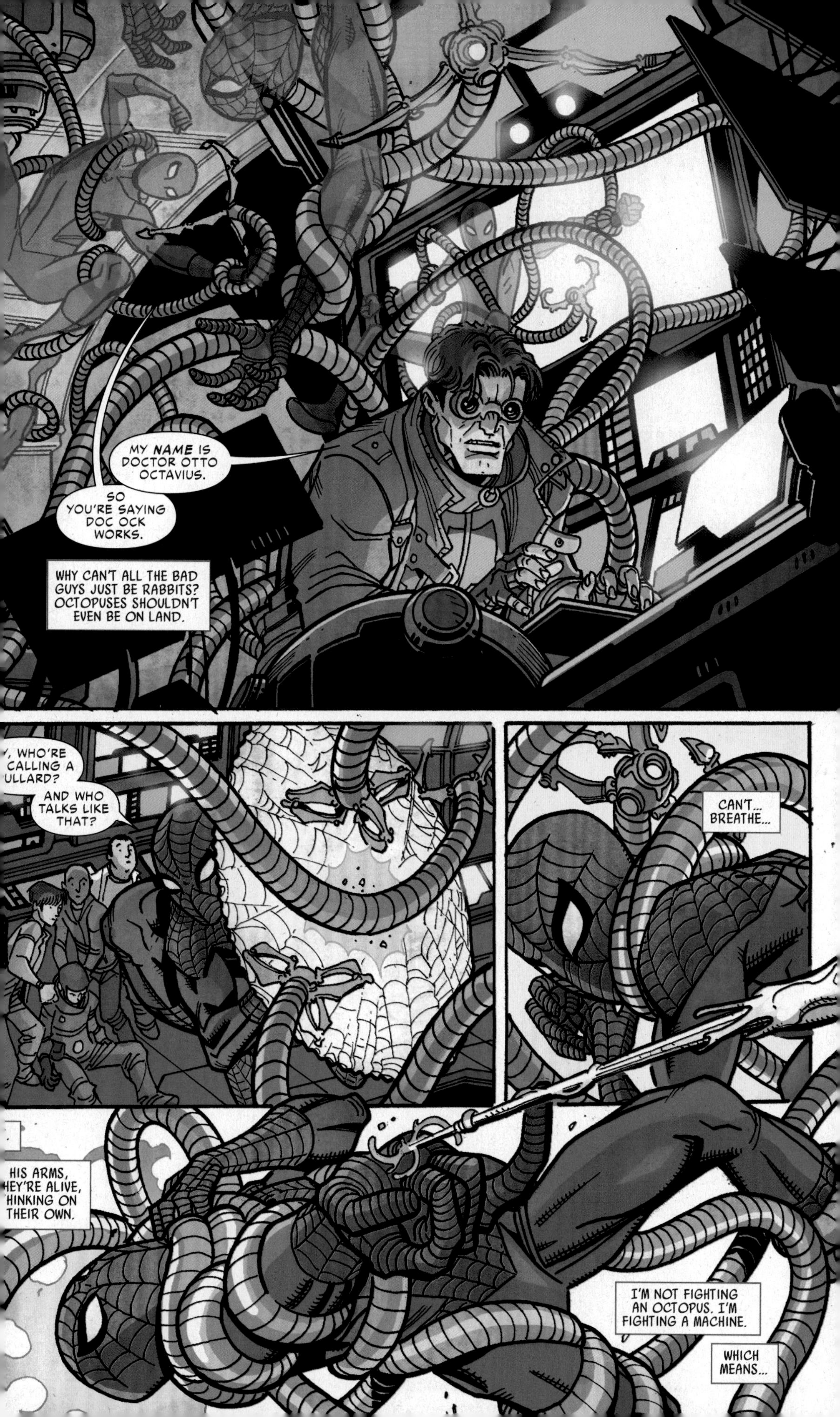
MY NAME IS DOCTOR OTTO OCTAVIUS.
SO YOU'RE SAYING DOC OCK WORKS.
WHY CAN'T ALL THE BAD GUYS JUST BE RABBITS? OCTOPUSES SHOULDN'T EVEN BE ON LAND.
, WHO'RE CALLING A ULLARD?
AND WHO TALKS LIKE THAT?
CAN'T... BREATHE...
HIS ARMS, HEY'RE ALIVE, HINKING ON THEIR OWN.
I'M NOT FIGHTING AN OCTOPUS. I'M FIGHTING A MACHINE.
WHICH MEANS...

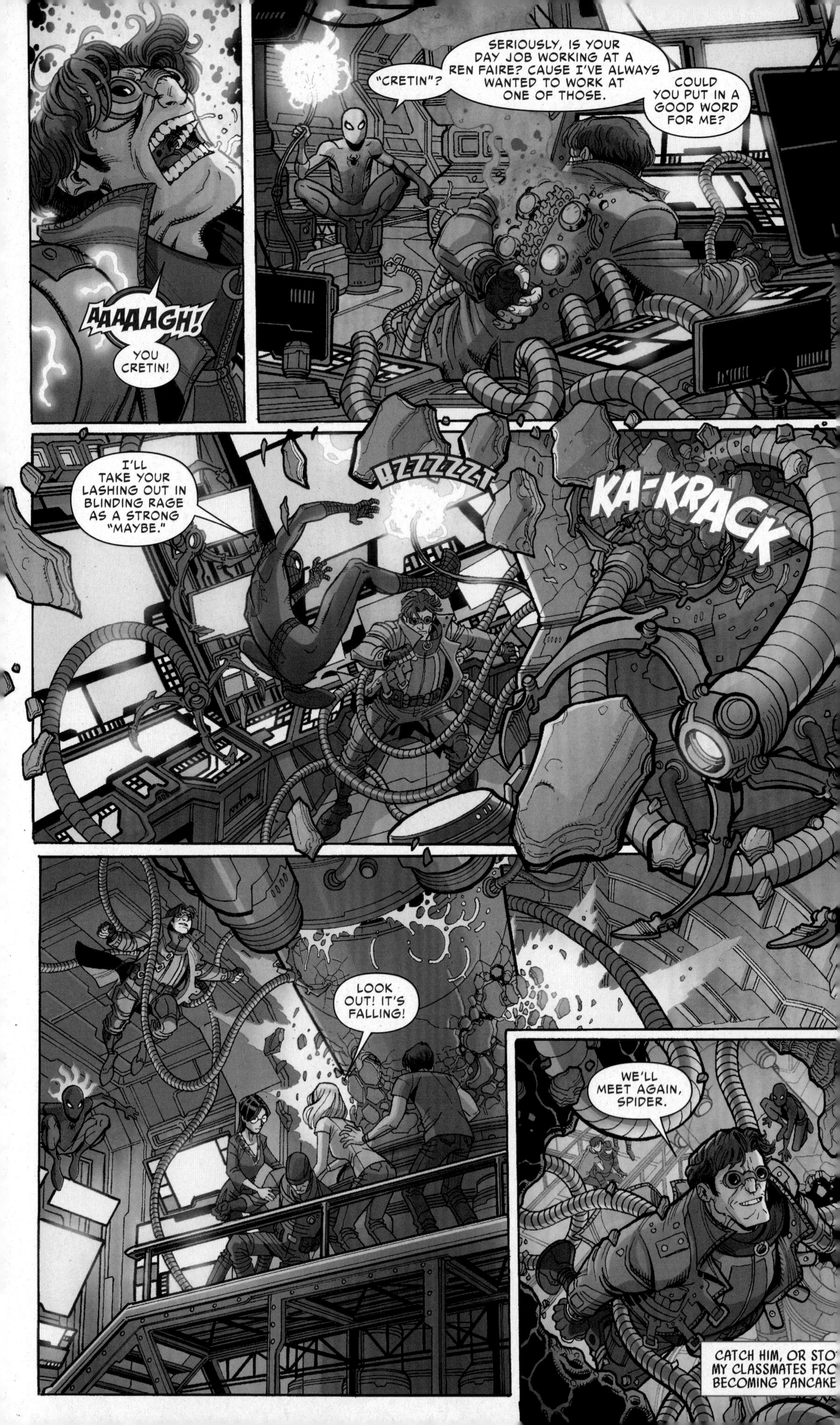
AAAAAGH!
YOU CRETIN!
"CRETIN"?
SERIOUSLY, IS YOUR DAY JOB WORKING AT A REN FAIRE? CAUSE I'VE ALWAYS WANTED TO WORK AT ONE OF THOSE.
COULD YOU PUT IN A GOOD WORD FOR ME?
I'LL TAKE YOUR LASHING OUT IN BLINDING RAGE AS A STRONG "MAYBE."
BZZZZZT
KA-KRACK
LOOK OUT! IT'S FALLING!
WE'LL MEET AGAIN, SPIDER.
CATCH HIM, OR STO
MY CLASSMATES FRO
BECOMING PANCAKE

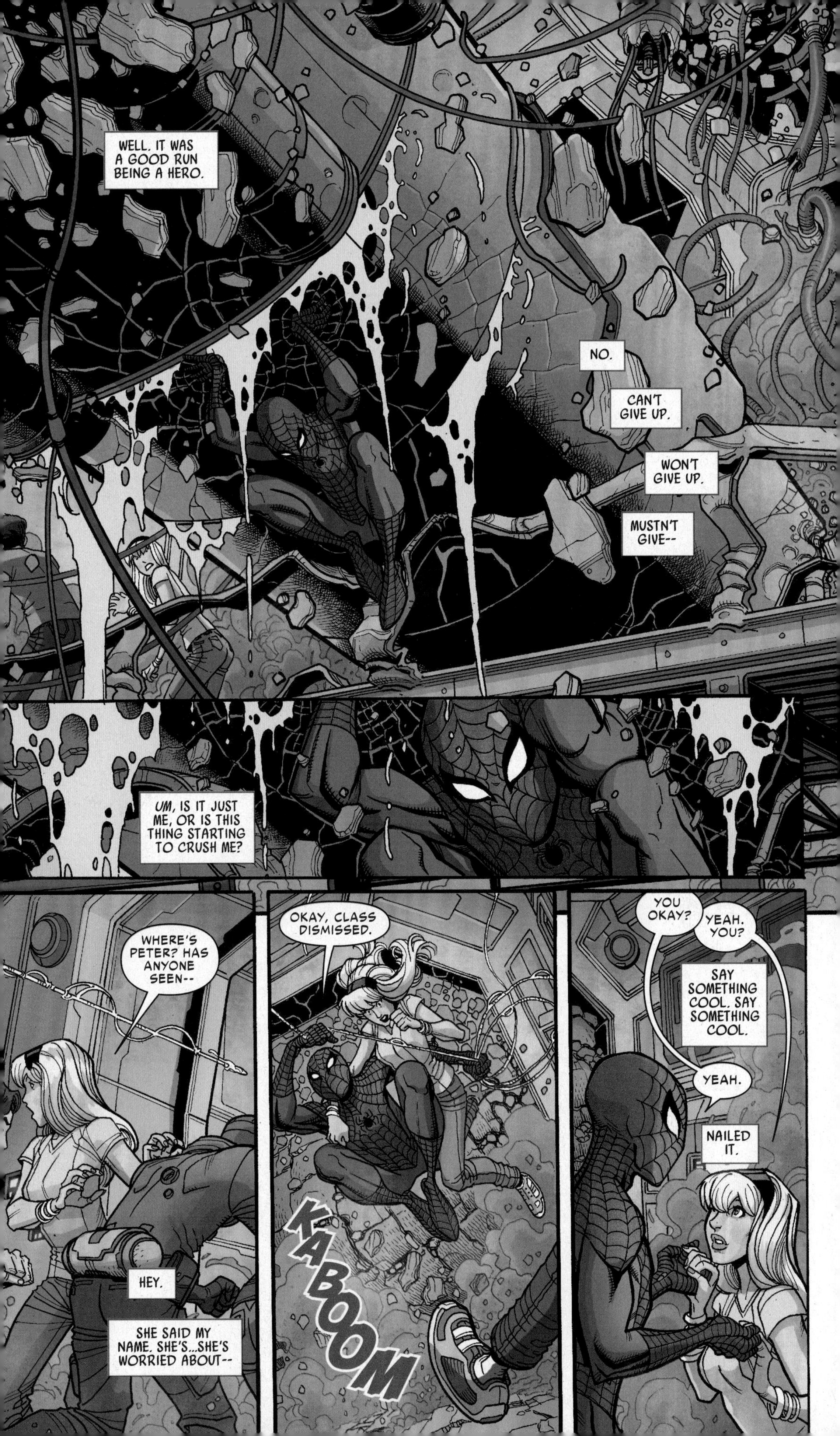
WELL. IT WAS A GOOD RUN BEING A HERO.
NO.
CAN'T GIVE UP.
WON'T GIVE UP.
MUSTN'T GIVE--
UM, IS IT JUST ME, OR IS THIS THING STARTING TO CRUSH ME?
WHERE'S PETER? HAS ANYONE SEEN--
HEY.
SHE SAID MY NAME. SHE'S...SHE'S WORRIED ABOUT--
OKAY, CLASS DISMISSED.
KABOOM
YOU OKAY?
YEAH. YOU?
SAY SOMETHING COOL. SAY SOMETHING COOL.
YEAH.
NAILED IT.

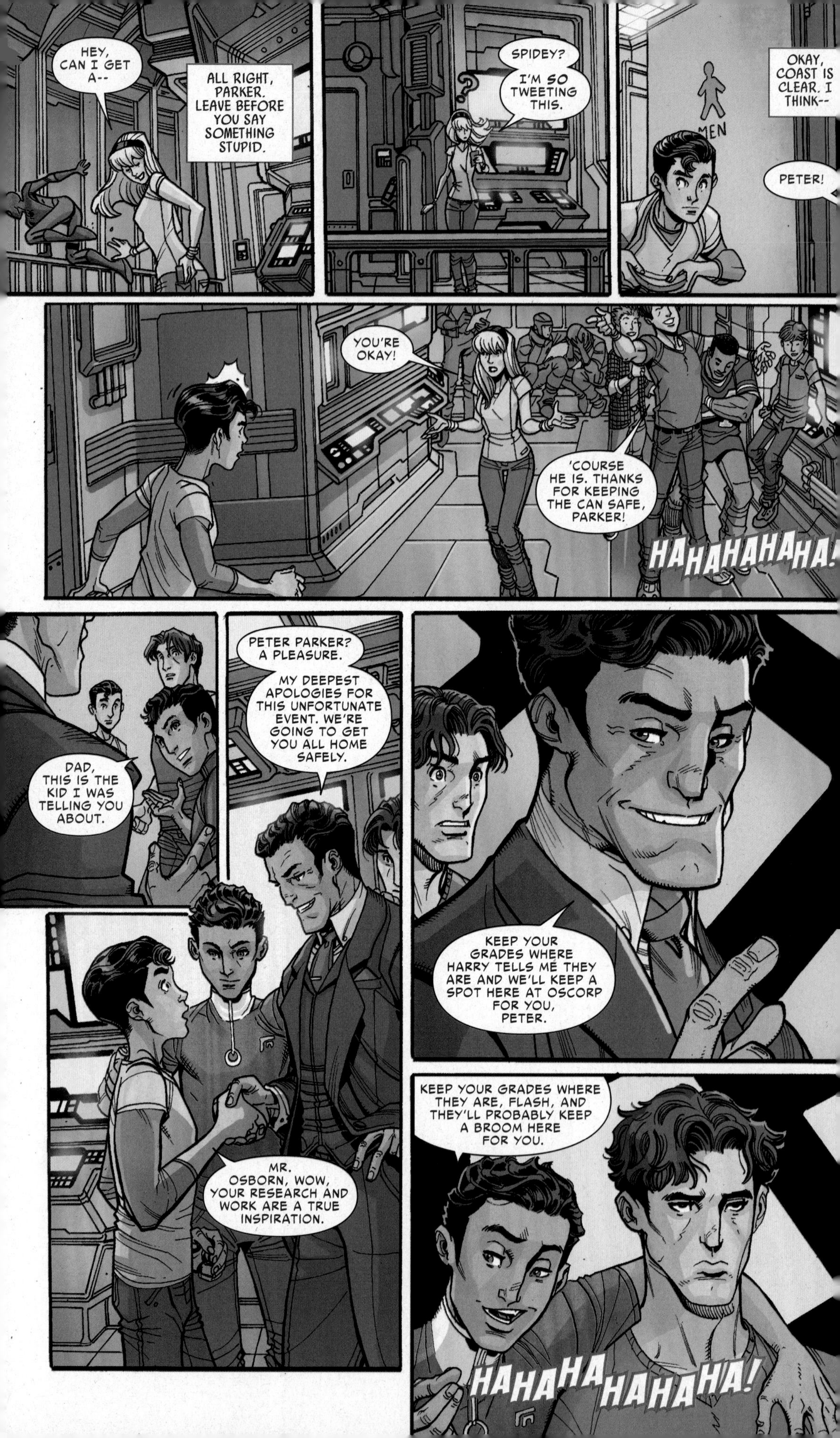
HEY, CAN I GET A--
ALL RIGHT, PARKER. LEAVE BEFORE YOU SAY SOMETHING STUPID.
SPIDEY?
I'M SO TWEETING THIS.
MEN
OKAY, COAST IS CLEAR. I THINK--
PETER!
YOU'RE OKAY!
'COURSE HE IS. THANKS FOR KEEPING THE CAN SAFE, PARKER!
HAHAHAHAHA!
DAD, THIS IS THE KID I WAS TELLING YOU ABOUT.
PETER PARKER? A PLEASURE.
MY DEEPEST APOLOGIES FOR THIS UNFORTUNATE EVENT. WE'RE GOING TO GET YOU ALL HOME SAFELY.
MR. OSBORN, WOW, YOUR RESEARCH AND WORK ARE A TRUE INSPIRATION.
KEEP YOUR GRADES WHERE HARRY TELLS ME THEY ARE AND WE'LL KEEP A SPOT HERE AT OSCORP FOR YOU, PETER.
KEEP YOUR GRADES WHERE THEY ARE, FLASH, AND THEY'LL PROBABLY KEEP A BROOM HERE FOR YOU.
HAHAHA HAHAHA!

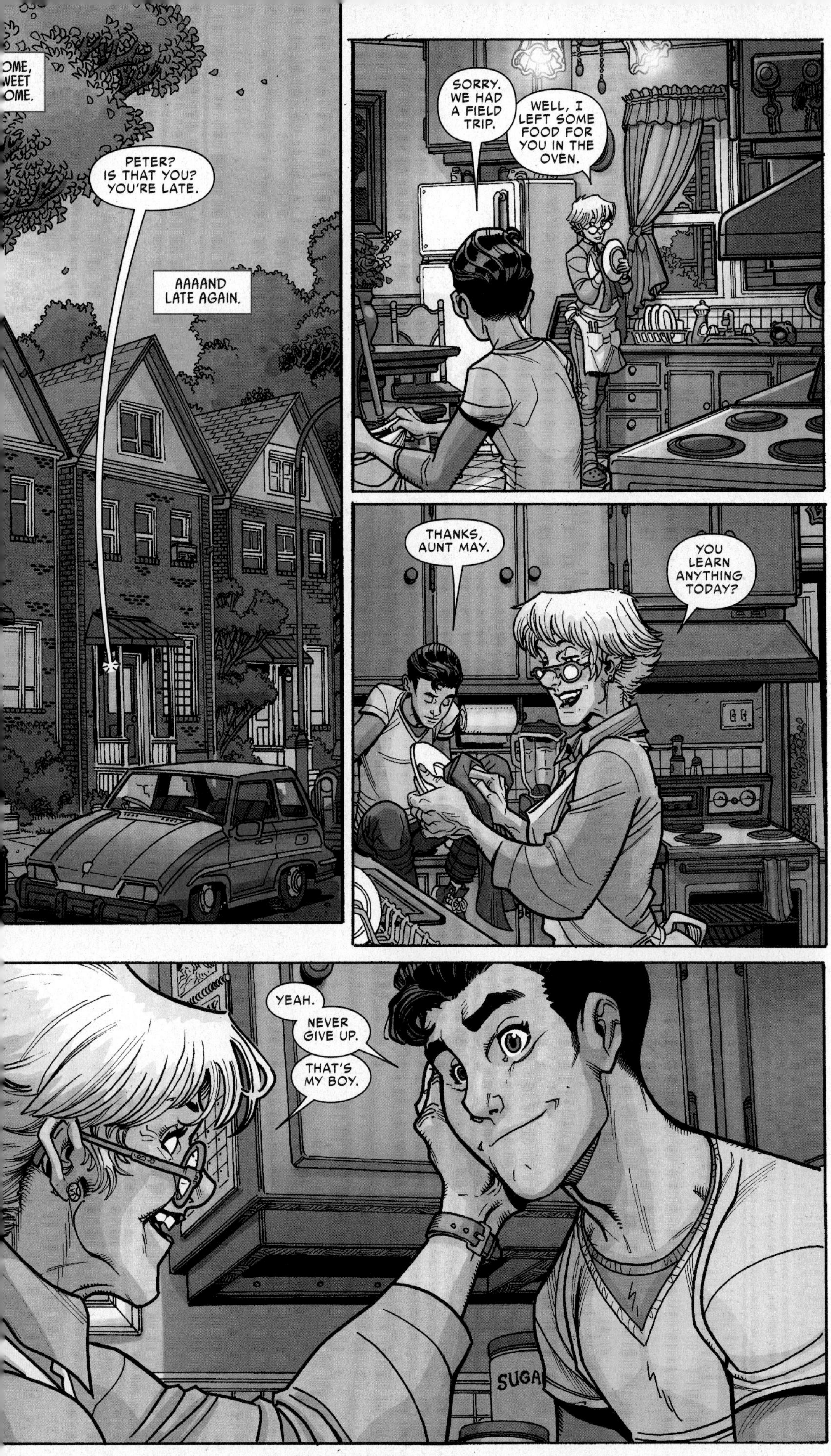
OME,
WEET
OME.
PETER? IS THAT YOU? YOU'RE LATE.
AAAAND LATE AGAIN.
SORRY. WE HAD A FIELD TRIP.
WELL, I LEFT SOME FOOD FOR YOU IN THE OVEN.
THANKS, AUNT MAY.
YOU LEARN ANYTHING TODAY?
YEAH.
NEVER GIVE UP.
THAT'S MY BOY.
SUGA

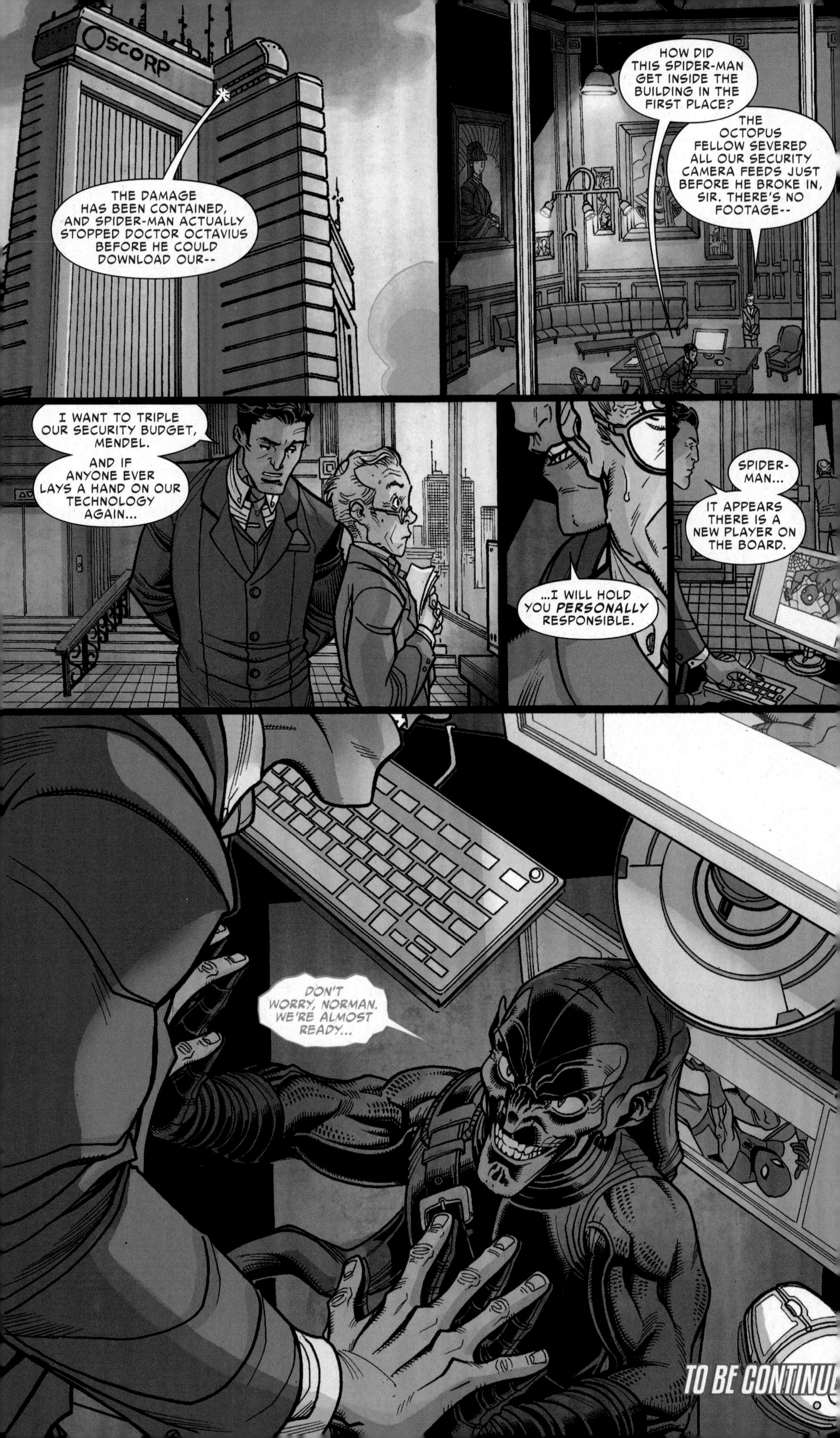

OSCORP
THE DAMAGE HAS BEEN CONTAINED, AND SPIDER-MAN ACTUALLY STOPPED DOCTOR OCTAVIUS BEFORE HE COULD DOWNLOAD OUR--
HOW DID THIS SPIDER-MAN GET INSIDE THE BUILDING IN THE FIRST PLACE?
THE OCTOPUS FELLOW SEVERED ALL OUR SECURITY CAMERA FEEDS JUST BEFORE HE BROKE IN, SIR. THERE'S NO FOOTAGE--
I WANT TO TRIPLE OUR SECURITY BUDGET, MENDEL.
AND IF ANYONE EVER LAYS A HAND ON OUR TECHNOLOGY AGAIN...
...I WILL HOLD YOU PERSONALLY RESPONSIBLE.
SPIDER-MAN...
IT APPEARS THERE IS A NEW PLAYER ON THE BOARD.
DON'T WORRY, NORMAN. WE'RE ALMOST READY...
TO BE CONTINU

SPIDEY VOL. 1: FIRST DAY
ISBN: 978-0-7851-9675-4

PENCILS BY NEIL EDWARDS

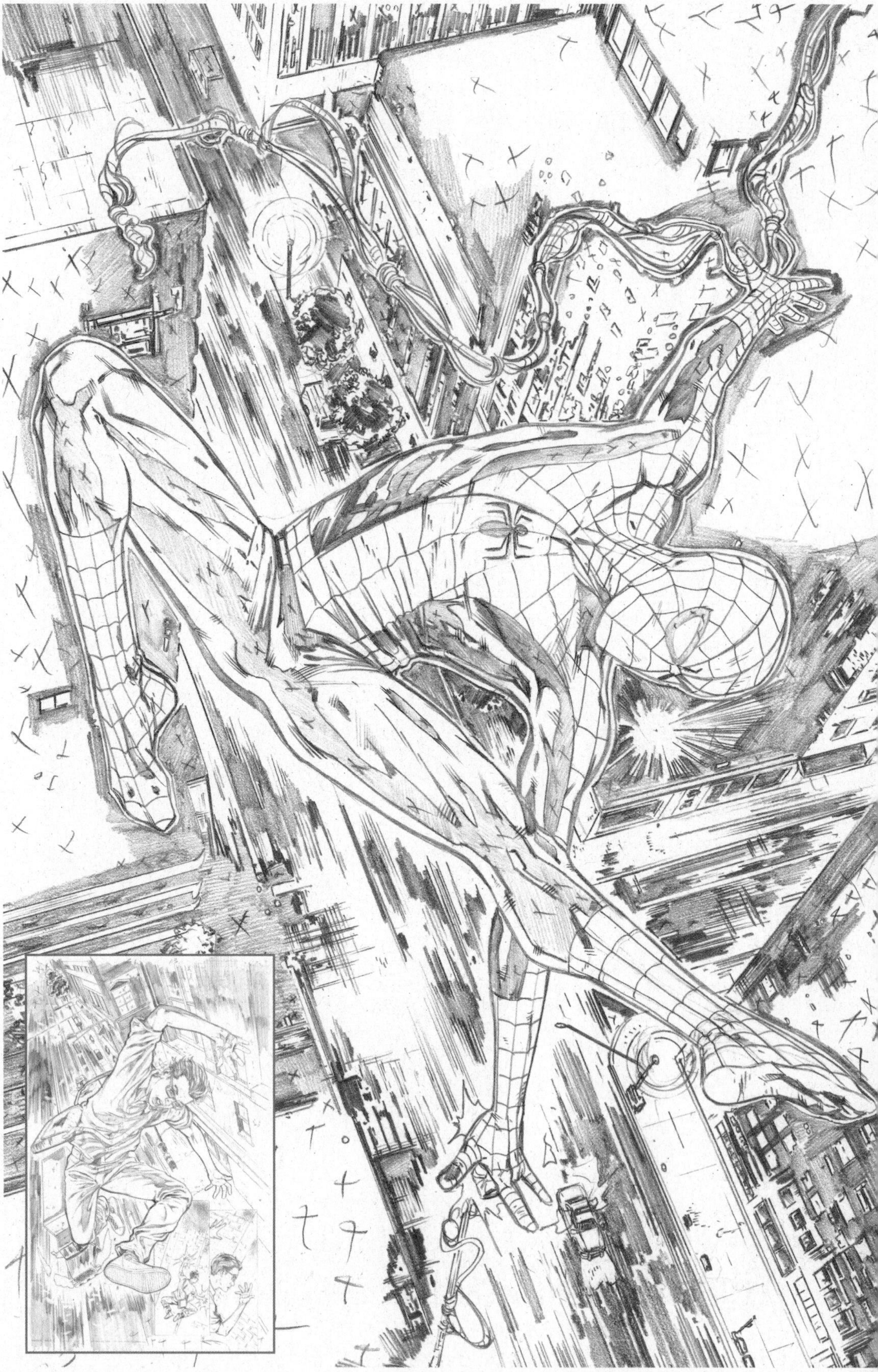

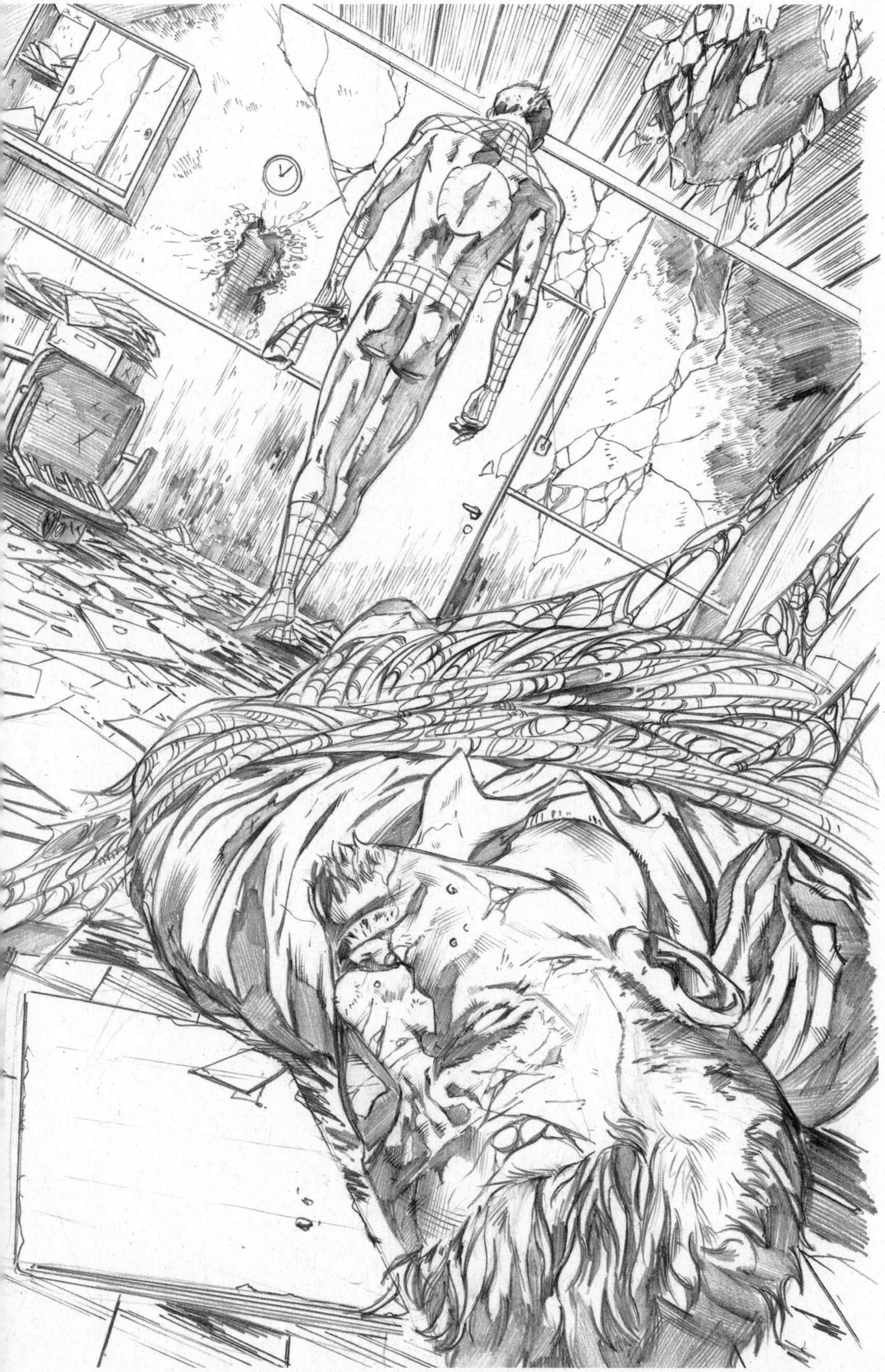

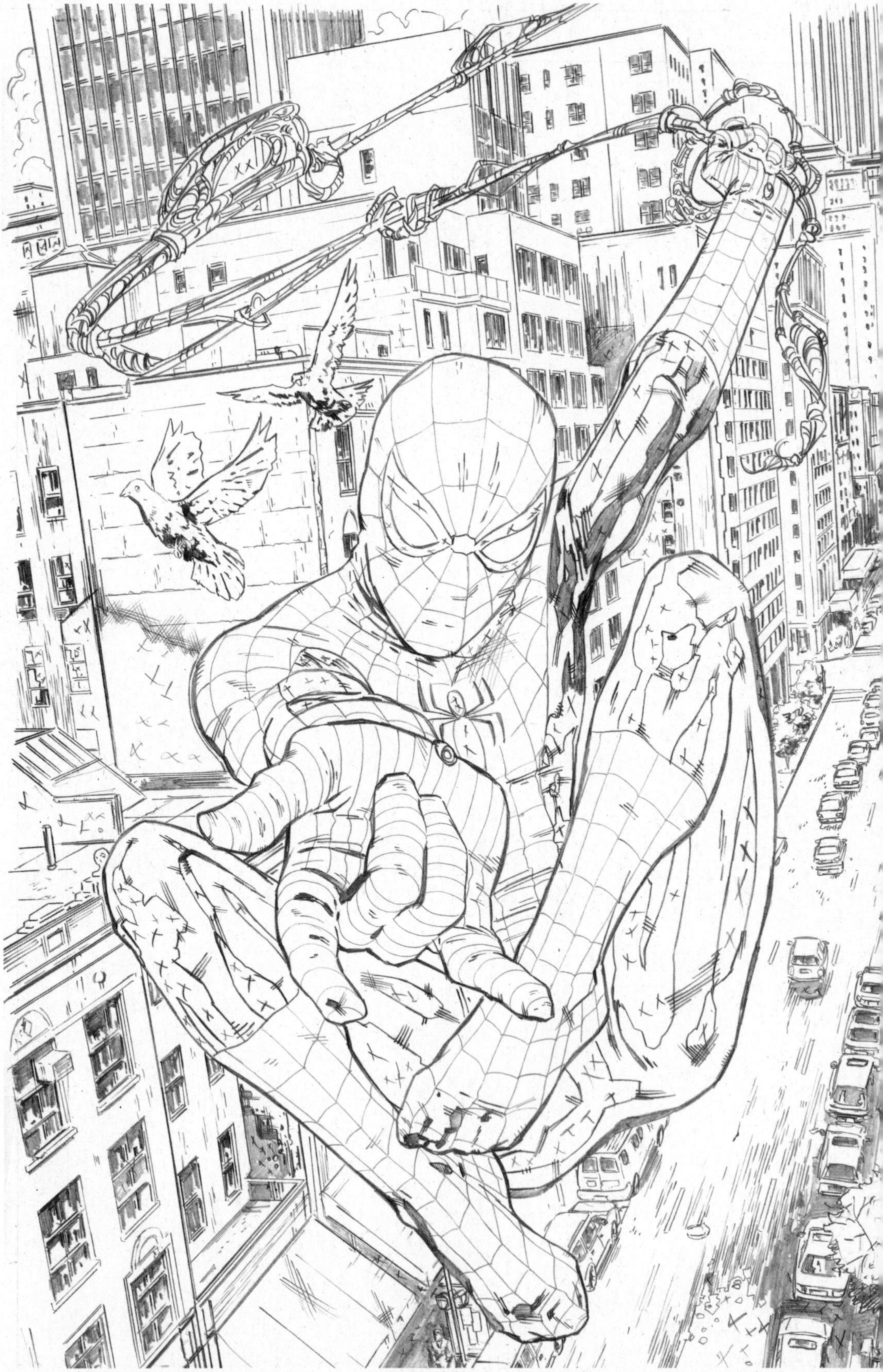